OPERATION IRONMAN
One Man's Four Month Journey from Hospital Bed to
Ironman Triathlon
George Mahood

Operation Ironman
George Mahood

www.facebook.com/georgemahood
twitter: @georgemahood
www.georgemahood.com

To medical staff everywhere.
Thank you.

1

Even the sunflowers had admitted defeat. Either side of me, fields of them stretched to the horizon, their leaves shrivelled and dried, and their once vibrant yellow petals now a shade of rusty brown. The heat was too much and they hung their heads in resignation.

I was taking part in an Ironman triathlon in France. I had cycled 80 of the 112 miles in the bike leg, but things had started to go horribly wrong. I had not seen another cyclist in a long time. I had surely taken a wrong turn somewhere and was cycling off into the French countryside, away from the race and all the other competitors. Both of my water bottles were empty and the temperature had reached 40°C with a vicious headwind. I had been suffering from hallucinations on and off for about half an hour, my head pulsating in the heat. I kept seeing water stations in the distance, only for them to vaporise into nothing as I approached.

Four months previously I had been lying in a hospital bed, having had a tumour removed from my spinal cord. I signed up for the Ironman as an incentive to get fit and encourage my rehabilitation. It had proved to be a challenge too far. I had put up a good fight, but I had nothing left to give. Even if I were to complete the remaining 32 miles, I still had a 26.2 mile run to contend with and, based on my current state, there was not a chance in hell that would be possible.

I thought of the many cyclists I had seen; their bodies littering the roadside, sheltering under the little shade they could find. I thought of the ambulances that had sped past, whisking away many of these competitors to receive further medical attention. That would soon be me. I would find a tree, lie beneath it, and wait for help to arrive.

A shape took form further up the road ahead. Shimmering in the heat. A mirage surely? It was a man. In his late fifties. Perhaps older. His weather-beaten face unfazed by the scorching heat. He stepped into the middle of the road, raised his arm in front, and pointed a gun at my head. This was it. There was nowhere for me to go, and I didn't have the energy to try to negotiate. I continued pedalling towards him, hoping that he was just another figment of my imagination and I would pass straight through him. But the closer I got the more lifelike he became. He was real, and there was no chance of an escape.

I took my hands off the handlebars and sat back in my saddle. I raised both arms in the air in defeat.

'Shootez moi, monsieur!' I shouted in Franglais, as my bike careered towards him. 'S'il vous plaît,' I added, not wanting my final words on this earth to be considered impolite.

A toothy grin spread across his wrinkled face. He tilted his head back and roared with laughter. If this had been a film, his gold tooth would have glinted in the sunlight. But this wasn't a film. This was real life. He looked me straight in the eye. And then he pulled the trigger.

It was a long old journey that ended with me cycling through the French countryside as part of an Ironman triathlon in France. It was a journey that began almost a year and a half earlier, when I first started to notice a pain in my back.

It was March 2014 and it was just a slight niggling ache towards the bottom of my spine. It got steadily worse over the following weeks, and the pain spread to other parts of my back and to my legs. I went to see my GP and he referred me to a physiotherapist and offered to review me again a few weeks later if there was no improvement.

A couple of sessions of physiotherapy had no effect and the symptoms got progressively more painful. In early July I was referred for an MRI scan, with a suspected slipped/herniated disc in my lower back.

In August 2014 I went for my first MRI scan at Derriford Hospital in Plymouth. It was six weeks before I got the results, and my GP phoned to say that the MRI scan had picked up a slight abnormality in my spine. What appeared to be a 'fatty cyst' was present on the scan, but they would need to scan me again with a contrast dye to get a better look at it.

I began Googling spinal cysts (it's not a hobby I would recommend) and found that they were a fairly common side-effect of a herniated disc. I was happy with the logic that I had simply slipped a disc and had developed a cyst as a result. It was nothing serious and easily treatable.

By the end of the summer I struggled with any form of physical activity as it was far too painful. When I played 5-a-side football I spent more time doubled over in pain than playing. Running was impossible. Cycling was just about bearable along flat ground, but there is no flat ground where we live in south Devon. So I tried swimming. I thought swimming would be the answer. It would keep me fit, and provide good all round exercise for my body. But it was also far too uncomfortable. I could only swim breaststroke at the time, and the forced curvature of my spine exerted too much pressure on my lower back so I had to stop that too. Also, in my first (and last) session in the pool, I managed to split my swimming shorts and kick an old lady in the head. Swimming was not for me.

In October 2014 I went for my second MRI scan. Again, I had to wait six weeks for the results, which although mildly frustrating, was not overly concerning because I had already self-diagnosed on Google.

A phone call in mid-November 2014 changed all that. My wife Rachel was at work, and I was in the process of collecting our children from school. Kitty, our youngest – aged 3 – had fallen asleep in the car on the way to pick up the older two, and because of my bad back, I was unable to lift her from her car seat. I managed to wake her and persuade her to walk, but she was extremely grumpy.

I retrieved Leo – aged 4 – from his teacher and we waited for our eldest daughter Layla – aged 7 – to come out of her class. It was pouring with rain, extremely windy and miserably cold. My phone rang.

'Mr Mahood. It's Dr Ramesh from the medical centre,' said a female voice. 'Is now a good time to talk?'

It could not have been much of a worse time, but I had waited so long to get my results that I didn't want to drag it out any longer.

'Yes, perfect,' I said.

'Ok. Well, the results from your recent MRI scan have been reviewed by the neurology and oncology departments and they seem to suggest that...'

But I already had a feeling I knew what she was going to say. Oncology? At no point in my previous meetings with doctors had oncology been mentioned. I knew that oncology dealt with cancer.

She paused.

'...they think, Mr Mahood... that you have a tumour growing in your spinal cord.'

I felt my legs turn to jelly beneath me and a feeling of nausea swept over me. I squeezed Kitty's hand a little tighter.

'Ow, Daddy, you're hurting me,' she shouted.

'We don't know for certain that it's a tumour, and it might just be a red herring. And there's a very good chance that it is benign, but it will definitely need further investigation.'

'Ok,' I said, taking a deep breath. 'What happens now?'

'I will arrange an appointment for you to meet with a neurologist who will be able to discuss it with you further and talk you through how we proceed from here.'

A few days later I received a letter from the doctor confirming my appointment with a neurologist. The date and time of the appointment were written in bold in the middle of the letter, but after skim reading the rest of the page, two words made an impact more than any others: *'suspected cancer'*. Suspected cancer? Doctor Ramesh hadn't actually mentioned anything about cancer. She had even said there was a very good chance that the tumour was benign, and that it might be a red herring and not a tumour at all. But now it was being labelled as *'suspected cancer'*.

'Everything alright?' asked Rachel, noticing the look of terror on my face as I read the letter.

'Yes, fine. I've got a date to see a neurologist,' I said, folding up the letter and stuffing it quickly into my pocket. I phoned my doctor's surgery to discuss it and had a call back from my usual GP later that day.

'Hopefully it's nothing to worry about,' he said.

'But the letter says 'suspected cancer',' I said. 'How am I supposed to not be worried about that?'

'Yes, I'm sorry. The letter is a bit misleading. Basically anything that presents as a tumour has to be treated as a suspected cancer in order for a quick and correct diagnosis. We can't take any chances.'

'So that doesn't mean that they think it IS cancer?'

'No, it just means that your scans are showing what appears to be a spinal cord tumour, and it could potentially be cancerous, so it will require further investigations and tests.'

'Ok.'

'I'm sorry. It was a bad choice of words in the letter. We don't want to cause unnecessary concern, but things like this need to be taken very seriously.'

Two weeks later I was sitting in the office of a neurologist awaiting his verdict. He sat in front of me going through my scans for the first time and reading the radiology notes.

'Yes, I think what you have is an ependymoma on your conus medullaris or filum terminale.'

'I'm sorry… An appendy-what? On my what?'

'An ependymoma. It's a fairly rare type of tumour that grows either in the brain or spinal cord. The type you have grows exclusively at the conus, which is the very base of the spinal cord, where all the nerve endings exit the spinal cord.'

'Is it… cancerous?' I asked.

'No. At least, I don't think so. It's impossible to tell at this stage, but I think it's very unlikely. Most ependymomas are benign.'

I breathed a sigh of relief.

'Most, but not all?' I asked.

'No, not all, and the fact that it appears to be growing inside the spinal column is a slight cause for concern.'

'Why is that?'

'Because cells can potentially spread through the spinal fluid, and it also makes surgical resection more complicated.'

'So what happens now?'

'I will book an appointment with you to meet with one of our neurosurgery team, and they will discuss the options.'

'How long will that take?'

'You should get to see someone within the next month.'

'A month? But isn't this thing dangerous?'

'It's very slow growing so it is unlikely to change too much in a month.'

My symptoms did get increasingly worse over the following weeks. Looking back, I don't think I helped my situation by abstaining from most physical activity. I've always been quite a determined person, and even when I've had an injury in the past, I have always done as much as I could to recover and get active again. Having a tumour was different. While it was still there I knew that I couldn't physically beat it. It wasn't going to disappear and it wasn't going to get any smaller. My symptoms were certainly not going to improve, and, as it grew bigger, they were only going to get worse. It affected me emotionally and I found it very hard to deal with. I was used to being mobile and active, and as I became more and more sedate, my back started to seize up due to lack of activity. The less I did, the worse it got. And the worse it got, the more I convinced myself that the tumour was growing at a rapid rate.

I never once believed that I wouldn't eventually recover. I had every faith and confidence that I would be eligible for surgery and then make a full recovery following the removal of the tumour. But while it was still growing inside of me, it was beating me, both physically and psychologically. Days turned into weeks and the weeks turned into months as I waited for results and scan dates to come round.

The location of the tumour was such that it was pressing on nerves that affected my legs. I had permanent pins and needles in both legs – most noticeably in my feet. Both thighs felt like they were suffering from a dead leg (or a *'Charley horse'*, as they are obscurely called in America. Or a *'corky'* in Australia.) There were a couple of areas on my thighs that had no sensation whatsoever. I could put an ice cube on a particular spot of my left leg and not feel anything at all.

The tumour had so far not affected me neurologically and apart from the occasional moment of foot drop when walking downhill, my legs still operated as normal.

Before moving to Devon two years ago, my wife Rachel had never shown any interest in sport or exercise. She had managed to get out of almost all PE lessons at secondary school with the commonly used excuse of *'girl problems'*, and ever since had shown a complete disinterest in physical activity.

Things changed after we moved house. She started running and weirdly seemed to enjoy it. She completed a 10k in late 2013, a half-marathon in June the following year, and another half marathon in October, just as my back was rendering me almost unable to do anything. On one hand I was delighted to see Rachel's enthusiasm about running, and the immense enjoyment she was getting out of it. But it made things increasingly difficult for me to cope with. She would come home smiling after a 13 mile run, marvelling at how great she felt and how wonderful it was to be out and about in the open air. I stood there wincing in pain having walked across the kitchen.

I had gone from a physically active person, to someone who had difficulty standing or walking in a relatively short space of time. My back and leg muscles, previously used on a daily basis, became more redundant as I moved less, and used my back less. Muscles weakened, my posture changed and both my physical health and emotional well-being deteriorated.

On December 21st, 2014, as everyone was preparing for Christmas, I went for my appointment with the neurosurgeon. During the drive there, I started to feel a slight tingling and a sensation of numbness in my left hand. It was something I had never experienced before, and I became convinced that it was caused by the tumour, and that it was beginning to affect other parts of my body too.

When I described my symptoms to the neurosurgeon he and his assistant looked at me with emotionless expressions. I realised that they had their doubts.

'Mr Mahood, it's not possible for you to be experiencing any problems with your arms or hands based on the location of the tumour,' said Mr H, the young smooth-looking neurosurgeon.

'Oh. Ok.'

'Looking at your scan results, I would agree with the neurologist that you have what's called a myxopapillary ependymoma. I don't know how much you know about these tumours?'

'I've done a tiny bit of Googling,' I lied. I had spent so much time on the internet that I probably knew more about spinal cord tumours than he did.

'Right, well you'll know that they occur exclusively in the conus medullaris, which is the very base of the spinal cord. It's where all the nerve endings leave the spinal cord and spread throughout your lower body.'

'Ok,' I nodded.

'So, because of the location, and the fact that it can press on lots of different nerves, it would explain all of your symptoms such as the leg pain, the pins and needles, the numbness and the foot drop. They are all symptoms common with a myxopapillary ependymoma.'

'But not the tingling in my hand?' I said sheepishly, realising that it had disappeared as soon as I had got out of the car.

'No, not the hand. I think perhaps that must be psychosomatic. Do you have any issues with your bladder or bowels?'

'Not really.'

'What do you mean?'

'Well my bladder and bowels have never been great anyway. When I've got to go, I've got to go.'

'Ok. But it hasn't got any worse since the tumour?'

'No.'

'That's good. Any loss of sexual function?'

'No.'

'Ok. Well those are all symptoms that you might experience as the tumour grows.'

'So the tumour is not going to go away by itself, is it?'

'No, it won't.'

'So will I have to have surgery?'

'Not necessarily. Although it is causing lots of pain and discomfort, all of your reflexes and muscles seem to be operating fine, and it's not causing you any neurological problems at the moment.'

'But that could change as the tumour grows?'

'Yes, it could, but surgery carries with it a lot of risks and often people end up worse off after surgery than before.'

'So what do you suggest?'

'Well we are not going to do anything before Christmas, so you should just monitor how things go for the next month or two, and if symptoms get worse then we can consider the options.'

'So, I just have to leave it there?'

'For now, yes. It's not causing any major problems and the potential risks of surgery are too high.'

'Ok.'

'I will book you in for a brain scan in the New Year, too?'

'Wait... WHAT? A BRAIN SCAN?'

'Yes, it's just routine. Because you have a tumour in your central nervous system, we have to scan the rest of your spine and brain just to rule out any other tumours. I'm sure it will all be fine. Have a great Christmas!'

I had entered his office with high expectations of being given a date for surgery, told it would be a straightforward procedure, and that I would make a full recovery. I left knowing that they weren't going to do anything about the tumour for now, that surgery was very high-risk, and that I was going to be having a brain scan in the New Year to check for other tumours.

Christmas was a welcome distraction from my back pain. But worse than the pain was the now almost constant fear that I also had a brain tumour. Every slight headache, every momentary pain in the upper body, every brief dizzy spell I put down to my possible brain tumour. I managed to block it out of my mind as much as possible, and still had an immensely enjoyable Christmas. I even managed to join in our now traditional Christmas Day sea swim (does one year count as traditional?). The intense cold of the English Channel on December 25th numbed any pain present in my back and I felt surprisingly invigorated.

I tried my best not to let my back issues affect family life, but it had become increasingly hard to hide it. It was noticeable to the three children in my lack of activity and my inability to play with them as much as I used to. I was unable to carry them, play football, run after them, spin them around, give them piggy backs or go on the trampoline.

The trampoline had come to represent a symbol of my back problems. I knew I would not be completely better until I was able to go back on the trampoline with my children. I pointed out to them that Rachel didn't have any back problems and was perfectly capable of bouncing with them in my absence, and that trampolines can still be plenty of fun without grownups.

'But Mummy's not as bouncy as you,' moaned Layla.

'What do you mean?'

'Mummy just bounces on the trampoline. You REALLY bounce. It's more fun with you on it.'

'But every single time I go on the trampoline someone bangs their head, or hurts their arm or gets elbowed in the face, and it always ends in tears.'

'We don't mind,' said Layla.

'Yeah, we don't mind,' said Kitty.

'So when you next come back from hospital will you be able to go on the trampoline?' asked Leo.

'It will take me a little while to get fully better. I will probably have to see a few more doctors and go to hospital a few more times before it gets better.'

'How long?'

'I don't know. A few weeks. Maybe months.'

'Ohhhhhh. That's SO long,' said Leo.

'See, I'm their favourite trampoliner,' I said to Rachel, later that evening.

'Isn't it trampolinist?'

'I prefer trampoliner.'

'They only like you better because you're heavier,' she replied.

'Are you calling me biggishly built again?' I said, referring to a time a couple of years ago when she made up the term '*biggishly built*' to describe my frame, kick-starting me to lose some weight.

'I never said that. You're obviously just bouncier than me.'

'Oh I'm big and bouncy am I?'

'Stop it. You know what I mean.'

After the children returned to school following the Christmas break they all seemed slightly subdued; Leo in particular. Leo is quite a sensitive five year old and tends to

16

struggle with his emotions. His teacher asked to speak to us a few days after he had been back, and said that Leo was finding it a bit difficult at school, and didn't quite seem himself. When we asked if Leo had given any indication as to why he was subdued he had told his teacher that he was 'worried about Daddy's back'. It made me realise how important it was for me to keep a positive attitude, however bad things got. I couldn't let whatever was growing inside me affect the way my children perceived me.

2

'Is this your first MRI?' asked the radiographer, as I rested my head inside the U-shaped brace on the scanner table. It was February 6th, and the brain scan promised for early January had dragged on into February, causing me a further four weeks of worry.

'No, this is my third time,' I said.

'Ah, so you're a bit of a pro.'

'Yeah, I can't get enough of them.'

'Do you normally listen to music when you're in the scanner?'

'Music? No, I didn't even know that was an option.'

'Yes, you'll be in there for nearly an hour for this one. What would you like?'

'Whatever you've got. Thanks very much.'

'How about *Indie Hits of the 90s*?'

'Sounds perfect.' I said.

I closed my eyes as the table slid inside the MRI machine. The roof of the scanner is only a few inches in front of your face, and it can feel very claustrophobic, especially when you are in there for an hour. By closing my eyes, I could try and pretend I wasn't there.

'And there's no clothes I can buy make me feel like myself,' he said,' began the song. It was one of my favourites from my teenage years. *She Said* by The Longpigs.

'So I put on clothes to make me look like someone else, insteeeeeaad.'

This was going to be awesome. An hour lying down reliving my youth, listening to songs I hadn't heard in years.

And then they switched the MRI machine on.

JUNG JUNG JUNG JUNG JUNG JUNG it pounded.

And for the next hour I was in a 90s rave, listening to barely audible indie classics overdubbed with a pulsating beat that drowned out almost everything. I occasionally heard snippets of songs during the few seconds' interval when the scanner moved position to a different part of my body.

Dodgy's *Stayin Out For the Summer.*
'If I ever see you again, I will tell you whyyyyyy'
JUNG JUNG JUNG JUNG JUNG JUNG
Cast's *Fine Time.*
'I do believe you read the words'
JUNG JUNG JUNG JUNG JUNG JUNG

'All done,' she said, taking the cannula from the vein in my arm where they had injected a contrast die midway through the scan.

'Thanks. Any idea how long it will take for the results to be available?'

'I've emailed them over to Mr H just now, so he has them already.'

'Wow, that was quick. Thank you,' I said, wanting to probe further and trying to detect suggestions in her mannerisms that would indicate whether I had a brain tumour or not. But I knew it wasn't her job to say and she would not have been able to comment even if I had asked. Still, Mr H had my results so he would be able to tell me very soon. Or so I hoped.

I phoned his secretary a couple of days later, hoping that this would allow him plenty of time to have looked at the results. She told me that they were on his desk and he would report on them very soon. I called back a couple of days later. I got the same reply. Then the following week, and then the next, each time phoning two or three times per week.

Each time I called I was polite and courteous, but on the final time – five and a half weeks after my scan – I eventually lost my cool.

I began sobbing down the phone and I told the secretary that I had been given the same response every time I had spoken to her.

'Ok, Mr Mahood, I can see that you're a little emotional about this,' she said calmly.

'That's because I had my first MRI scan in AUGUST last year. It is now MARCH. That's SEVEN months since my first scan, and I still don't have a diagnosis. Whatever it is growing on my spinal cord is probably getting bigger, and I still don't know whether there are others I should be worried about too.'

'I will make sure Mr H reports on your scans today and I will call you back tomorrow. Ok, Mr Mahood?'

'Yes.... please,' I sobbed. 'That would be great, thank you.'

As promised, Mr H's secretary called me the following morning. It was good news. The scans showed no other tumours on my brain or the rest of my central nervous system. The tumour on my lower spine had changed its presentation, though. The radiologist who had also analysed the scan now believed it was a nerve sheath tumour, rather than an ependymoma. This was the reason the reporting had taken so long, as there had been a conflict of opinion. It didn't make much difference to me what type of tumour it was, as my main concern had been the possibility of further tumours to my brain and spine.

If it was a nerve sheath tumour then it was potentially easier to remove as it would be growing on the nerves leading off the spinal cord, rather than in the cord itself. It was still, in all likelihood, benign and slow growing.

'So what happens now?' I asked the secretary.

'Well, it will all be in a letter that will be sent out to you in the next few days, but I can read what the letter says to you now if you like.'

'Yes please,' I said, not wanting to wait any longer.

The letter laid out two options. I could opt to have surgery, for which there were many potential risks. Or, I could choose to leave it for now and have another scan in six months time, to monitor whether the tumour had grown.

'I would like to have surgery please,' I said immediately.

'Ok, well when you've received the letter you can have a think about it and see what option works best.'

'Thanks, but I've already thought about it. I would like to have surgery please.'

'Are you sure?'

'I'm sure. Thanks.'

'Well in that case I will let Mr H know and you will receive a letter confirming your date.'

'Thank you. Do you know roughly what the waiting time for surgery is like at the moment?'

'It's hard to say. As you probably know, the hospital is going through a very difficult time at the moment and we are being forced to cancel a lot of operations due to bed shortages. But what I can say is that spinal cord tumours are considered high priority, so that is definitely in your favour.'

'So are we talking weeks or months?'

'I would say somewhere between 4-6 weeks.'

'Ok, that's great. Thank you.'

I regretted losing my temper with the secretary. But I needed to shout and cry at someone. I needed to tell someone I was scared. I needed to tell someone I wasn't as strong as I was pretending to be. It wasn't ideal that it should have been a secretary at the other end of a telephone line, but she happened to be the one that took the brunt of my frustrations.

21

I felt a huge sense of both relief and release after that phone call. Relief that I didn't have a brain tumour, and release that I was finally getting towards a resolution.

For me, despite the risks, surgery was the only possible way to get things back to normal. A date soon followed and four weeks later Rachel and I made our way to Derriford Hospital at 6.30am on Friday, April 10th.

I sat in Fal Ward's waiting room dressed in my theatre gown covered with my brand new dressing gown over the top. It's not everyday you get to go into hospital for major surgery, so I thought I would treat myself. Also, I didn't actually own a dressing gown and it was one of the very few things on the list of required items to bring with me.

The registrar called me into his room to go through all the details.

After confirming the procedure that they were going to do, he then went through the possible complications of spinal surgery. These ranged from the neurosurgeon being unable to remove the tumour at all due to it being entangled with nerves, to the tumour being partially removed and then growing back, to the tumour being completely removed but nerve damage causing symptoms worse than before – symptoms that could include total or partial paralysis. Infection was also a possible complication – either internal or external – and if not treatable with antibiotics it would require further surgery. Blood clots and deep vein thrombosis were also concerns, especially if the tumour turned out to be inside the spinal canal which would require me to lie on my back for three days. A dural tear – or a tear of the sac containing the spinal cord and nerves – was another possibility. As was a cerebrospinal fluid leak, facial sores from lying face down on the operating table for several hours, and also, in some cases, blindness. Death wasn't completely avoidable either. The anaesthesia alone was a potential killer.

Each complication that the registrar talked through had a statistic next to it, representing the chances of it occurring. Most of these were extremely rare, and, being a relatively young patient, the odds for me were even better. The number of possible complications, however, was so vast, that my brain began to try and work out what the chances of me suffering at least one major complication would be. My poor mathematical skills convinced me that I was odds-on to suffer at least one of the many complications.

The registrar was extremely reassuring and put me at ease, and, to my surprise, he didn't try to talk me out of the surgery. He never once suggested that if I wasn't completely comfortable then we could leave it for six months and see if the tumour had grown. He knew as well as I did that I had made the right choice. I had made the only choice. I had a tumour in my spine and it needed to be removed.

The anaesthetist was a young, smiling man with a charismatic demeanour. He ushered Rachel and me into a screen-partitioned area of the ward where we sat down and he went through a few details with me.

'So, what do you do for a living, George?' he asked, presumably making small talk, although it's possible it affects the dosage of anaesthetic.

'Er, well I'm an author,' I said.

It was the first time I had said that out loud to anybody. I had been a wedding photographer for the best part of ten years, but had photographed my last wedding almost six months previously. I was still putting together wedding albums for couples who had been slow to get back to me with their feedback, but there was no denying it any longer. I was an author.

'Wow, that's amazing. Tell me about your books?'

And so we chatted for a few minutes about my books and he seemed genuinely interested in hearing about them. I was then told to go and sit in the waiting room where I would shortly be called through to surgery.

I would be in the operating theatre for several hours, so Rachel planned to drive into Plymouth to kill some time and then come back later.

'Drive carefully,' I said to her.

'Don't worry about me. I hope everything goes well during the operation. I'll be thinking of you the whole time you are in there and I can't wait to see you in a few hours.'

I could see that she was fighting to hold back the tears.

'I'll be fine, I promise,' I said. 'I'll be back to normal in no time. Please make sure you drive carefully.'

'Why do you keep telling me to drive carefully?'

'Because I am worried about waking up from the surgery and being told that it all went really well, but that something bad had happened to you.'

'That's very sweet, but I'm only going a couple of miles into Plymouth. I'll be fine.'

'I love you,' I said, as a nurse ushered me towards the door.

'I love you, too.'

'Drive carefully,' I called after her.

As I walked through the doors to the anaesthesia room, the anaesthetist and his three assistants were there to greet me.

'Here's our world famous author,' he said. 'We've never had a world famous author in here.'

'Ha, thanks. But I'm far from world famous. In fact, you were the first person I have ever told I am an author.'

'Well, I don't think we've ever had an author in here before. Lie down on the bed here please. We've warmed it up for you.'

He didn't mean that they had been lying in the bed before me to warm it up (at least, I don't think he did) but the bed did feel particularly warm. It was a strange spongy bed with sheets made from crepe paper. The kind of thing I imagine they would have on a space station. Disposable paper bedding is the way forward. It's not very environmentally friendly, but it was extremely comfortable.

I knew that the comfort would be short lived because as soon as I was under anaesthetic I would be flipped onto my front so that they could operate on my spine. Unless, of course, the neurosurgeon was planning to operate from underneath the table, which seemed highly unlikely. These poor people were going to get a sight of my hairy arse for the next four hours.

'So, who are your books published by?' the anaesthetist asked.

'I actually published them myself.'

'Oh,' he said, and I could tell instantly that his eyes had glazed over. He had clocked that I wasn't a 'real' author.

'What are your books about?' asked a young blond female assistant.

'Well, my first one, and probably my best one, is about a bike ride that my friend and I did, from Land's End to John O'Groats. We set off...'

'I'm just going to put this over your mouth,' said the anaesthetist, slipping an oxygen mask over my face as I was mid-sentence.

Not wanting to be deterred, I continued.

'...fwom Land's End wiv nuffing bwut a pwair of bwoxer shorts...'

'And relax,' he said. 'Just breathe nice and slowly.'

'...we had no mwoney.... no.... cwoves.... and.... no....'

Gone.

A week later (*SPOILER ALERT* I survived the operation) I was followed on Twitter by a lady whose bio mentioned that she was from Plymouth and was an anaesthetist's assistant. I clicked on her profile and scrolled through her recent tweets. The previous day, she had posted two that caught my eye. The first said:

A patient in surgery last week was a writer. I bought one of his books and I've laughed and cried in the first two chptrs.

And then, ever the professional, and adhering to her strict patient confidentiality rules, she posted:

I wish I could tell you the name, but I can't. It's really really good though.

It was one of the proudest moments of my life. I had sold a book to someone as I was being anaesthetised.

Waking from a general anaesthetic is a strange experience. You don't dream whilst anaesthetised. At least, I didn't. The only other time I have had a general anaesthetic was for a ruptured appendix when I was 13. I remember waking from surgery and asking the nurse if something had gone wrong because I was awake so soon. There is no sense of time passing, but on this occasion when I woke I knew I had had the surgery. Something felt different.

'I can wiggle my toes,' I shouted as a smiling nurse leaned over me.

'Hello,' she said. 'You're in the recovery room. How do you feel?'

'Great thanks. I'm alive!'

'You certainly are. I will tell the neurosurgeon that you are awake.'

'How did it all go?' I asked her.

'Very well, as far as I know. Mr H will be along shortly.'

I drifted off to sleep again, and a short while later I could make out the form of Mr H standing over me.

'No, no, please don't sit up,' he said, as I reached to try and shake his hand. 'You're going to need to stay lying down for a while, I'm afraid.'

'Is there something wrong? Did something happen during the surgery?'

'No, it all went to plan. I got the whole tumour out, and you shouldn't have any lasting nerve damage.'

'That's amazing news. Thank you so much.'

'It turns out it was a myxopapillary ependymoma, which means it was actually growing in the spinal cord. It is what I had originally diagnosed, but I was overruled by the radiologist after your last scan.'

'Ok, is that why I have to stay on my back?'

'That's right. You will need to stay horizontal for about 72 hours to ensure the incision is fully healed. If you sit up then it will increase the pressure of spinal fluid at the bottom of your spinal cord and you run the risk of leaking fluid. If that happens then we would probably have to operate again.'

'I'm happy to lie here for as long as it takes. Thank you so much for everything. You don't know how grateful I am. It feels so good to be alive.'

'You're welcome. I'll come and see you on the ward in a few days. The staff there will take great care of you.'

'Thanks again.'

After a while, they moved me down the corridor and into a ward. As we entered, I caught sight of Rachel sitting in the waiting room.

'Hello,' she squealed. 'How are you?'

'I'm alive!' I said. 'You're alive too. Hooray.'

I was wheeled into a room full of elderly men, most of whom were fast asleep in their beds.

'Room 7 is now free. Mr Johnson was discharged this morning,' called an older nurse.

'That's good timing. It looks like it's your lucky day,' said the porter, who turned my bed around, wheeled me out of the room, and pushed me further down the corridor. 'You've got yourself your own room.'

'Wow, thanks. I am lucky.'

'It's so good to see you,' said Rachel, leaning over and giving me a kiss. 'I've been so worried.'

'It's great to see you, too.'

'How do you feel?'

'I feel pretty good. How do I look?'

'You look... good.'

'Why did you pause?'

'Did I?'

'Yes, do I look awful?'

'No, you look fine.'

'What?'

'It's just that your face looks… a bit... well... massive. Is that normal?'

'Here we go again. I've just come out of a major operation and you're telling me I am biggishly built.'

'You're not biggishly built. It's just your face looks a bit... weird. And massive.'

'I have a massive weird face?' I laughed. 'Thanks a lot.'

'Well, yes. A bit. Sorry.'

'I think it's normal. They did warn me that I might look a bit puffy for a while. It's because I had to lie on my front for four hours with my head through one of those holes. I'm sure it will settle down soon. Anyway, how are you? How was Plymouth?'

28

'Plymouth was fine thanks,' she said, changing the subject suspiciously quickly. 'I'm so pleased the operation was such a great success. So Mr H said that he got the entire tumour out?'

'Yes, it sounds that way.'

'That's amazing. I've been so worried about it all.'

'Me too.'

She gripped her hand tightly on mine.

'What happens if you need to go to the toilet?' she then said.

'I've got a catheter, I think.'

'What happens if you need to... you know... do a poo?'

'I don't know. I guess I'll worry about that when it happens.'

Rachel stayed with me for most of the afternoon. My parents were looking after Layla, Leo and Kitty, and we both agreed that there was no point in them coming to visit me while I was in hospital. Unable to sit up, and attached to various tubes and bags, I didn't look in the best shape. The operation had been a great success, and I would make a full recovery, but to them I would have appeared ill and vulnerable. It would be better for them to see me when I was back on my feet.

3

My first thoughts of taking part in an Ironman entered my head during those first few hours on the ward. I was lying on my back, unable to sit up, yet I knew that things were going to be ok. I was going to make a full recovery, and if I put my mind to it, I could come back stronger and fitter than I had ever been before. It didn't matter that I was in a hospital bed. This was all part of the required recovery. It was just a minor phase that I would have to endure on the road to where I wanted to be.

I wanted to set myself some form of physical challenge. I had been sedate and inactive for so long and I had a lot of catching up to do. Whether I completed my challenge or not didn't matter. But I needed to have that goal. Without it, I knew that I ran the risk of sitting around and feeling sorry for myself, constantly aware that my back was not as strong as it once was. It would take a while for the muscles to heal, but structurally, my back hadn't altered, so there was no reason that it couldn't be as strong as it once was. In fact there was no reason that it couldn't be stronger.

I considered a long distance bike ride. But there would not have been any way for me to judge my improvement, since cycling had caused me the least amount of pain before the surgery.

I considered a long distance run, but I really hate running. And I knew that running puts a great deal of strain on the back and would be one of the last things I could do during my recuperation. Training for a long distance run would be a little complicated if I wasn't allowed to actually run during the training.

So I decided on a triathlon. Once the seed had been planted in my mind to attempt a triathlon, there was only ever one type of triathlon that I considered. An IRONMAN. The Daddy of all triathlons. Any distance of triathlon after back surgery would have been a challenge, but I wanted to aim high.

There was something about the Ironman. It's an event I had heard of long before I actually knew what it entailed. It carries with it an air of mystique. It was a thing for crazy people – super humans that aren't like you and me. I knew that it involved swimming, cycling and running, and over a stupidly long way, and whatever the specific distances of this mysterious Ironman, I always thought of it as something way beyond anything that I could ever achieve.

The idea of the first Ironman triathlon was conceived one evening in 1977 during the awards ceremony for the Oahu Perimeter Relay in Hawaii. Members of both the Mid-Pacific Road Runners and the Waikiki Swim Club were present and they started up their regular argument about who was fitter – runners or swimmers? A U.S. Navy Commander named John Collins added cyclists to the debate, after reading an article in Sports Illustrated magazine that claimed Belgian cyclist Eddy Merckx had recorded the highest 'oxygen uptake' of any athlete ever tested.

Commander Collins had taken part in a few triathlons in California so suggested that they settle the debate once and for all with an extreme distance triathlon. They would combine three established endurance races on the Hawaiian island of Oahu: the Waikiki Roughwater Swim (2.4 mi./3.86 km), the Around-Oahu Bike Race (115 mi./185.07 km – previously raced over two-days) and the Honolulu Marathon (26.219 mi./42.195 km). By shaving three miles off the bike route, they were able to make it start at the swim exit and end at the traditional start of the marathon. The first person to cross the finish line would be known as the Iron Man.

On February 18th the following year, 15 men lined up for the start of the very first Ironman. Commander Collins gave each competitor three pieces of paper with a few basic rules and a description of the course. On the final page, he had handwritten the line:

'Swim 2.4 miles, bike 112 miles, run 26.2 miles- BRAG FOR THE REST OF YOUR LIFE.'

This is now a registered trademark under the Ironman brand. 12 of the 15 completed the race; the winner, Gordon Haller – a US Navy Communications Specialist – finishing in a time of 11 hours and 46 minutes. Collins crossed the line after 17 hours, establishing the now mandatory 17 hour cut-off time.

The race steadily increased in popularity over the next few years, but it wasn't until television footage of Julie Moss taking part in the Ironman of 1982 was shown around the world that Ironman became a globally recognised event. Julie Moss was an American college student who took part in the 1982 Ironman as part of her research for her thesis on exercise physiology. She was leading the race, but, suffering from severe dehydration and fatigue, she collapsed just yards from the finish line. Whilst lying on the floor she was overtaken by Kathleen McCartney who claimed the women's title. But Julie Moss carried on fighting and heroically crawled the final few yards to the finish line. The following year's race sold out instantly and the prestige of the Ironman was established.

(Throughout this book I will refer to Ironman and Ironmen, and never Ironwoman or Ironwomen. Ironman events are open to both sexes, and all those who complete it – regardless of their sex – are referred to as an Ironman. It is not a sexist term. It is just a title, and I am yet to meet a female Ironman who would rather be known as Ironwoman.)

I remember hearing the Ironman distances for the first time a couple of years ago. The concept of swimming and cycling any distance before running was unfathomable, but when I heard that the swim was 2.4 miles, in open water, and the bike ride was 112 miles, with a marathon just to cap it off, I honestly could not get my head around it. Not once did I think *'I'd love to do that'*, not once did I think it would be something I would ever even aspire to. I just asked myself, *'why?'* Why would anyone want to put themselves through something like that? And there I was, lying on a hospital bed, incredibly excited about the prospect of putting myself through something like that. Why? Because I needed to.

It had to be an Ironman, and it had to be this year. I could have applied for something in a year or 18 months time, but that would have given me too much time. I understood that training for an Ironman would require a lot of sacrifices and determination. I was prepared to do that for a few months, but I didn't want to spend a year or more obsessing about something that I might not even be able to complete. It had to be this year.

For the first few hours of being in hospital I thought, *'This is ace.'* I had food delivered to my bed, free WiFi, on-demand drugs, and I didn't even have to get out of bed to take a leak. I even enjoyed the novelty of sucking tea through the spout of a plastic beaker.

But the feeling didn't last. That first night I didn't sleep at all. Nurses came in regularly to check my blood pressure and temperature, to look for symptoms of a spinal fluid leak. To minimise the risk of deep vein thrombosis, I was told to try and alternate my sleeping position regularly. I was allowed to lie on my side, providing I stayed horizontal. My back was fairly comfortable providing I didn't move, but rolling from one position to the other was agony, and each time I felt pain I was convinced that I was opening up the wound and causing a fluid leak.

I longed for morning and eventually they switched the corridor lights on and the ward came to life. Everything felt a bit better in the daytime.

The following day I was in good spirits and ambitiously ordered steak pasty, mash and beans for lunch, forgetting that I couldn't sit up. Eating beans whilst lying down is quite a challenge, and its one that I failed at miserably. I didn't learn my lesson and ordered meatballs and peas for dinner. I kept finding peas in my bed for the remainder of my stay in hospital.

There was a change of shifts midway through the afternoon and a new nurse arrived.

'How are you feeling?' she asked.

'I'm ok thanks. It's a bit uncomfortable lying flat all the time, though.'

'I can sort that out for you,' she said, taking the hand control for the electric bed and pressing a button. The bed began to rise up at the head and the legs lowered.

'What are you doing?' I said with panic rising in my voice. 'I need to stay flat.'

'It's ok, your body will still be straight. But your head will be higher than your feet.'

'NO!' I shouted. 'Please, put me back as I was. I have to be horizontal.'

'Your body will be horizontal,' she said, as the bed continued to rise.

'It needs to horizontal to the floor. If I'm tilted up then the pressure of the spinal fluid could cause a leak in my spinal cord.'

'Oh, I've never heard of that before,' she said. 'Sorry, I don't usually work on this ward.'

She moved the bed back to how it was and I breathed a sigh of relief, hoping she hadn't done me any harm.

'Have you had to go to the toilet yet?' asked Rachel, later that day.

'No. I still don't know what happens when I do need to go. I'm going to try and hold it until I get home.'

'But that might be four days.'

'I don't care. It sounds like too much of an ordeal.'

My second night in hospital was one of the worst I have ever known. Sleep deprivation had started to mess with my mind, and I became quite delusional. Every time I closed my eyes I could see flashing lights and it was impossible to escape them. I started to sense a feeling of water in my ears, like you get after swimming, and when I put a finger in my ear I was certain it was coming out wet. I was convinced I had a spinal fluid leak. Your spinal cord runs all the way up into your brain, so it seemed plausible that if my cord had leaked at the bottom, the fluid could have somehow drained down my spinal canal and was exiting via my ears.

It was 2am and I pressed the call button. The nurse was in my room within seconds.

'How can I help, dear?'

'There's water coming out my ear,' I said. 'I think I've got a spinal fluid leak.'

'Ok, I will go and speak to the doctor who is on duty. She's in with another patient at the moment.'

'Please hurry.'

She returned a few minutes later.

'Is she on her way?' I asked.

'I've spoken to the doctor and she said it's not possible for the fluid to be leaking out of your ear. She said it is most likely just perspiration and that you should try to get some sleep. She will call in to see you when she gets a chance.'

On assessing me an hour later, the doctor decided I was probably suffering an adverse side effect of the morphine. That, combined with the lack of sleep, was causing the hallucinations and anxiety. She agreed to stop the morphine immediately.

I managed a few hours sleep and felt significantly better the following morning. Coming off the morphine had made me feel a lot more human.

'Is everything ok?' I asked Rachel when she came to visit in the afternoon.

'Yes, fine. Why?'

'You look a bit pre-occupied. Is something the matter?'

'No. Everything is fine,' she said in the way that meant everything was not fine.

'Tell me what it is. I can tell something is up.'

'It's nothing.'

'Tell me.'

'I can't. You'll be really angry with me.'

'Why would I be angry? What is it?'

'Nothing. I wasn't going to tell you until you were out of hospital.'

'Tell me what?'

'Do you promise you won't hate me?'

'Of course I won't hate you. What is it?'

'Well, I... er... I sort of crashed the car a bit.'

'You crashed the car? Are you ok? Are the children ok?'

'Everyone is fine. The children weren't even there. There weren't even any other cars involved.'

'What happened?'

'It was just after you went into surgery. I was really upset and scared about the whole thing. I got into the car in the multi-storey car park and then reversed into this big concrete pillar. It left quite a big dent in the back of the car. I'm really sorry.'

'Don't be silly. It doesn't matter. At least nobody was hurt.'

'I really am sorry. As soon as it happened I suddenly realised why you had kept telling me to drive carefully.'

'That's ok. I knew you would be a bit emotional. I'm just glad you're ok. It's only a car.'

'Well, there is another thing.'

'What?'

'Our other car is kind of broken too. The power steering stopped working and it's going to cost over £400 to fix it. And the boiler doesn't work. And the cat's gone missing.'

All of these things would have felt quite important on a normal day. But things felt different in hospital.

'I'll be home soon. It will all be fine, I promise.'

I was feeling so positive about life that I confidently ordered chicken pie with peas, sweet corn AND GRAVY for dinner. Needless to say, almost all of it ended up around my neck.

I started Googling different Ironmans. I learned for the first time that Ironman is a brand name. It is a registered trademark of the World Triathlon Federation. There are many other 'iron-distance' triathlons around the world. These are exactly the same as an Ironman in almost every way. They are every bit as long, every bit a tough, and every bit as an accomplishment to finish. The only difference being you haven't technically completed an 'Ironman', so therefore you can't call yourself an Ironman. People of course do, and, in my opinion, have every right to do so. So why was I only interested in an official Ironman event? I don't consider myself a materialistic person, and I usually shun brand names in favour of cheaper equivalents. The truth was that I had become suckered in by the marketing buzz. Ironman had cast a spell over me. I wanted the official medal. I wanted the official t-shirt, and I wanted someone to shout those six magical words that would potentially change my life: 'GEORGE MAHOOD, YOU ARE AN IRONMAN!'

My Ironman credentials didn't look particularly promising.

I couldn't swim front crawl/freestyle. My stroke of choice since learning to swim had always been a slow and steady breaststroke. If I really pushed myself I could probably manage a single 25 metre length of crawl, but nothing more.

I can ride a bike. Not particularly fast, or for any great distance, but I know which way to turn the pedals, and I don't need stabilisers. I have never ridden a proper road bike, though, and I have never worn Lycra.

I am a reluctant runner. I ran the London Marathon in 2009 and, despite hating it, decided to try and run one marathon a year for as long as I could. I kept this up for five years – my finishing times getting steadily worse over the years – but my annual marathon challenge came to a premature end due to my back problems, and 2014 ended without a marathon medal.

The UK currently hosts two official full Ironman events each year. One takes place in Bolton in the middle of July. The other takes place in Tenby in Wales in the middle of September. It was already the middle of April, so July was far too soon. It didn't allow enough time for me to even recover fully from the surgery, let alone get fit enough to attempt an Ironman. The middle of September, on the other hand, was perfect. Five months should allow me enough time to build up my fitness and stand a realistic chance of at least getting to the start line. Plus, having been on a family holiday to Tenby a couple of years ago, I knew what a stunning location it would be. So it was decided. IRONMAN WALES, BABY!

Only it wasn't to be. Ironman Wales was already full. In fact, the event was so popular that it had sold out last year within hours of places going on sale.

So had Ironman UK in Bolton. The lure of Ironman is so great that people are happy to add to their suffering by travelling all the way to Bolton.

I put down my phone and resigned myself to the fact I would have to consider a non-branded 'iron-distance' triathlon instead. Nobody else would care, so why should I? Signing up for something when I was still unable to get out of bed was probably a bad idea anyway. I would wait until I got home before deciding on an event to enter. Plus, the hospital's WiFi was particularly shit.

The physiotherapist arrived on the morning of the fourth day.

'So we're going to try and get you moving today,' she said.

I had been looking forward to this moment from the second I woke up after surgery. All of the pain and frustration from the previous year was over, and this was the true start of my recovery.

'I want you to sit up gradually, and then just sit with your legs hanging over the side of the bed for a few minutes. You are probably going to feel very light-headed because you have been lying down for so long.'

'Ok.'

'So, whenever you're ready, try and get yourself into a sitting position.'

I raised myself onto my elbows and the pain shot through my back. I then grabbed hold of the bar on the bed and slowly pulled myself up into a sitting position. The pain was excruciating. You don't realise how much you actually use your back muscles until you've had a scalpel cut through them.

I kept holding tight to the bed as I tried to steady myself. I felt faint and the room span uncontrollably around me.

'Ok, just take a few minutes, and when you're ready, try to stand up. You can use the chair to support you.'

As I tried to haul myself up, the pain in my back was too much. Perhaps coming off the morphine was a bad idea. I slumped back down on the bed.

'That's ok, take your time,' she said.

I tried again. Again, the moment I tensed my back to try and get off the bed, the pain in my back caused my muscles to spasm and I could feel my entire body contracting. I felt thoroughly defeated. This had been the moment when I was going to turn the corner and start making progress towards a full recovery. Only I couldn't even get off the bed.

I had expected it to be painful, but I didn't think it was going to be this bad. All I wanted to do was lie back down on the bed and cry.

'You can do it,' said the physiotherapist. 'The pain won't be nearly as bad once you are on your feet.'

'I'm worried about opening up the wound,' I said.

'You won't do it any damage. The muscles are all tightly sutured together inside.'

I decided that I was going to get to my feet this time, however painful. I just reminded myself that this was as bad as it was going to be. It was only going to get easier from now on.

I leaned forward, grabbed the back of the chair and went for it. As soon as my feet hit the ground, I transferred the weight from my back onto my legs and pushed myself upright using my thigh muscles. The pain instantly subsided.

'Well done,' she said. 'How does that feel?'

'Amazing,' I said.

'Great. Do you want to try walking down the corridor?'

'Let's do it.'

I waddled slowly towards the door. She held my arm lightly in case I stumbled, but I felt pretty good. Once out in the corridor I had to grip her arm briefly because I felt extremely dizzy. Being in the same small room for four days, my eyes had not been required to focus on anything further than two metres away. Now, on a long, brightly lit corridor, they were taking a moment to adapt.

I felt a little unsteady on my feet, but my legs felt great; lighter than they had done in months.

I beamed at everyone I passed like a child taking their first ever steps. We reached the reception desk at the far end – a distance of about 30 metres – and I expected to turn around and walk back to my room.

'How do you feel about trying the stairs?' she said.

'Ha ha,' I laughed. Only she wasn't smiling. 'Are you serious?'

'Sure, why not? You're looking good.'

'Well, I didn't think I would be going upstairs for several days.'

'It's entirely up to you. I would walk right behind you and there's a handrail the whole way. It won't do you any harm.'

'Ok then. Let's give it a go.'

'Great, that's the spirit. I'll just go and ask another member of staff to come along too.'

The three of us exited the ward and turned left where the staircase stretched up like the Matterhorn in front of me. Only minutes earlier I had been unable to get off the bed.

It felt incredible to be on my feet. My legs felt fresh and full of energy and I wanted to jog up the stairs. I made it to the top without a problem and then came cautiously back down.

'That was brilliant,' she said. 'Well done.'

'Thanks. I never thought I would enjoy climbing stairs so much. Can we go again?'

'I think that's enough for today. We'll walk back to your room now.'

'Am I allowed to get out of bed and walk about on my own?'

'Yes, of course, providing you don't overdo it. Your body has been through a lot in the last few days and it's going to take several weeks for it to get back to normal.'

I returned to my room and sat in the chair for five minutes, but then I was up again and did another lap of the ward. I sat down, had a cup of tea, did some reading and then did another lap. My final night in hospital was actually quite enjoyable. The mealtimes were so much better (and far less messy) once I was able to sit in the chair, and drinking tea out of a mug had never tasted so good.

I had been told that Mr H was coming to visit me in the afternoon and would, in all likelihood, allow me to be discharged the following morning. 9pm came and went and there had been no visit. At 9.40pm, as the ward nurses were doing their final rounds of the evening, in walked Mr H and two of his neurosurgery team, still wearing their green scrubs and surgical hats.

'Sorry I'm late,' he said. 'We've only just finished in theatre.'

In that moment I had an understanding of the demands of a neurosurgeon in a busy city hospital. He had been in theatre since 7am, carrying out life-saving operations, and was still doing ward rounds at 9.40pm.

He asked me a few questions about my pain, described again in brief detail about the procedure he had done and then said:

'In a few weeks, you won't even know we've been in there,' before firing two imaginary finger guns at me and blowing the smoke away. He then left the ward through a cloud of smoke like a Wild West gunslinger, his two assistants by his side. That might not have all actually happened, but because of my respect and admiration towards Mr H, it is certainly how it felt.

On the morning of the fifth day I was allowed to go home. Rachel had to work so my Mum and Kitty came to pick me up from hospital. It was amazing to see Kitty and she gripped my hand tightly as we made the long walk from the ward to the car park.

'I missed you, Daddy,' she said as I climbed into the car.

'I missed you too. What did you miss most about me?'

'The same thing we always miss about you, silly.'

'Remind me, what is that?'

'Mummy doesn't know how to work Netflix, remember?'

'Ah, yes, of course. Well I'll get that sorted as soon as we get home.'

'Daddy's home!' shouted Layla, when my mum returned from picking her and Leo up from school later that day.

'Can you go on the trampoline now?' asked Leo.

'It's great to see you both. I've missed you all so much,' I said, squeezing them both tightly.

'Well? Can you go on the trampoline now?' asked Leo again.

'Not yet I'm afraid. My back is better but it will take a few weeks for it to heal after my operation.'

'A few WEEKS? Ohhhh. That's SO long.'

'How many weeks do you think, Daddy?' asked Layla.

'I don't really know. We'll have to see how it all goes.'

'Will you be able to go on the trampoline on my birthday?'

'How many weeks away is that?'

'Ten and a bit.'

'Yes, I think I should be ready by then.'

'Promise?'

'Promise.'

4

'What can I get you?' asked Rachel, once the children had gone to bed.

'I would love a beer.'

'Are you allowed to drink while on medication?'

'I don't know. They didn't say anything.'

I had been prescribed codeine just before being discharged and had taken some in the morning before leaving hospital but had not yet had my evening dose. I read the small print. *'Side effects of drinking alcohol while taking this medication may include: drowsiness, dizziness, light-headedness, difficulty concentrating, and impairment in thinking and judgment, low blood pressure, respiratory distress, fainting, coma, or even DEATH.'*

Most of them didn't seem too bad, but a coma or death seemed like a bit of a severe price to pay. I couldn't risk it. So I made the sensible decision. I did the right thing. I stopped taking the codeine and opted for a beer instead. It would help numb the pain anyway.

That first night I was home I managed to get myself onto the sofa and lie down across the three seats. Once in position I felt fairly comfortable and I lay there for several hours in absolute bliss. I was so happy to be home, alive and on the road to recovery. The cat had returned, I had fixed the boiler (I turned it off and turned it back on again) and the dent in the back of the car was not as bad as Rachel had made out. We did have to pay the £400 to get the power steering fixed, but things were certainly looking up.

And then I tried to get off the sofa.

I dropped my legs over the side and managed to haul myself up into a sitting position easily enough. But I couldn't stand up. The seat of the sofa was so soft and sagging that my bum was significantly lower than my knees. It was not possible to transfer any weight to my thighs to get them to do the work. All of the pressure and movement had to go through my back, and that wasn't possible.

Rachel then tried to help me up. She put her arms under mine and tried to lift me into a standing position, but again my back was strained too much – this time from above – because my knees were too high to be able to support my weight.

She let go and I slumped back into the depths of the sofa. She then burst out laughing at me.

'What's so funny?' I said, trying to stifle my own laughter.

'Sorry, it's just you. Look at you.'

'I can't get off the sofa.'

We tried again, but again my back and legs could not coordinate for me to get into a standing position. Again I flopped back down into the sofa.

This time I couldn't control my own laughter and began snorting like I hadn't done for months. It turns out that laughing requires considerable use of your back muscles. The more I laughed, the more it hurt, but, sadistically, the more it hurt the more I couldn't stop laughing. My laughter then reached the stage where I had a minor coughing fit, which then exacerbated the pain even more, which in turn moved the laughter up a notch.

Rachel stood there, tears rolling down her face, and I lay slumped on the sofa with tears of pain rolling down mine. It was good to be home.

'I think I'll just have to bring you a duvet down and you can sleep here,' she said, once she had caught her breath.

'But I'm bursting for a wee.'

'I can get you a bottle.'

'No. I'm determined to get off this bloody sofa.'

At this stage, I hadn't told Rachel I was considering signing up for an Ironman. Based on my current situation, I don't think she would have held out much hope.

'Hold on, I've got an idea,' I announced.

I lay down on the sofa on my back, then slowly rolled over and dropped off the edge. I had planned to make this a controlled fall, but it didn't quite go to plan and the impact caused considerable pain as I face planted into the carpet. A moment later, whilst lying on my side, I brought my knees up alongside me, and then managed to push myself into a kneeling position, before getting myself into a standing position relying solely on my legs.

'Hooray, you did it, well done,' said Rachel, giving me a hug.

'Arghh, not too tight,' I said.

'Sorry, I forgot.'

After conquering the sofa, my thoughts turned once again to the Ironman. An Ironman seemed like the next logical step after the sofa. I looked around for other iron-distance triathlons. There were plenty in the UK, but most were scheduled during the summer months. I had my heart set on September or even October.

Out of curiosity I clicked onto the Ironman website again so see where else in Europe Ironman branded events were held. There were plenty all over Europe, but, as with both of the UK Ironmans, they had sold out months ago. And then I spotted Ironman Vichy. Vichy is a city in the Auvergne region of central France. Ironman's other French event in Nice is extremely popular so I assumed that Vichy would be oversubscribed too. I clicked on the *Register* button and to my surprise there were still spaces available. A little further research showed that Vichy had been an iron-distance triathlon operated under another brand called Challenge for the previous few years. Earlier in the year, Ironman had bought the rights to Challenge Vichy and this would be its first year under the Ironman brand. Because the rights were only recently acquired, most people had already planned their race season, which was why there were still spaces available.

The swim took place in the freshwater of Lake Allier, meaning I would not have to contend with waves, sharks or jellyfish. The bike leg consisted of two 56 miles laps through the relatively flat French countryside, with a few climbs. The run was four laps of the lake, with virtually no elevation gain. On paper, it almost looked like the perfect Ironman course.

There were a couple of disadvantages, however. Firstly, it was in France. I love France, but it wasn't somewhere I could just nip to for an Ironman, unlike Tenby or Bolton. It would be a lot more costly and time-consuming.

The second reason against it was that Ironman Vichy was scheduled to take place in August. The 30th August, to be exact, but August nevertheless. I thought that September would be fairly ambitious to get fit for, so surely August was completely unrealistic.

I considered the possibility of combining it with a family holiday. We had often talked about going camping in France, and had never been for a family holiday abroad. This could be the perfect opportunity. Being in France for the final week of the school holidays made Ironman Vichy a far more attractive proposition. It would take quite a lot of work to convince Rachel that an Ironman was a sensible idea, but tying it in with the incentive of a family holiday might be just what was needed. If my training didn't go to plan, and I was unable to get fit enough to even attempt the Ironman, at least we could still enjoy a nice week's camping in France. It would leave me a little over four months to get from a post-op hobbler, who took nearly half an hour to get off a sofa, to an Ironman. Could it be done?

April 18th

I had been home four days when Rachel and I were woken in the night by a loud squeaking noise from the bathroom.

Our young cat, Moomin, had been going through a phase of catching lots of mice and bringing them upstairs to leave outside our bedroom door as presents for us. So thoughtful.

'What is that noise?' asked Rachel.

'The cat's probably just got a mouse. Let's just leave it. It will probably be too late to save it.'

The noise gradually got louder and more frequent. Whatever the cat had caught was putting up a brave fight and it was not going to concede defeat easily.

'That doesn't sound like a mouse. Can mice make a noise that loud?' asked Rachel.

'I don't know. Just go back to sleep.'

Another burst of shrieking followed, and, with that, Rachel sprang out of bed, opened the bedroom door and went to investigate.

'Oh My God!' she screamed.

'What is it?'

'Whatever it is, it's huge,' she said, returning to the bedroom and shutting the door behind her.

'How big? What was it?'

'I don't know. I didn't turn the light on, but it was big – almost as big as the cat – and it ran behind the door.'

'A mouse as big as a cat? Was it a rat?'

'I don't know. Maybe. Go and check. Please.'

'Really? Can't we let the cat sort it out and deal with it in the morning?'

'No. I won't be able to sleep when I know it's in there.'

'Fine,' I sighed, rolling onto my side, sliding my legs off the edge of the bed and then slowly propping myself up. It was a technique that I was beginning to master.

I staggered into the bathroom, flicked on the light, and peered cautiously behind the door. There, squashed into the gap between the door and the wall was a rabbit. It was a young one, but still a decent size.

'It's a rabbit,' I called to Rachel. 'It's alive and looks ok.'

'Poor thing. How are you going to get rid of it?'

'How am I going to get rid of? I can't do anything. I'm not allowed to bend or lift.'

'Well there's no way I can go anywhere near it. You know how freaked out I get by things like that.'

'It's just a bunny.'

'I know but what if it hops or bites, or both? I'm not doing it. You'll have to.'

'I'm not allowed.'

'What does it say in your post-surgery booklet?'

'About catching rabbits in the middle of the night? Funnily enough that wasn't mentioned.'

'But what would doctors suggest?'

'I doubt it's anything that a patient has ever asked. *Ok, doc, so I have to wait four weeks before I can go on a bicycle, ten weeks before I go running, but how long before I can catch a rabbit with my bare hands?*'

'You know what I mean. I mean that sort of domestic chore. It says you can do things like cleaning after a while, doesn't it?'

'It's hardly a domestic chore. Hanging out some washing is a bit different to catching a rabbit. You'll have to do it, I'm afraid. Just put a towel over it and then carry it outside.'

'I can't do it. Sorry.'

'Are you really going to make me do this?'

'Yes. Sorry. I really can't.'

So there I was, less than a week after returning home from spinal surgery, standing in the bathroom in a pair of boxer shorts, clutching a towel with two hands, trying to catch a rabbit. I locked both cats downstairs, knelt down and edged closer to the rabbit. It hopped and thrashed frantically as I reached for it, but once I placed the towel over it, it calmed down.

'Have you got it?' asked Rachel from the other side of the door.

'Yes.'

'Well done. What are you going to do with it now?'

'I don't know. I can't get up. Can you help me please?'

Putting a hand under each of my arms, Rachel helped hoist me into a standing position and I took the rabbit into the garden, out of the gate and into the neighbours' garden. The neighbours were away, or at least I hoped they were. It was 2am and the sight of a partially dressed man in their garden in the middle of the night with a rabbit wrapped in a towel would have been a little disconcerting. I placed the rabbit under a bush and it looked up at me in surprise, surveyed its surroundings, realised it was free, and then hopped off into the undergrowth.

I limped back up to bed.

'I'm very proud of you,' said Rachel. 'Look how far you've come in a week.'

'What do you mean?'

'Well, this time last week you couldn't even walk, let alone catch a rabbit. You are making great progress.'

April 19th

Over the following days I gradually built up my walking distance. After a wet and miserable winter, my recuperation had coincided with the best spell of weather we had had all year. It was wonderful to be outside enjoying the fresh air and appreciating the countryside at a slow, leisurely pace. Lambs in the fields, flowers blossoming in the hedgerow, and the first swallow I had seen of the year, swooping low over my head before coming to rest on the telephone wire. These were all things I wouldn't normally have paid much attention to, but I had developed a new appreciation for the world around me.

Each time I set off from the front door I would go a little bit further than the time before. Once back home I would be eager to head out the door again, but I was determined to recover properly and not to do things too quickly. I made sure to sit down and relax for a few hours, read a book or watch some daytime TV before heading off for another short walk.

'Can I come too?' asked Layla, as I was heading out the door.

'Yes, you can if you want. It will be quite boring, though. I'm not actually going anywhere. Just walking down the road and then back again.'

'That's fine. I want to come.'

It was another beautiful day; one of the warmest of the year so far. I don't think I had been for a walk with just Layla since she was a toddler. It was a lovely experience to spend time alone with just her, and it made my daily walk far more enjoyable. That was until she started covering me from head to toe in stickyweed or goose-grass or Galium aparine or cleavers, clivers, catchweed, grip grass, or robin-run-the-hedge, velcro weed, sticky willy (yes, really), sticky willow or whatever you want to call it.

We walked about 1.5 miles to a nearby creek, following a quiet country road, and then turned around and walked back. It was tempting to go a bit further but three miles was my longest walk by far.

We passed a friend of Rachel's who was out on her final training run before the London Marathon. I had not seen her since my surgery. Layla had momentarily popped into a field to replenish her stash of stickyweed.

'Hi George. You're looking... er...' she said, looking at me aghast. I was standing on my own on a country road covered from head to toe in stickyweed. 'How are you feeling?'

'I feel great. Yeah, really good thanks.'

'That's good. Did the operation go well?' she said, in a way that implied *'did something happen to your BRAIN?'*

'The neurosurgeon said it couldn't have gone better.'

At this point Layla reappeared from the field and plastered another arm full of the stuff onto my back. A wave of relief swept over Emma's face as she realised that I hadn't lost the plot completely.

'Ah, that's great to hear. Hi Layla. Well, it's really good to see you both. Say hello to Rachel for me.'

'Will do. Good luck in the marathon next week.'

April 20th

The following morning I walked a little further. This time I covered a 4.5 mile loop that took me round and into town and then home. There was a slight discomfort in my back, but it was manageable, and I could feel the walking getting easier the more I did it.

I passed a man walking the opposite way to me. He was in his seventies with a big grey beard and a baseball cap perched on his head. A pair of binoculars hung around his neck.

'Beautiful day,' he said.

'Gorgeous,' I said.

'I've just seen the first swallow of the spring,' he said. 'It's perched on a telephone wire just up the road. You might still catch it if you hurry.'

'That's nice. I saw my first one a couple of days ago,' I said.

'No, they only arrived back today.'

'Well, I definitely saw one a couple of days ago. And another one yesterday. Although it might have been the same one, I guess.'

'Perhaps it was a swift,' he said. 'I've been along here everyday and that's the first I've seen.'

'Well, I've been along here every day, too, and I can assure you that...' and then I stopped as I clocked the look of pride and mild disappointment on his face. 'Actually, come to think of it. It might have been a swift. I'm not too good with birds.'

'Yes, I thought so. It's an easy mistake to make. Anyway, it was nice to meet you.'

'Nice to meet you, too,' I said, and he strode off up the road, hands clutching tightly to his binoculars.

'Good walk?' asked Rachel, when I returned home.

'Yes thanks. I nearly got into a fight with a 70 year old birdwatcher.'

'What about?'

'Swallows.'

'You've changed.'

April 21st

I was still unable to drive, so on the days on which Rachel was working, my mum would come over to help with the school drop off. I would go with her in the car, walk the children in to school and then walk home to get some exercise.

'How are you feeling?' asked one of Rachel's friends at the school gate.

'Pretty good thanks.'

'And how about your other problem?'

'What other problem?'

'Rachel mentioned that you were a little... constipated?'

This was an understatement. I hadn't been to the toilet since before my surgery. Twelve days ago. My body had fought so hard against going to the toilet whilst in hospital, that it now seemed to be on permanent strike.

'Did she now? That was good of her.'

'It just came up in conversation. So, any progress?'

'No. Nothing to report,' I said, skulking off in embarrassment.

On the way home I caught up with another friend of Rachel's who had just dropped her kids off at school, too.

'Have you had any success with your other matter?'

'Has Rachel been chatting to you too?'

'Well, it got mentioned in a conversation, yes.'

'How many of you were in this conversation?'

'Not many. Only a group of six or seven of us.'

'That's great,' I laughed. 'Well, it's lovely to have so much interest in my bowel movements. There are no updates, I'm afraid. I'm sure Rachel will let you all know as soon as anything happens. Look out for an announcement in the school newsletter.'

'It just sort of came up in conversation at pickup the other day,' said Rachel, when I questioned her later that evening why all the parents seemed to know about my bowel movements, or lack of.

'How does something like that just come up in conversation?'

'Someone asked me what happened if you needed to go to the toilet when you were in hospital. I said you hadn't had to worry about that yet. And then it just sort of continued from there.'

'Thanks. Were you discussing my catheter too?'

'No, of course not. Well, only briefly.'

The following day, things finally started to happen. After almost two weeks of waiting, I had some action. Rachel soon circulated the news, and at school pickup the following morning I saw a couple of knowing smiles from the other mums directed my way, as they mouthed the words *'well done'*.

A week later I was able to drive for the first time since surgery. I drove the kids to school and had no problems at all on the way there. On the way home, I met another car on a narrow lane. An old lady sat behind the wheel and she looked at me, completely emotionless, showing no intention of being the one to reverse back into a passing space.

I knew there was a passing space a little way back up the road behind me, so technically it was my responsibility to be the one to reverse. I am used to turning my head when I reverse as I find I can get a much better gauge of the road behind me, rather than relying solely on mirrors. I went to turn my head to look over my left shoulder but the pain was too much, and I had been advised not to do any twisting for the first few weeks. I wanted to wind down my window and shout to the old lady that I had recently had back surgery, but I don't think she would have heard me, and she looked like the sort of person who, had she been able to hear me, would not have cared in the slightest.

Instead I inched back slowly using the mirrors. Each time I glanced forward, the old lady had edged up to my front bumper. After an excruciatingly long time, I pulled back into the passing space, and I rolled down my window to apologise and to tell her about my surgery, in an attempt to make her feel bad, but she sped past and just glared at me muttering something under her breath. Damn granny racers.

5

I had been out of hospital for two weeks when I woke up with a pain in my chest. It didn't concern me too much to begin with as I was feeling otherwise great. But it didn't go away and when I woke up the following morning the pain had got worse. I knew it was foolish of me to ignore something that could potentially be very serious. I Googled *'chest pain'* and was directed to an NHS online questionnaire called *'Are you about to die?'* or something like that.

I answered the questions truthfully, expecting it to tell me to have a cup of tea and to go to bed and that my symptoms would be better in the morning. Instead, I clicked *submit,* and large writing on the screen read *CALL AN AMBULANCE NOW!!*

I still didn't feel cause for concern, but phoned my GP surgery, and the doctor phoned back ten minutes later.

'I think you'd better come down and see me,' he said.

I was in his office ten minutes later, being checked over and then strapped to an ECG machine. Everything appeared fine, but there was still the possibility that – because of being in a hospital bed for four days – I might be at risk of suffering a pulmonary embolism, when blood flow to the lungs is blocked by a clot in an artery. He did a blood test to check my d-dimer levels. D-dimer is a substance detected within the blood if a blood clot is present. He warned me that people often have a high d-dimer count after surgery, so if the test came back stating such, then it didn't necessarily mean there was cause of concern.

The blood samples were taken by motorbike courier from the surgery that afternoon and processed the same day. The results showed that I did have a high d-dimer count so was required to go to the hospital in Plymouth the following day for further tests, to rule out a pulmonary embolism. My GP also asked me to drive to see him again that evening, just as the surgery was shutting up for the day, so that he could give me an injection of the anticoagulant drug *heparin*, to minimise the risk of any potential clot causing damage in the meantime.

The following day I was back at Derriford Hospital having a series of tests. First up was an X-ray to rule out any lung abnormalities. I then had to be injected with some radioactive agent and have a VQ scan that uses the radioactive material to compare blood flow and air flow from the lungs.

'Did you run the Cornish Marathon a couple of years ago?' asked the nuclear medicine technologist.

'Yes, how did you....' I started, before realising I was wearing a Cornish Marathon 2013 hoodie. 'Oh yes. Did you do it too?'

'Yes, I did it last year as well.'

'I couldn't do it because I had problems with my back. What colour was the hoodie? I only entered it for the hoodie.'

'It was white,' she said. 'It was a bit gross.'

'I'm glad I missed that one. Are you doing it in November this year too?'

'Yes, probably. I assume you won't be running?' she said, adjusting the scanner slightly.

'I'm hoping to. But I've got an Ironman to get through before then.'

She just laughed and didn't take me seriously.

I didn't try to push it any further, because at this stage I found it difficult to believe myself.

After a couple of hours back on the ward a doctor approached my bed.

'Mr Mahood,' she said, 'please follow me.'

She led me down the hallway and into an empty office.

'Please, take a seat.'

There was an anxious pause while she flicked through a file that sat on her lap.

She looked at me with a very concerned expression.

'We've got your results back,' she said.

'Ok. What's the verdict?'

'It's not good news I'm afraid...' she said, looking at me with doleful eyes. '... it's GREAT news! The tests were all clear. You're free to go home.'

She didn't give me the results EXACTLY like that, but it really wasn't far off. The long, drawn out nature of her delivery, her deadpan expression and the awkward pauses made it feel like I was a contestant about to be booted off the X Factor.

'That's brilliant. Thanks very much. I'm sorry for wasting everyone's time.'

'Not at all, Mr Mahood. Just take it easy. Try not to overdo your recovery.'

I reduced my walking distances over the next couple of days and when I needed to use the car I took the longer routes, avoiding narrow lanes as much as possible, so that I wouldn't have to do too much reversing. Thankfully I had no more encounters with that evil granny racer.

'I'm thinking of entering an event that I have to train for,' I said to Rachel as we drove to the theatre in Plymouth (I know, get us!).

'That's a really good idea,' she said. 'It's good to have something to aim for.'

'That's what I thought.'

'What are you thinking of doing? A 10k or something?'

'I was thinking of entering an Ironman.'

'Very funny,' she said, looking over at me in the passenger seat and realising that I wasn't laughing. 'You're serious, aren't you? An Ironman?'

'Yes, why not? I might not finish it but it's something to aim for.'

'When is it?'

'The end of August.'

'August this year?'

'Yes. I've found one in France. I thought we could all go over there for a camping holiday, like we keep talking about.'

'An Ironman! Are you serious?' she said, shaking her head. 'You've just had a tumour removed from your spinal cord and you want to enter an Ironman?'

'I know, but I'm making good progress.'

'You had to go and get checked out for a pulmonary embolism a couple of days ago.'

'Yes, that's true, but I was fine. I won't overdo it. I promise to stick to the physiotherapist's guidelines.'

'What does an Ironman involve anyway?'

'Just a bit of swimming, cycling and running. Nothing major.'

'I know what it is, but how far to you have to swim, cycle and run?'

'2.4 mile swim. 112 mile bike ride. Then a full marathon.'

She didn't say anything. Instead she just sat there with her eyes fixed firmly on the road ahead and slowly shook her head.

'Well, what do you think?' I asked.

She continued to shake her head, and a glimmer of a smile spread across her face.

'I think you are completely crazy,' she said. 'But I think it's a brilliant idea. You should go for it.'

Later that evening, I entered my details into an online form, made a huge dent in my bank account, and signed up for Ironman Vichy.

The first rule of training for an Ironman, or any endurance event for that matter, is to have a training plan. A training plan allows you to map out your goals in advance and see how your fitness is going to progress over the coming weeks. A training plan is usually put together by an expert in the field; someone who has been through it all many times before and knows how the body adapts and changes, allowing plenty of recovery time to ensure that the body reaches its peak condition just before race day.

A training plan shows commitment and dedication. A training plan is arguably the most important element in training for an Ironman.

It was also the first of many rules that I decided to ignore completely.

If you search for Ironman training plans on the internet, most are set out over at least six months. Many are upwards of a year. I had four months, and for two of those I wouldn't even be allowed to run.

Also, because I wasn't in the best physical state when I entered the Ironman, I genuinely didn't know how my training and fitness would progress over the weeks. I couldn't swim front crawl, I had never ridden a proper road bike, and I wasn't allowed to run for a couple of months, and once I could, I had no idea how my back would cope after the surgery. Setting a training plan would only prove to be disheartening. Missing a day, failing to make the targeted distance, or slipping way behind schedule would just be demoralising for me.

Instead I drew up a simple training plan in my head. It was short, adaptable, yet set out my goals clearly.

Learn to swim front crawl.
Get fit enough to cycle 112 miles.
Hope I have enough left to run/walk a marathon.

As many people had told me, when it comes to triathlons, it's all about the bike. Often at least half of the entire total race time is spent on the bike. The difference between a good and a bad Ironman swim time might be half an hour at most. The difference between a good and a bad bike section can be as much as four hours.

But I didn't necessarily want to get very fast at cycling. Speed was not going to be my priority. My priority, and main intention, was to get fit enough at cycling so that I could cycle 112 miles without it completely destroying me. I knew that my run training was going to be seriously neglected, so the only way to help my chances would be to allow enough left in the tank to attempt to get round the marathon course.

I liked my training plan. It had realistic, achievable goals, and it allowed for plenty of setbacks and gaps in training along the way. If I missed a few weeks here and there, there would be no blob on my training plan. If I cycled 100 miles one week and then only 5 the next, then so be it. And if I achieved everything on my training plan, then I would be an Ironman.

Ironman races have a strict cut-off time of 17 hours. Anyone completing the distance in anything over this time is marked down as *DNF* (did not finish) on the race results, and they don't get a medal. It sounds harsh, but if Ironman events were made too easy, then they would lose some of their charm. A cut-off time needs to be in place otherwise there would be nothing to stop people completing the distance over several days.

As well as the 17 hour overall cut-off, there are separate cut-off times imposed on the different legs. 2 hours and 20 minute for the swim and 10.5 hours for the swim plus the bike. There are even more specific cut-off times for various points on both the bike and the run, but I won't bore you with those here. 17 hours didn't sound like a huge amount of time to complete three gruelling disciplines, but when I broke it down it became a little more manageable.

If I allowed 2 hours for the swim (which was potentially achievable, providing I could learn how to swim), then 8.5 hours for the bike (which didn't sound too bad, providing I could learn how to cycle over a long distance at a faster average speed than I'd ever cycled before), that would leave me 6.5 hours to run/walk a marathon (which would maybe be enough time, providing I survived both the swim and bike, and providing that my legs still functioned and I had enough energy to keep myself moving).

I had never been much of a swimmer. My breaststroke had always been ok, but my front crawl was non-existent. Layla, aged 7, could swim four lengths of front crawl in the pool without stopping. I could manage one at a push. In order to stand any chance of completing the Ironman swim, I needed to learn front crawl. Breaststroke is not only too slow, but it is too reliant on the legs, wearing them out before the long cycle and run.

My recollections of learning to swim as a child are not particularly fond. One of my strongest memories is of the fear of the purple cloud in the water if I ever released even the slightest bit of urine into the pool. I spent most of my childhood swimming lessons trying desperately to hold in any remote feeling that I might need a wee.

'What happens if anyone gets caught weeing in the pool?' I remember asking an older kid.

'I don't know, but I promise you you'll never see them at this pool again.'

Years later when I found out it was an urban myth and that the purple cloud didn't actually exist, I still had my suspicions. Even now, as an adult, I still have a slight panic of the purple cloud. Not that I make a habit of weeing in swimming pools, you understand.

But my main overriding memory of swimming as a child is just that I was rubbish at it. Matters weren't helped by my sister – 18 months my junior – being a very talented swimmer.

It took me a long time to progress from Stroke Development 1 (the bottom group) to Stroke Development 2, by which point my sister had progressed through all of the Stroke Development stages (they went up to Stroke Development 4) and then moved into Dolphins. By the time I reached Stroke Development 3 – another two years later – my sister had gone from Dolphins to Seals, to Piranhas, and was now in Orcas. Each time she moved group, she seemed to move to a different pool in the county, which was somehow deeper and longer than the one before. I had every single one of my swimming lessons in the same pool. It was a pool where the 'deep end' came up to my waist. I was there for so many years that I'm surprised I didn't get my own locker.

After several years, I eventually moved to Stroke Development 4, by which time my sister had moved from Orcas to Barracudas, to Stingrays, to Sharks-With-Frickin-Laser-Beams-Attached-To-Their-Heads, and was swimming four times a week, including lessons before school.

I was the oldest in my group by several years, but I tried not to let it deter me. I kept plodding on regardless. Perhaps that's where I was going wrong. That's the disadvantage of a pool that was waist deep.

It's a contentious issue with my family about what happened next. I maintain, vehemently, that I eventually moved up to Dolphins. After years of frustration and effort, I had clawed my way out of the Stroke Development chasm, and had moved into the lofty heights of Dolphins; a group at a pool with a slightly deeper deep end. A pool that took more than five strokes to reach the other end. A group with different coloured swim caps. Even if it was a group of children all still several years younger than me.

My parents and sister all claim this never happened. They still mock me to this day, and claim that my swimming education ended in Stroke Development 4. Admittedly, I never actually attended a single Dolphins lesson. Once I had been promoted, I felt like my work was done. I hated swimming, and felt like I had earned the right to quit.

I decided to stick to land based activities from then on, so started tennis lessons instead; a sport which became even more humiliating than swimming once I started getting routinely beaten by 9 year old girls at the age of 15.

If only my Stroke Development 4 coach could see me now! Ok, so I hadn't improved since those days, and, if anything, I had regressed considerably. But I had entered an Ironman, goddammit.

I phoned my sister for a chat.

'Mum told me you've entered an Ironman. Is that for real?' she said.

'Yes, well, I've entered. I don't know if I'll actually do it though. It's something to aim for.'

'Cool. What are the distances?'

'A 2.4 mile open water swim, 112 mile bike ride, then a full marathon.'

'Oh my god, that sounds crazy. A 2.4 mile SWIM? Aren't you in Stroke Development 4 still?'

'Oh shut up. I got to Dolphins!'

'Yeah, yeah, whatever.'

'I did!'

'Anyway, I'm very impressed. I think it's a great challenge. I spoke to Mum earlier.'

'Oh. What did she say? Is she worried about me?'

'What do you think? Of course she is. I don't think she's slept much since you told her. She's worried you're going to really hurt yourself training.'

Later that day I had an email from my dad.

Hi Dord (Dord is the name I used to call myself as a child when I couldn't pronounce 'George'. My family still call me it. Or they use the extended Dordie Wardie, for some strange reason).

I was thinking about your Ironman, and wondered if you knew that it was possible to do a half-ironman too? It might perhaps be a more sensible option as a stepping stone before doing the full distance? I've pasted a couple of links below to some half-distance ones that I found.

Love,
Dad

I replied.

Hi Dad,

Thanks for the links. I've already paid my entry fee. I'm assuming Mum asked you to email me? Tell her I promise I'll be sensible.

Love
DW

6

The doctor had told me that I could start swimming once my surgical wound had healed, and now, three weeks post-surgery, the external butterfly stitches had all peeled off and the site of the surgery looked nice and neat.

I assumed that a lane session at the local pool on a weekday during term time would be almost empty. I was wrong, and a quick scan of the swimmers suggested that I was the youngest swimmer by some way. Each of the lanes was marked according to speed: *Slow, Medium, Medium Fast, Fast*. I instantly ruled out the *Fast* lane, but decided that I would probably be an adequate fit for the *Medium Fast* lane. *My front crawl can't be THAT bad*, I thought, as I watched middle-aged men swim slowly up and down. I knew my arms moved a lot quicker than theirs, so assumed it meant I was faster. I lowered myself into the pool, and pushed off from the side, my arms flailing frantically as I tried to pull myself through the water.

I am a sinker. There are slabs of concrete that have more buoyancy than me, and my main focus was just to stay afloat. As I reached for the wall at the end of the first length, I noticed the man who had been swimming midway down the pool towards me when I set off was now inches from my feet.

'Do you mind if I go?' he asked, as I panted, still holding onto the side.

'No, please do. I've just had back surgery,' I said, trying to justify my swimming inadequacies. The truth was that my back felt absolutely fine. It was the rest of my body, mostly my lungs, which were in agony.

I switched to the *Medium* lane, which was occupied by two middle-aged women. One was swimming backstroke and the other was swimming with a float using just her legs. It was embarrassing for me to admit, but they looked to be more my standard.

Only they were also too quick for me. Due to my inability to complete more than one length without stopping, each time I paused for breath, I was caught up by either the backstroke lady or the float lady, or often both, and I would have to let them pass.

I ducked my head under the lane rope and moved reluctantly into the *Slow* lane which was occupied by one lone man. He was in his 70s, and seemed to be using swimming as a form of rehabilitation as he inched his way forwards, his legs dragging motionless beneath him. I began swimming and by the end of my second length I had overtaken him. I paused for a quick breather and set off before he got to me. By the end of my third length I was so exhausted that by the time I had got my breath back, the man had completed his length, and because he wasn't pausing between lengths, I had to let him through. This pattern continued for ten minutes. Although I could complete a length in the time it took him to swim half a length, because of my lack of stamina and technique, we had completed the same amount of lengths in the same amount of time.

I climbed out of the pool and walked ashamedly to the changing rooms. 2.4 miles was a seemingly impossible distance for me to ever be able to swim. My family were right. I was never good enough to be a Dolphin. I was still very much in Stroke Development.

A couple of weeks later I was allowed to begin cycling. I have always secretly wanted to be a cyclist. I love riding bikes, but have never made the transition from someone that uses their bike occasionally, to someone who actively goes for bike rides.

It was almost nine years ago that a friend and I cycled from Land's End to John O'Groats. We completed the trip on completely inadequate bikes, spreading out the mileage over almost three weeks (the world record is 41 hours), and using every available second of daylight to cover our meagre daily distances.

I planned to keep up the cycling afterwards, but the bicycle rarely became more than an environmentally friendly method for me to nip to the shops to buy milk. In the years since our end-to-end trip, I have been for bike rides of further than ten miles on about half a dozen occasions. I am also slightly intimidated by 'proper' cyclists, with their elite-looking road bikes, their complicated-looking cycle computers... and their Lycra. I have never even sat on a proper road bike, let alone owned one, and I wasn't yet ready to become a MAMIL (middle aged man in Lycra).

I do love bikes, though and have owned several during my life. Each made its mark in its own special way:

Banger Bike

The first bike I ever owned as a child was a maroon coloured piece of crap we affectionately referred to as Banger Bike. It was a bullet proof little machine with tyres made from solid rubber; the benefit being that they never punctured. The disadvantage being that it was too heavy for a three year old to even lift. It was also incredibly uncomfortable to ride. Every stone or groove in the ground would send tremors up through the bike's frame, shaking the rider to the bone. My sister learned to ride on Banger Bike too, and as many other bikes came and went over the years, trusty Banger Bike remained.

The Dirt Burner

The Dirt Burner was my first proper big boy's bike. It was a hand-me-down from a friend. Made by an American company called Iron Horse, the Dirt Burner was the coolest bike ever manufactured. That's how it felt at the time, and looking at pictures of it now, I believe it still holds that accolade. The name alone oozed cool. Who wouldn't want a BMX that could burn dirt? But its coolness didn't end with the name. Everything about this bike was amazing. For a start, it was bright red and yellow. It had yellow plastic tyre rims, yellow saddle and red tyres. Yes, red TYRES. Every other bike in town had traditional black tyres. The Dirt Burner really was revolutionary.

The Raleigh Grifter

I eventually outgrew the Dirt Burner, and when an advert appeared in the village newsletter for a Raleigh Grifter, we were knocking on the door of the neighbour's house that same morning. The Raleigh Grifter was the younger (much better, in my opinion) brother of the Chopper. It was a beast of a bike, dark blue, with fat tyres and a saddle that was twice the width of anything I had ridden before.

It was the first bike that I ever owned with gears. But the Grifter wasn't like its counterparts. It had a special twist-grip gear system, which felt ground-breaking at the time. I used to make the sound of a motorbike whenever I twisted the handlebar grip, and if you cleverly folded the front mud guard under itself, the plastic would rub against the front tyre as you cycled along, making the experience even more authentic. When combined with the gigantic seat and the chunky frame, the Grifter did feel more like a motorbike than a bike.

The Raleigh mountain bike

For years I wanted a racing bike like my dad's.

'But you don't do any races,' said Dad.

'Nor do you.'

'That's different.'

'Why?'

'Because it is.'

I eventually went off the idea of a racing bike and decided I wanted a mountain bike instead.

'But there aren't any mountains in Northamptonshire,' said Dad.

I eventually got my first mountain bike as a teenager. It was bought second hand but looked almost new, and its unblemished shiny white paint gleamed. It had 18 gears which completely blew my mind. The bike was so pristine and shiny that I was reluctant to ever get it dirty, lifting it over puddles and avoiding any mud.

I then went off to University and spent a year travelling and was without a bike for four years.

The Cycle King mountain bike

After Rachel and I first moved in together, in downtown Northampton, I thought that a bike would be useful to get in and out of town. I bought a brand new shiny mountain bike from Cycle King at the end of our road. It was a cheap and cheerful bike, with no suspension, but I had no plans to cycle down any actual mountains (there are no mountains in Northamptonshire, as my dad has rightly said) and it served its purpose. It was the only bike I had ever owned from new. It lasted 6 months.

I cycled to the pub to watch a Champions League football match one evening, and chained my bike to the fence outside. When I returned to it later that night, the chain lay broken on the ground, and the bike had gone.

I phoned our home insurance the following day. The excess I would have to pay was £100. The bike had cost me £99.99. I didn't make a claim.

The Dawes Street Motion

When a family friend sadly died in 2005, his wife offered me his old bike. It was a huge hybrid called a Dawes Street Motion. It was way too big for me, and was at least 15 years old when I received it, but it seemed indestructible and it remains my bike to this day. I took it to be serviced a couple of years ago, and the man replaced a few parts, made a few adjustments, but told me not to spend any more money on the bike in the future. It had almost reached the end of its life.

The Falcon

When my friend Ben and I set off on our Land's End to John O'Groats adventure we didn't have bikes, but acquired a few different steeds during our 1000 mile journey. The Falcon was a 5-speed junior racing bike that we were given by a legend of a man named Roger Badcock in a small village in deepest darkest Cornwall. I became slightly obsessed with the bike and stubbornly rode it all the way to Scotland. I still can't bear to part with it, and it sits gathering dust in the shed.

I do take it out for a spin very occasionally, and I used it for my first and only ever triathlon – the short 'sprint distance' Roade (that's the name of the village, not a misspelling of the surface) triathlon in Northamptonshire in 2012. The bike caused lots of taunts from marshals and spectators, but it got me round the course.

The Street Motion and The Falcon were the only two bikes I owned, and neither of them was suitable for completing an Ironman. The Ironman rules strictly state that the bike must be 'roadworthy', so that instantly ruled them both out. Neither was fast nor reliable enough to give me a chance of completing the course inside the required time. For the Ironman, I would need to ride a road bike.

The roads around where we live in Devon are not really suitable for road bikes. Lots of steep country lanes caked in mud and gravel from tractors, makes braking with slick tyres a liability. I also planned to tackle The Dartmoor Way during my training. The Dartmoor Way is a cycle route mostly on roads and cycle paths, but there are a few sections along rocky paths and bridleways that require something a bit sturdier than a road bike.

A hybrid bike, like my trusty Dawes Street Motion, would have been the obvious choice for a bike to train on, but it would not allow me any practice at using drop handlebars. The seating position of a road bike is very different to a hybrid, too, and I needed to get used to spending many hours in that position.

Following a suggestion from a friend, I decided on a cyclocross bike. Cyclocross is a sport which has gained in popularity over recent years. It involves racing around a muddy circuit on a bike as quickly as possible. Many of the sections are so steep, or have obstacles, that riders are forced to dismount their bikes and then sling them over their shoulders while they run, before mounting again once they are able to.

I had no intention of taking part in any cyclocross races, but the style of bike suited my needs perfectly. A cyclocross bike – or CX bike – has drop handlebars and looks like a road bike, but with fatter tyres, and a chunkier frame.

The man in the bike shop told me that the one I had chosen was good because it had a particularly stiff frame. I didn't know what this meant, but I was relieved because I didn't like the sound of buying a bendy bike.

I made a promise to myself that I was going to look after this bike, but also, I was not going to make the same mistake that I did with my white Raleigh mountain bike. This bad boy would not be side-stepping any mud or puddles.

7

'How was your day? What have you been up to?' asked Rachel.

'This and that. I've watched a lot of swimming videos on the internet.'

'Were they useful?'

'I'm not sure yet. I haven't tried out what I learned.'

'What did you learn?'

'I've learned that I've been swimming front crawl completely wrong all these years.'

'I thought you couldn't swim front crawl?'

'I can't. But I thought I at least knew HOW to swim it. It turns out I don't.'

'So what have you been doing wrong?'

'Everything. Kicking too hard, paddling too fast, breathing too often or not often enough. I've pretty much got to start from scratch.'

'You mean go back to Stroke Development 1?'

'Very funny.'

'Maybe they taught proper front crawl when people moved up to Dolphins?'

'I DID get to Dolphins, alright. I just didn't go to any of the lessons.'

'If you say so,' she laughed. Rachel has always sided with my parents and sister and refused to acknowledge that I ever progressed beyond Stroke Development 4.

'I'll show you. And all of you doubters.'

'I'm not doubting you at all. I'm only joking. I'm sure you'll master it. Just please don't drown trying.'

Layla was performing with her school choir at an outdoor concert about 15 miles from our house. I thought it would be a good opportunity to go for my first ride on my new bike. It had been six weeks since my surgery and I was told that I could ride my bike after five.

It was great to be out on the bike, and after a little pain getting onto my trusty new steed, I felt fairly comfortable once seated. A 30 mile round trip was, in hindsight, way too ambitious for a first bike ride, but having driven the route many times, I thought it was a relatively flat loop. Hills never seem too problematic in a car, though, and I reached the concert just before it started, feeling like I had just circumnavigated the globe.

Rachel had driven there and I would have gladly thrown my bike in the back of the car and gone home with her, but she had to leave two minutes into Layla's school's first song in order to get back in time to collect Kitty from pre-school. I felt a duty to stick it out until the end, which meant I would be cycling home.

The ride home took me a long time, and I arrived back feeling thoroughly miserable. My neck hurt from the unfamiliar riding position, my back ached, but most frustrating of all was how tired and generally unfit I felt. I had cycled as quickly as I could, and maintained what I thought was a decent speed, but checking my stats proved otherwise. I had averaged a little over 10mph for the 30 miles. In order to complete the 112 mile bike leg of the Ironman inside the cut-off, I needed to be averaging 14mph at the absolute minimum, over nearly four times the distance, and with a difficult swim before it, and a difficult run after. I had a very long way to go.

8

For Christmas, I bought Rachel a place in the Edinburgh Marathon as a surprise. Since taking up running 18 months previously she had completed a 10k and a couple of half marathons. Each time I suggested that she enter a marathon she just laughed and said there was no way she could ever complete a marathon. I knew she could. A friend of hers whom she ran with regularly – the one who saw me covered in stickyweed – had a place in the London Marathon in April, so Rachel was going to be doing all the training anyway. She might as well have the satisfaction of a medal at the end of it.

So I bought her a place. This was back in early December and I signed me up too, optimistically hoping that I might have surgery in January or February and miraculously recover in time for the marathon on May 31st. That didn't happen, but I was excited about a child-free weekend in Edinburgh anyway, and was looking forward to it even more knowing that I didn't have to run a marathon.

Rachel was initially shocked by her 'present' but gradually warmed to the idea, and by the time May came around she was more than ready. I was about seven weeks post-surgery and had been riding a bike for a week, so thought it would be a good idea for me to incorporate some cycle training into my spectator duties.

The Edinburgh Marathon course is not very spectator friendly. It starts conveniently in the centre of Edinburgh, but then traverses the edge of the Firth of Forth, out into East Lothian and Musselburgh, with very few access points for the spectators along the way. The route then does an about turn and follows the same road back, but finishing in Musselburgh, about eight miles outside Edinburgh.

I looked for bike rental places in Edinburgh, but couldn't find any that opened early enough on the Sunday for me to pick one up before the start of the marathon. The reserved bike spaces on our train had already been pre-booked, and I didn't want to risk being turned away at the station, so I had what I thought was the genius idea of buying a fold-up bike for the weekend. I could buy a second hand one cheaply, and then sell it afterwards, hopefully recouping most of my money.

'I've been thinking about the Edinburgh Marathon,' I said to Rachel.

'You're not thinking of running it, are you?'

'No, no, of course not.'

'Good.'

'I was thinking of cycling it.'

'What do you mean? Like cycling around the course with me?'

'Well, no, not alongside you. But I mean I could use a bike to get around the course so that I could see you a few different times.'

'Hmmm,' she said, with none of the enthusiasm I had hoped.

'Why are you hmmming?'

'No reason.'

'Go on. Tell me.'

'No offence, but I'm not sure I like the idea of you popping up every few hundred metres. It wouldn't feel like I was making much progress.'

'I wouldn't 'pop up' every few hundred metres. Just every few miles or so. I've looked at the route map and I don't think there's really any other way for me to see you between the start and the finish without having a car. Even getting to the finish line will be quite tricky.'

'Ok, I suppose it's a good idea then. Are you sure you're ok to cycle?'

'I'll be fine. It can't be any tougher than the ride I did to Layla's concert.'

'You should do it then.'

'Great, because I've just bought a fold-up bike off eBay.'

I found one for £40 that was being auctioned by a charity shop via their eBay page (charity shops are so down with the kids these days). Not only was I getting a bargain bike, but I was making a generous donation to charity, too. Bonus. There was one small problem, though. The bike didn't have a saddle. Or a seat post. Still, saddles were very easy to buy and fit. Or so I thought.

After collecting the bike from Plymouth, I tried borrowing the seat posts from all other bikes that we owned, but they were either too big or too narrow. I assumed there would only be a couple of different sizes of seat post, but it turns out that seat posts are measured by the tenth of a millimetre, and there are many different sizes on the market. My fold up bike was no longer in production and spare parts had been discontinued. I contacted the manufacturer to see if they had a record of the seat post dimensions for this model. They didn't. So I tried measuring the hole with a ruler. Rulers aren't great for measuring tenths of millimetres, but I took a guess and ordered a cheap seat post and saddle on the internet. It fitted perfectly... providing I didn't put my full weight on it. If I did, then over time, no matter how tight I had screwed the bracket, the saddle would gradually sink down to the frame. And the frame of a fold up bike is a very long way from where the saddle should be. So I had to ride it in a sort of squat position, which for someone who had recently had back surgery, was not ideal. Still, I had a fold up bike!

For a portable bike, it was stupidly heavy and cumbersome. Even when folded up. In fact, for some reason, it felt like it was even bigger when it was folded than when it was assembled. At least when erected it could be wheeled around. Collapsed, it was an unwieldy, awkward, oily tangle of heavy metal and rubber. But I hoped it would at least get me around the marathon course, and it would also be allowed on the train, which were the only two reasons I bought it.

The train from Devon to Edinburgh took eight hours. To people without young children, this might seem incredibly tedious. If you have young children, you will understand that this is heaven. Eight hours of peace and quiet. I read an entire book from start to finish. The book was called *Eat and Run*, by Scott Jurek, in case you are wondering. It's a book about eating and running.

When Scott Jurek took part in the Western States Endurance Run – a brutal 100 mile run through the mountains and canyons of California – he didn't just want to complete the race, he wanted to win it. Not only win it, he wanted to set a new course record. So he wrote down all of the timing splits for the current record on the back of his hand. That was his motivation. As he passed through each timing checkpoint, he was able to assess how far off the current record he was. Jurek went on to win the Western States Endurance Run a record seven consecutive times, eventually breaking the course record on his sixth attempt. His own record stood for six more years.

'What are you writing?' I asked Rachel, who was sitting next to me on the train, scribbling numbers onto the back of her hand.

'Toilet stops on the course.'

'What do you mean?'

'I am worried about needing the toilet during the run.'

'Can't you just do a Paula Radcliffe?'

'No, I will not 'do a Paula'.'

Poor Paula Radcliffe. One of the greatest long-distance runners the world has ever seen – marathon world record holder, three time winner of the London Marathon, three time winner of the New York Marathon, and countless other medals and accolades – yet she is often remembered most famously for 'doing a Paula' during the London Marathon in 2005, when she was forced to take evasive action in the street when her bowels got the better of her.

'So what do those numbers on your hand actually mean?' I asked Rachel.

'They are the mile markers where all the portable toilets are. I am copying them down from this route map.'

The disparity between elite runners and everyday runners could not have been more apparent. On the pages of the book I was reading, a man writing down the course record splits on his hand, to my right, my wife – a marathon first-timer – writing down the toilet stops.

We arrived in Edinburgh late afternoon and walked to the small flat that we had rented for a couple of nights. I offered to take my fold up bike on a trial run and go and get us some dinner. I was under strict instructions from Rachel to not get anything too flavoursome or spicy that might cause an upset stomach and force her to 'do a Paula'.

I bought a cheese and tomato pizza and two packets of instant rice. One was Mediterranean Vegetable flavour, the other was Lemon and Coriander.

'Sorry, I don't think I can eat any of that,' said Rachel when I returned to the flat.

'Why not? This is about as simple as food gets.'

'The pizza has cheese on and I don't think that would be great to eat the night before a marathon.'

'Why not?'

'I've heard that it's not recommended to eat dairy food before a long run.'

'Really? Ok. What about the rice then?'

'That Mediterranean one has paprika listed as an ingredient.'

'And?'

'Well that's sort of a spice.'

'It's not going to be spicy though, is it? It's instant rice.'

'I don't know if I want to risk it.'

'Oh come on! You're not Mo Farah, you know.'

'I know, I'm sorry.'

'What about this one? Lemon and Coriander. There's no paprika in this one.'

'But coriander is used in spicy dishes.'

'Yes, but it's a herb. There are NO spices in it.'

'I just don't want to take any risks.'

'Risks? It's a packet of instant rice. You're hardly living on the edge.'

'Don't worry about it then. I'm not that hungry anyway.'

'You've got to eat something. What would you eat in an ideal world?'

'Probably just some plain pasta.'

'Pasta? No sauce or cheese or anything?'

'No, just pasta.'

'Ok, fine. I'll be back in about 20 minutes.'

'I'm sorry for being so annoying. I love you.'

So I made a second trip to the supermarket, this time following Rachel's exact instructions, and came home and cooked her a bowl of plain pasta. I ate the pizza and both packets of instant rice. I like to live dangerously.

As Rachel lined up on the start line the following morning I had expected to feel a pang of jealousy. This was a race I had hoped to be running too, but I didn't feel any envy whatsoever.

I was excited for her, and eager to see her completing her first ever marathon. I was also excited by the prospect of my day. Only a few weeks previously I had been unable to walk, and now I was in Edinburgh going to cycle around a marathon route on a fold-up bicycle. Life was pretty damn good.

'Don't go off too quickly,' I said. 'Try and stick to your pace, ok?'

'I'll try,' she said.

I waved her off and then went to retrieve my bike which I had propped up by a portable toilet. It was so crap looking I knew nobody would consider stealing it.

The marathon runners did a lap of the streets of Edinburgh's old town, before turning out towards the Firth of Forth. I headed off along Leith Walk down towards the docks to try to get ahead of them.

My bike had just one gear. And I soon discovered that it was one particularly shite gear. Once the bike was travelling at any sort of speed, on even the most gentle of descents, the pedalling had no effect whatsoever. Even on the flat, my legs had to spin at approximately 200 rpm in order to get any traction. I didn't care. I was having the most fun I had had in a long time.

The roads were relatively quiet as it was a Sunday morning, and I raced down the pothole ridden Leith Walk, the bike shuddering and vibrating the entire way. My back was a little sore, but I felt far more comfortable on the bike than I would have done standing or walking.

By the time I reached the water's edge by the four mile point, the lead runners had already passed through. The road was closed to traffic so I was the only spectator along this section. It was a beautiful sunny day, and the forecast stormy weather had so far avoided us.

Rachel passed me after another ten minutes, smiling and looking good, as she usually does when running. I continued onwards a couple of miles, not wanting to piss her off by popping up every few hundred metres. I had to stop frequently to raise the saddle up, as it slowly slipped down so that my knees were pedalling level with my head.

Rachel came through the halfway point far quicker than she had planned, and even quicker than her previous half marathons. She was grinning manically and waved when she saw me.

'This is such fun!' she shouted.

'Well done. You're doing really well.'

'I love it!'

'You are going quite quickly,' I said, cautiously.

'Too quickly?' she asked.

'Well, yes, probably. There's still a very long way to go.'

'But I feel really good. It's SO flat!'

'Ok then,' I said, gritting my teeth. 'See you in a bit.'

I was stopped by a marshal just after the 14 mile point.

'You can't cycle any further on the road. The leaders will be heading back on this side soon, so you won't be able to get through.'

'Oh, how can I get further up the course?' I asked.

'You'll have to head back the way you've come, about a mile or so, then follow the road up to the main road and turn left and continue that way.'

'How far is that?'

'Well it's a long old way, but there's no other way through.'

By this point, another cyclist had joined me. He was about the same age as me, but wearing a big thick coat, which seemed quite impractical for riding a bike on a nice sunny day in May.

'Are yous trying to get up there too?' he asked, in an Irish accent.

'Yes, are you watching the marathon?'

'Trying to. I want to get up to the 18 mile point where they turn around.'

'Me too. Looks like we'll have to take a bit of a detour if we want to get there. It's going to be pushing it a bit to get there in time.'

'Excuse me,' said the man to the marshal. 'Can we keep going this way if we cycle along the grass verge and not the road?'

'Err... I don't see why not. But stay off the road. You can't get in the way of the runners.'

'Good man. We'll be no bother.'

I decided to join him, as it sounded a much more sensible idea than the other option.

The grass verge was fairly flat and easy enough to cycle along. But only for the first couple of hundred metres. It then became narrower, and more uneven. My new Irish friend was on a decent mountain bike. I was on a shitty fold up bike, but I was doing my best to keep up, my body bouncing all over the place. After another mile or so, the grass verge became a steep grass bank and it was impossible for either of us to cycle along so we were forced to get off and push.

It was very slow progress, and we were caught in no-man's land. Rachel would not be passing through here for over an hour, but if we wanted to get any further up the course then we needed to hurry. We reached a caravan park with an entrance from the road we were on.

'I'm going to head up through here and hope I can get to the main road the other side,' I said.

'Mind if I tag along?'

'Sure. But don't wait for me. I'll be much slower than you.'

Despite being on a fold up bike with one gear, and a stupidly annoying self-adjusting saddle, I was able to match him for pace over the first mile. He then started to flag on his mountain bike, realising that his Arctic coat was probably a bad idea. It was cutting it fine whether I could make it to the viewing point further up the course before Rachel went past, and as much as I liked my new Irish friend, I had to say goodbye and push on ahead. He's probably still cycling around East Lothian looking for the marathon route. Don't feel too sorry for him, though; he's got a nice warm coat on.

I had to cycle an additional loop of about four miles, including a long section on a busy A-road, before descending a big hill into the village of Longniddry to rejoin the race route just after the 19 mile point. I made it just in time, as soon after discarding my bike in a bush, I saw Rachel approaching. I offered her a handful of Jelly Babies and two pieces of flapjack that I had in my rucksack. She took everything I had.

'I've been dreaming about this,' she said, not looking as cheerful as she had done earlier.

'How are you feeling?'

'I was ok until the turnaround, but the wind is awful now. It's starting to feel much tougher.'

'You're doing brilliantly. Keep it up. Not long to go now.'

The forecast bad weather had finally hit, and as I retraced my route up the big hill and along the A-road, it was a real battle to cycle into the brutal headwind. I rejoined the marathon route at about the 21 mile mark.

'Only 5 miles to go,' I said cheerily to Rachel as she ran past me moments after I arrived.

She didn't say anything and just glared at me.

'5 miles!' I said cheerily. 'That's all. You're almost there.'

She still didn't say anything.

This was the first time I had ever seen Rachel looking miserable whilst running. I decided to give her some space, so set off to cycle further up the field. The wind was so strong, my bike so crap, and my legs so tired, that it was difficult to go faster than the runners. I had an awkward few moments when I was trying frantically to get ahead, but actually cycling alongside Rachel. I eventually put some distance between us, and after a couple of miles I pulled over to wait for her to pass again.

'Just three miles to go,' I said.

She didn't even look at me this time. She had 'the rage'.

I didn't say anything else, as she clearly wasn't in the mood and I wasn't helping the situation.

In a strange, sadistic sort of way, I was secretly relieved that the marathon had broken Rachel. I could never understand her love and enjoyment of running, as it is something I have never experienced. How could she go out on a hilly 22 mile training run and come home smiling and saying what a great time she'd had? It's just not right. This was more like it. She was clearly suffering, but that's what marathons do to you.

At one point, my bike decided to fold itself in half, as I was riding it. I had pulled off the road at a vantage point by the water. The wind had really picked up and the waves were smashing against the shore. I cycled along a cobbled pathway and went to turn around a corner, but as I turned, the bike just kept on turning so that it had folded back on itself, like a malfunctioning bendy bus. I was going fairly slowly at the time, but I still fell into a crumpled heap on top of the bike. The vibration of the cobbles had undone the bolt that held it together. Fortunately, only one old lady was nearby and she just chuckled to herself and carried on walking.

Rachel's mood hadn't improved much when I saw her next with a little over a mile to go. She was still running, but obviously struggling. I tried again to boost her spirits and miserably failed. She gave me a look as though I was to blame for her suffering, which in many ways I was. I felt momentarily guilty for entering her into the event, and then remembered how horrible and painful the marathons I have run had been. I could understand what she was going through. But I also knew that whatever pain and suffering she was experiencing would instantly vanish the moment she crossed the finish line and be replaced with an immense feeling of joy and elation. All that effort would be rewarded. She just didn't know that yet.

'It will all be worth it,' I said, as I tried to cycle off.

She just grunted.

'I promise you, when you cross the line all of this will be a distant memory. You have done amazingly. You are so close.'

She grunted again.

I pedalled my crappy bike the final mile to the finishing straight, where the crowd were packed several people deep at the barriers. I stood on tiptoes and could just about make out the runners coming past and entering the final straight. Eventually I saw Rachel approaching. Her speed had increased and she had a little more spring in her step. I called out her name. She didn't look up and I don't think she would have been able to see me anyway, but there did look to be the slightest glimmer of a smile. There was the sense that she knew the misery was almost over.

When I met her a few minutes later outside the finishers' enclosure, she was a different person. Proudly wearing her medal and finishers' t-shirt and clutching her disappointingly sparse goody bag.

'I did it!' she beamed.

'I knew you would,' I said, squeezing her tightly. 'I'm so proud of you. Just think months ago you could barely run a mile. Now you're a marathon runner.'

'I'm a marathon runner!' she squealed.

'It's great to see you so happy.'

'Yeah, sorry for being so grumpy and miserable with you.'

'That's ok.'

'How do you always manage to smile when you've done races?'

'I don't know. I guess because however painful it is, I always remember that's it's all self-inflicted. I chose to put myself through it.'

'Ah, that would explain it. YOU entered me into the marathon. I didn't inflict this on myself.'

'Oh. Yeah, that's true. But are you glad I did?'

'Very,' she said, putting her arms around me. 'Thank you.'

I gave her an official Edinburgh Marathon hoodie that I had secretly ordered for her. Souvenir t-shirts are all well and good, but a hoodie is way better. Plus I was getting fed up with her stealing mine.

Far from feeling despondent that I hadn't been able to compete, I was delighted with my own achievement. I had cycled 26 miles – possibly more – on a rubbish fold up bike with one stupid gear and a self-adjusting seat post in extremely windy conditions. I didn't need a medal around my neck. I knew I was making progress.

We both limped home towards the train station, which was almost two miles from the race finish. It was a choice of this, or walk almost a mile to the bus stop and then join a queue that snaked for eternity.

Whilst Rachel was queuing in a coffee shop, I phoned some local taxi companies, and after waking up a man who I assume was the owner of a single driver taxi company, he reluctantly agreed to pick us up in five minutes.

Rachel emerged from the coffee shop clutching her coffee, and shuffling at an incredibly slow pace.

'Right, I'm ready. Let's get to that train station,' she said.

'I've booked us a taxi,' I said. 'It will be here in five minutes.'

'Oh wow! Thank you. Is this because you're feeling guilty because of what you put me through?'

'Yes, partly. But my legs are knackered too.'

We had planned to enjoy a long, fun night out in Edinburgh, taking advantage of our child free weekend, and exploring the many different bars around the city, but it proved to be too much for either of us to manage. After a huge meal of burgers, ribs and chicken wings, washed down with a couple of beers, we had an early night.

I awoke the following morning at 5am. The curtains in our flat were made of tissue paper and the early morning sun blazed through the window. There was no use trying to get back to sleep. It was morning.

I knew Rachel would be in no state to do much in the way of energetic sightseeing, so I saw it as the perfect opportunity to go and explore nearby Holyrood Park.

Holyrood Park is like a piece of the Scottish Highlands transplanted into the sprawling city of Edinburgh. It's a spectacularly rugged patchwork of hills, cliffs and lochs, with magnificent views across the whole of Edinburgh.

I was in the park by 5.30am and there was not another person in sight. The peak of Arthur's Seat loomed serenely above. Arthur's Seat – the highest point in Edinburgh – is the main peak in Holyrood Park. Some suggest it got its name because of a connection with King Arthur, while others have claimed it got its name after a variation of the name 'Archer's Seat'. The summit looked an awfully long way, but the walk took no more than half an hour, and I had the entire park to myself.

I sat on the top and looked down over the spectacular city of Edinburgh, the streets eerily quiet for a Monday morning. Any sound of the city waking up was drowned out by the ferocious wind that whipped around Arthur's Seat. The rugged beauty of Holyrood Park contrasted perfectly with the sprawling urbanisation below. Both looked magnificent in their own different way.

I recorded a quick video of me miming to The Proclaimers' *500 Miles* – it would have been rude not to – before beginning my descent. Just as I started down the path, I met an American climbing up. He had missed my singing by seconds.

'I'm suffering from jet lag, what's your excuse for being up here so early?' he asked.

'I couldn't sleep either. It looks like we picked the best time of the day to be up here,' I said.

'It's awesome. What a view!'

'Hold on tight, it's a bit windy up there.'

'Will do, thanks. Have a nice day.'

I visited the impressive ruins of St Anthony's Chapel on the way down, with its views over St Margaret's Loch. I then added a longer loop that incorporated the Salisbury Crags over the other side of Arthur's Seat, and as I neared the bottom, a number of dog walkers, runners and cyclists were starting to fill the park. I felt oddly privileged that I had been the day's first visitor.

I retrieved my bike from outside our flat and cycled to a nearby shop and bought pastries, fruit salad, and coffee, and by the time I got back to the flat, Rachel had surfaced.

Our train home wasn't until 2pm so we had several hours to explore Edinburgh. Its steep streets and Rachel's post marathon legs didn't make a great combination, but she gallantly walked up and down the Royal Mile several times, all the way up to the entrance to the castle, where we decided that all the rampart steps would be too difficult, and then down the hill and along Princes Street.

I had haggis, neeps and tatties for lunch (neeps and tatties – Scottish for turnip and potatoes, both served mashed. Haggis – strange creature with two legs longer than the other two that runs around hills in Scotland). To top off my culinary tour of Scotland, I had my very first (and last) deep fried Mars Bar. I had known about the legend of the deep fried Mars Bar since I was a child. It sounded like food heaven. A Mars Bar, covered in crispy delicious batter! What's not to love?

Well, all of it, it turns out. It was a huge disappointment, but I have since been told that I probably got a bad one.

Firstly, it wasn't crispy. The batter was pale and spongy and clung loosely to the Mars Bar like a fresh scab. Secondly, Mars Bars taste fairly sickly on their own, but when melted and covered in batter they are taken to a whole new level of indulgence. Thirdly, and most disconcerting, was that it tasted of fish. Apparently it is not traditional for the Mars Bar to be deep fried in the same fryer as the cod, but this particular establishment didn't get that memo. The smell lingered for the entire train journey home.

9

Back home my swimming had improved slightly and I began to feel like I was making a little progress. I still couldn't swim more than a couple of lengths front crawl without stopping, but my stroke felt marginally easier than it had done.

I booked myself into an adult group swimming lesson at the local swimming pool. They didn't distinguish between the standard of swimmers, and adults of all abilities were lumped together into one group.

Malcolm was a kind-faced, mild mannered man in his forties. I explained that I had come along to see if group lessons would be of any benefit to me.

'So is it all the strokes you would like to improve?' he asked.

'Just front crawl please.'

'Right, ok then. Well to start with, why don't you swim two lengths so I can take a look at you?'

I set off, acutely aware that every element of my stroke was being scrutinised. Was I going too quickly? Were my legs kicking enough? Was I rolling too far onto my side to breathe?

I reached the end of the pool and then realised I was completely out of breath. I paused for a moment, adjusting my goggles to provide justification for stopping, and then swam back down to the other end.

'On the whole it looks ok, but there are definitely a few things we can work on,' said Malcolm. 'Just do a few more lengths while I go and see to this lady.'

He rushed off to the aid of a middle-aged lady in the shallow end who seemed to be drowning. I swam a couple more lengths, throwing in a bit of breaststroke to keep myself going, and then Malcolm reappeared.

'Right, the first thing I noticed is your legs. They are just dragging behind you at the moment.'

'Yes, I'm hoping to do a triathlon, and I heard it was a good idea to save your legs for the cycling and running.'

'That's true, but if you don't use them at all then they just sink, which creates more resistance and it will only slow you down. You don't have to kick them frantically, but they need to at least be moving.'

'Ok, thanks. What else?'

'Your breathing. Make sure you've fully emptied your lungs when your face is in the water. At the moment you aren't, so that means you have to breathe out and then breathe in each time you come up for air. There isn't time to do both effectively. It's far more difficult to fill your lungs with air, if you haven't exhaled properly first. Always breathe out fully underwater.'

'Great advice, thanks.'

'I do have a few other pointers. You practice those things for a few lengths while I'll go and see to these boys.'

He then rushed around to the deep end, where two teenagers dressed in pyjamas were retrieving bricks from the bottom of the pool. Meanwhile, the middle-aged lady was splashing around frantically again in the shallow end.

'You can touch the bottom there, Debbie,' called Malcolm. 'Try not to panic. I'll be with you in a minute.'

I assumed that adult swimming lessons would be a group of adults all looking to improve their swimming. But it incorporated everyone from Debbie – the non-swimmer, to me – the improver, to teenagers learning life-saving skills, and poor old Malcolm had to look after us all.

'That was looking better,' said Malcolm, lowering himself into the water next to me. How he had had time to actually watch me whilst attending to the others I have no idea.

'It did feel a bit better,' I said. 'It still doesn't feel natural, though.'

'No. I think the main problem is that you're not swimming with your core.'

The 'core' was a word I had come to loathe over recent years. Mostly because I didn't understand what it meant. Most types of fitness these days seem to be about improving your CORE, or generating CORE STRENGTH. If you glance at the covers of any fitness magazines in a newsagent, it will almost always have the word CORE somewhere, in big bold letters. Where did this obsession with the core come from? I swear in all my years of PE at school, football training, tennis lessons, even Stroke Development, the word 'core' was never mentioned once. Nowadays it is all that is ever talked about. And, embarrassingly, I still didn't even know what it meant.

'Right. Ok,' I said. 'And how do I do that?'

'You just have to power your arms and legs using your core.'

'Right,' I nodded, not having the faintest idea what he was talking about.

'Like this,' he said, pushing off from the wall and swimming a few strokes up the pool. He did look very natural, but it was impossible to know what he was doing differently to me. Never mind his core, it looked to me like he was swimming with his arms and legs like I was. Only much better.

'You see?' he said.

'Er... yeah, I think so,' I lied.

'Ok, you give that a go. I'll be back in a bit.'

He swam off slightly frantically towards Debbie who had somehow drifted up towards the deep end and looked like she genuinely was drowning this time. Either that or she too was attempting to retrieve a brick from the bottom.

The lesson came to an end (because our half hour was up, not because Debbie drowned or anything) and Malcolm came over to speak to me.

'Sorry I didn't get a chance to spend much time with you,' he said.

'That's ok. Thanks very much for all the tips. It was really helpful.'

'To be honest, I don't know whether you would benefit much more from these group lessons. I mean, you can obviously swim. Your stroke just needs some work. You could perhaps have a think about some one-to-one lessons with me or one of the other instructors instead.'

'Yes, thanks. I will have a think about it. Private lessons are a bit expensive though.'

As I was speaking, I noticed a group of a dozen or so adults – male and female – all walking out of the changing rooms in their swimming kit.

'Is it open for public swimming now?' I asked Malcolm, thinking that I could perhaps do a few more lengths.

'No that's Simon's swimming class,' he said.

'What's that?'

'It's a sort of advanced adult swimming group, for swimmers to improve their technique and endurance.'

'That sounds good. Would I not be better suited to that?'

'Er... well... I think that it might be a bit too advanced for you. They do lots of swim sets, focussing on speed and technique.'

'Would I not be able to do that?'

'I think you might struggle a bit, to be honest. It's more a group for triathletes and endurance swimmers.'

'I've entered an Ironman,' I said.

'An Ironman? Really? Wow. When's that? Next year?'

'The end of August. This year.'

'Blimey. Ok, well maybe you should go and have chat with Simon then.'

Simon was very amused by the challenge I had set myself. It was reassuring that he didn't try and dissuade me, or suggest I was completely out of my depth. He had, however, been at the poolside during my last few lengths of Malcolm's lesson so had witnessed my swimming ability, or lack of.

'So, do you have to be a certain standard before joining this group?' I asked.

'No…' he said hesitantly. 'Not necessarily. But we do lots of drills and sets. It's fairly tough if you're not an experienced swimmer.'

He pointed at a whiteboard on the wall behind him, on which he had written a list of drills such as:

4 x 100m freestyle
4 x 100m breast
4 x 100m back
4 x 100m fly

'It is quite intensive,' he said, noticing the look of shock on my face. 'The group is full this week but you could ask at reception about next week and then come along and see how you get on.'

'Ok, great, thanks. I might just do that.'

I experienced a flashback from my childhood swimming days. This was the equivalent of me moving up to Dolphins. Did I have what it takes? Was I really ready to move up to the next level?

After getting changed I went up to the viewing gallery above the pool to watch some of Simon's class. They were all very good swimmers; seamlessly transitioning from one stroke to the next, complete with tumble turns at the end of each length, and not pausing for breath at the end of each length like me.

I would not have been able to manage the first drill. Two lengths of freestyle was my personal best. Simon wanted four. And then another four, and then another and then another. I would have still been working my way through the first set, when the others had finished their lesson. And the less said about my backstroke and butterfly the better.

I felt thoroughly demoralised. On one hand, Malcolm confirmed that I was too good to be in his adult beginners' lesson, which was some consolation. And at least I was better than Debbie. But on the other hand, I was completely inadequate for Simon's group; a group that was designed to help potential triathletes. Here I was, a few weeks away from attempting the Daddy of all triathlons, and I clearly wasn't good enough.

10

I was slowly getting used to my new bike. My neck no longer hurt when riding it and my body seemed to have adapted better to the new sitting position. The gear ratio (look at me using cycling lingo like I actually know what it means) was very different to what I was used to and required a lot more thought about the appropriate gear to use, depending on the speed and the gradient. I set myself a challenge to try and complete my shorter rides in the big front ring, meaning the tougher set of gears. It required more pushing to get up a lot of the hills, but it felt like I was working harder.

I then started reading some books about endurance sport and triathlons. The more I read, the more I understood that there are two distinct types of cyclist: mashers and spinners. Mashers grind along in a tough gear, using up energy extremely uneconomically for very little gain. Spinners pedal with a much faster cadence (revolutions of the pedals per minute), creating less resistance and requiring a far lower expenditure of energy. I realised to my shame that I was a masher. If I was to stand any chance of becoming an Ironman, I needed to become a spinner.

'Good bike ride?' asked Rachel when I returned from a quick 10 miler.

'Very good thanks. I've upped my cadence.'

'Great. What does that mean?'

'I'm trying to become a spinner, rather than a masher.'

'I still don't know what you are talking about.'

'Basically, I've been cycling wrong all this time.'

'Oh here we go again. You said that about swimming.'

'I know. And it's happened with cycling too.'

'But you're a fairly competent cyclist,' she said.

'I can ride a bike. But it turns out I've been riding it wrong.'

'Can you not ride your bike very well, Daddy?' asked Leo, who was doing some colouring at the kitchen table.

'I can, but I'm learning to ride it a bit differently.'

He looked at me with a puzzled face.

'You can use my old stabilisers, if you like,' he said. 'I don't need them any more.'

'Thanks, pal. That's very kind of you. I'll bear that in mind.'

A couple of days later, Rachel and Kitty had gone to the beach with some friends to enjoy the good weather, and I decided to incorporate a visit to see them (and a quick dip in the sea) into a bike ride.

I locked the bike to a lamppost in the car park by the beach, and then tried to retrieve my rucksack that was wedged under the back wheel. I pulled the bag free, but as I did so my hand pulled across the razor sharp teeth on the front cogs of my new bike. The oily metal teeth sliced effortlessly through the skin on the back of my right hand, leaving two inch long gashes that bled steadily across my knuckles.

I tried to stem the bleeding with my t-shirt and then made my way down onto the beach where I found Rachel and her friends sitting in the sun.

'Hello. It's nice seeing you here,' she said. 'Did you cycle here?'

'Yes. I fancied a quick swim in the sea.'

'How was your bike ride?'

'Good thanks. It's very hot though.'

'What have you done to your hand? Did you fall off your bike?' she asked in the patronising voice she sometimes uses to talk to the kids. Her friends laughed. 'Is this because of your new cycling technique?'

'No, it's nothing to do with that,' I said.

'Are you sure?' she said, and then turned to her friends and whispered 'George has apparently been cycling wrong all these years. He's trying out a new technique.'

They all laughed.

'I cut it on the chain cogs.'

'It looks nasty. Poor you. What were your hands doing down there? Did you fall off?'

'No. My rucksack was under my back wheel when I locked it up, and I caught my hand when I pulled it out.'

'Oh dear. Cycling sure is a dangerous sport.'

'I know. Luckily I was wearing a helmet.'

As I write this, five months later, I still have two very prominent scars on my right hand from my freak cycling accident. I just need to think of a better story of how they got there. Let's just keep the truth between me and you, ok?

11

During my swimming research, I found many articles and videos about a style of front crawl called Total Immersion. Total Immersion swimming is a freestyle technique created by American swimming coach Terry Laughlin. The method focuses on becoming as efficient as possible in the water, using the whole body to create a natural balance to the stroke.

It is a technique particularly popular with triathletes and endurance swimmers as it minimises energy loss. Watching Terry in action got me extremely excited (no, not like that). He made swimming look so easy and effortless. Despite the fact that he and I were both swimming the same stroke, we could not have looked more different. The principles of Total Immersion suited me perfectly, and I felt like I had found the style of stroke I wanted to replicate. All I needed to do now was learn how.

I watched all of Terry's videos on YouTube and then spent a few sessions in the pool trying out the different elements. Slowly, it felt like things were coming together. I was starting to feel like a proper swimmer. I hoped I was starting to look a bit like Terry.

12

In late 2014 I received a message from a stranger on Twitter:

'Entries open for the Dartmoor Classic today. Sold out in a day last year. Worth a look.'

I had never heard of the Dartmoor Classic. Further investigation (clicking on the link) revealed it to be a sportive. A sportive is an organised mass-participation cycling event of varying lengths and terrain. I had not taken part in a sportive before. The one and only mass-participation cycling event I had done was the London-Brighton charity ride, over 10 years previously.

It grabbed my interest from the start. If something is called a *'Classic'* then surely it must be amazing? I later found out that the event had only been going for a few years and was called a *Classic* at its inception.

Living so close to Dartmoor National Park, it seemed a good opportunity, and although I was finding any form of physical activity extremely painful at the time I received the message, I was optimistic that I would have made a full recovery by the time of the event so I clicked on the *Enter* button and paid my admission.

The Dartmoor Classic had three options: the 107 miles *Grande Route*, the 67 miles *Medio Route*, and the 35 miles *Debutante Route*. The *Debutante Route* was for females only so that ruled it out (the organisers have since scrapped this in favour of the *Piccolo Route*, open to anybody.) The *Grande Route* was too daunting for an inexperienced cyclist, so I signed up for the *Medio*. With over 6,500 feet of climbing over 67 miles, it would be far from easy.

I arrived early at the start at Newton Abbot Racecourse on June 20th, anticipating a queue for registration, but the event was incredibly well organised and I had received my number and timing chip within minutes. I was completely overwhelmed by the amount of Lycra on display. Every direction I looked, riders were fully kitted out in figure-hugging shorts and shirts of various degrees of garishness. I was wearing a souvenir t-shirt from my one and only sprint triathlon from three years ago with the logo badly peeling on the front, a pair of baggy shorts, and trainers.

I had assumed that being on Dartmoor the roads would be in varying states and therefore there would be a high proportion of people with mountain bikes and hybrids. In recent weeks, I had started to feel like a proper cyclist with my fancy new bike with drop down handlebars and tyres marginally thinner than a mountain bike, but standing there before the start of the Dartmoor Classic, I became acutely aware of what proper cyclists looked like. I felt incredibly out of my depth.

I joined my starting wave, and after a short race briefing, we were off. As all the Lycra clad cyclists clipped into their pedals on their sleek road bikes, I felt a bit of a fraud on my chunky cyclocross bike in my trainers. We left Newton Abbot Racecourse and skirted around the town of Kingsteignton at a manageable pace and I felt quite happy that I would be able to keep up with the others. I then realised that we had been following a pace car through the built up area, and after a mile or so, the car pulled over and the majority of the cyclists disappeared from view within seconds.

The road turned towards Bovey Tracey, and we began the climb up onto Dartmoor. The hill continued for 10 miles – the gradient reaching a brutal 20% in places. There was a mile long section of road on this stretch that had been assigned a *King of the Mountains* race. Any riders who signed up to the navigation tool Strava's GPS tracking could compare their time up this particular hill to that of other riders. I signed up beforehand but had no intention of actually racing.

But then I passed the *Start* sign and my competitive spirit kicked in and I couldn't resist. It was only a mile after all. How hard could it be?

I came out of my saddle and began pounding away on the pedals.

This section climbed from Beckaford to Haytor Down, ascending 313 ft in 0.9 miles. I was doing ok for the first half mile. I stayed to the right of the narrow lane, passing many struggling cyclists to my left, and only moving over when faster cyclists shouted at me to get out of their way. I felt like the King of the mountains.

And then I felt a burn in my thighs like never before. I gritted my teeth and tried to carry on regardless, but soon slumped back into my saddle, dropped into a lower gear and struggled up the remainder of the hill, as most of the slow and steady cyclists overtook me. It turns out a mile is a bloody long way when it's all uphill.

I eventually saw the *King of the Mountains Finish* sign and put in a final burst of energy before pulling over to the side of the road, dismounting my bike and lying down on the grass, my lungs burning and my body crying.

The winner of the *King of the Mountains* section would win an exclusive cycling kit, and although I knew I wasn't a contender, I hoped that I would have at least fared well against the others.

I checked my stats later in the day. 1597 people had signed up. I was ranked an abysmal 1172nd. I reminded myself that I was on a cyclocross bike, had no cycling shoes, and had only recently had back surgery. With better equipment, I think I could have potentially cracked the top 1000. I then looked at it another way. I beat 425 people up that hill. Admittedly many of those would have been more 'mature' riders, or cyclists simply not trying to bust themselves, but still.

I lay in a heap on Haytor Down and once I had got my breath back, I was able to fully appreciate the setting. I have spent a lot of time collapsed on grass verges during my lifetime, but none as picturesque as this. The climb up the hill had been shielded with high banked hedges and trees, but here, above the tree line, Dartmoor had opened up in front of us. Sheep grazed just metres away, more curious of the shiny, sweaty humans than we were of them, and the landscape – unchanged in centuries – stretched magnificently in every direction.

A long downhill stretch followed and the open moorland made the visibility of the road ahead much easier, so on some stretches it was possible to pick up lots of speed without the fear of meeting oncoming traffic. I approached a long open left hand bend on one steep descent, and could see far into the distance that it was free from vehicles. A sheep, happily grazing metres from the road, walked aimlessly from the grass to my left and then just stopped in the middle of the road, turned, and stared up at me. I didn't have time to stop before I got to it, so had to make a split-second decision whether to swerve to its right, hoping that I could nip in front of its path, or swerve behind it and hope that it didn't have a change of heart and turn back to where it had come from. I chose right, and fortunately the sheep stayed where it was. The cyclist behind me did the same, but by this point the sheep had decided to leisurely continue its journey. The rider was forced to take evasive action, swerving even further to the right and onto the grass on the roadside. He miraculously stayed upright and rejoined the road, having missed the sheep and some large rocks by inches.

The long slog up to Princetown (which roughly marked the halfway point) was relentless. The sun was out, but a fierce headwind had picked up. My back was aching and my body was completely drained. The road stretched off and up into the distance, and even the sections that levelled out required considerable effort to keep moving. The race signs didn't do much to ease the suffering.

Feed Station – 5 miles it taunted. 5 miles was nothing. I'd surely be there in 20 minutes. Twenty minutes passed and then another sign: *Feed Station – 3 miles*.

The road snaked its way behind us down the moor and, despite feeling a lack of progress, it was comforting to see how far we had come. I paused towards the top of one of the long uphill sections and decided to take a selfie with the road disappearing behind me. After putting my phone back into my pocket, I looked up and amongst a huddle of people about 10 metres further up the road sat one of the official photographers. He had his giant telephoto lens pointed straight at me.

'Oh bollocks,' I muttered.

As I went by, he kept his eye pressed to his camera's viewfinder but he had a big grin on his face.

'You didn't get a photo of me taking a selfie did you?' I asked.

'Sure did, buddy,' he said.

'Bastard.'

Sure enough, when I viewed the official photos a few days later, one is of me, paused by the side of the road, taking a selfie. You wouldn't catch Bradley Wiggins doing that.

I eventually turned the corner and savoured the brief section of downhill into Princetown. At 435 metres above sea level, Princetown is the highest settlement on Dartmoor and one of the highest in the UK. It is most famous for being the location of Dartmoor Prison. The prison was built during the Napoleonic Wars at the start of the 19th century for French prisoners of war, and later for American prisoners of war during the lesser known War of 1812 with the United States. The site was chosen due to its remote location, but despite its reputation I was relieved to hear that it is now a category C prison, housing non-violent criminals. Although dominated by the prison, the village of Princetown is very picturesque. But I only had eyes for the feed station.

All riders were required to turn off the main road into the feed station and ride over the timing mat. They could either take advantage of the food on offer, or loop straight back out onto the main course. I wasn't feeling particularly hungry but knew I needed to eat something to try and regain some energy. I lay my bike on the grass and went to see what was on offer, and perhaps force down an energy bar or something.

The organisers of the Dartmoor Classic had laid out a huge banquet. There were piles of bananas, bags of crisps, trays of sandwiches – of a variety of flavours – a weird looking vegetarian tart, chocolate brownies, cake and the legendary homity pie. I say 'legendary', but until the Dartmoor Classic, I had never heard of it.

Homity pie is an open pie, usually containing potatoes, leeks, onions and topped with cheese. It looks a little like a quiche. It is apparently a Devon speciality, and whilst the taste is fairly inoffensive, I can understand why its popularity hasn't spread outside of the county. Still, free food! I piled a plate high with all of it and sat down on the grass in the sun for at least 10 minutes.

'Not a bad way to spend a Sunday,' said the man next to me, who was lying down with his arms folded behind his head.

'Not bad at all,' I said. 'Shame we've still got another 35 miles to go.'

'I've still got over 70 to go,' he said. 'I'm doing the long route.'

'Ouch, good luck.'

'Thanks. It's not too bad though. In another 40 miles I get to come back here and have another feast.'

'That's true. If I'd known about the food on offer I would have signed up for the longer route, too.'

I had assumed that cycling into a headwind for most of the morning would mean the wind would be at our backs for the return to Newton Abbot, but it certainly didn't feel that way.

'Just one more hill to go,' said a rider as he passed me on the way into Moretonhampstead at about the 50 mile point.

'That's good news. Thanks,' I replied.

'But it's an absolute bastard,' he added.

And he was right. It was. This was the furthest I had cycled in many years, and my legs, lower back, buttocks and bollocks were really feeling the strain. I adjusted my seating position at every opportunity, sitting upright to try and stretch out my back and standing up on the pedals to ease the discomfort caused by my saddle. I had only been out of hospital nine weeks and this was proving to be a little too much too soon.

We navigated through a winding section of narrow roads, and, as we rounded one corner, shouts from the riders ahead ordered us to stop. We all skidded to a halt behind a huge group who were also stationary. Two cars had met each other on the narrow roads and, due to the number of cyclists, both were having trouble manoeuvring out of the way of the other. There was lots of chuffing from the riders around me, and anxious glances at their Garmins. I chuffed along in consolidation, but was secretly delighted to pause for a break. After another five minutes the cars eventually cleared and I reluctantly climbed back onto my saddle and continued onwards.

As the gradient eased, and we began the final stretch towards the finish at Newton Abbot Racecourse, more and more of the riders who were taking part in the 107 mile *Grandio* route overtook me. Assembled in pelotons, often more than 20 riders long, they snaked their way effortlessly through the Dartmoor countryside.

I decided to have a go at latching onto the back wheel of one such pack. Not literally, of course. As one group steamed past I began pedalling madly behind them. I was just inches away from the final rider's back wheel. *Look at me! I'm in a proper peloton!* I thought to myself. I continued to push hard and glanced down briefly at my feet, and by the time I looked up again I'd been dropped by about 10 metres. I had managed to keep up with them for approximately three seconds.

The final few miles followed main roads into Kingsteignton and then eventually for a spectacular grand stand finish at Newton Abbot Racecourse. I managed to muster a sprint finish and caught the guy in front of me just before the line. So what that he had cycled the longer 107 mile route in the same time as I'd cycled 67 miles? I kicked his sorry ass.

I completed the 67 miles in a time of 5 hours 42 minutes, which considering the conditions and the inferiority of my bike, I was delighted with. My average speed was about 12mph – far slower than would be required to make the cut-off for the Ironman, and over a significantly shorter distance, but it was definitely a step in the right direction.

I was awarded a bronze medal, which, in the world of sportives, means I finished in the third tier of finishing times. To discourage people from racing each other, riders are given a gold medal if they finish anywhere inside a certain time, a silver if they finish before another time, and a bronze if they make it inside the final cut-off time. All those riders who finish outside of this get given a big *'loser'* sticker on their forehead. Not really. There are no cut-off times in most sportives, which is what creates the fun mass-appeal.

'So you came third, Daddy?' said Layla, when I showed her my bronze medal.

'Well, not really,' I said.

'But the winner gets a gold, second place gets silver, and the third gets a bronze.'

'Yes, that's true.'

'So you came third?'

'Ok then. Yes, let's go with that. I came third.'

'Well done, Daddy.'

13

The day of Layla's birthday arrived. I was eleven weeks post surgery and I had set this as my target date to be trampoline fit. I hadn't mentioned it to Layla again, but after opening her presents before school she declared:

'Right, it's trampoline time now, Daddy.'

'Ok, I'm ready,' I said.

'Yeah! Come on, let's go.'

To me, bouncing on the trampoline that morning was a momentous occasion. Not only had I recovered well from the surgery, but I was now doing something that I couldn't physically do in the months before my operation. It certainly wasn't pain free, but it was a lot easier than it had been pre-surgery and I knew that things would only improve from this point onwards. It was also the happiest I had seen the children in a long time. I still don't understand why Rachel is exempt from being made to go on the trampoline, but to Layla, Leo and Kitty, it meant that Daddy was now properly fixed.

The second rule of training for an Ironman – or any other physical event, for that matter – is to find a training partner. Sharing the pain, frustration and elation with someone else makes it so much better. Better still, join a club. Surround yourself with like-minded people, and there will always be someone to aspire to, or even someone struggling more to help give you that much needed morale boost.

This was yet another training tip that I had to ignore. Not because I didn't want to have someone to train with, but because I would have been such an awful training partner.

Who would want an Ironman training partner who can't swim more than two lengths without stopping? Who would want an Ironman training partner who doesn't even own a road bike, yet still wants to cycle long distances at a nice leisurely pace? Who would want an Ironman training partner who can't yet do any running?

I was very much in this alone.

I knew that to get fitter and quicker at cycling I needed to have a more disciplined approach to my training. Everything I had heard and read talked about the benefits of interval training – meaning alternating the intensity of the ride with periods of high intensity and low intensity.

But I simply couldn't be bothered. I was enjoying just being out on the bike, and I was feeling fitter and quicker each time. I felt being governed by my stopwatch would strip all the fun out of my cycling.

Cycling in such a hilly county at Devon provided me with ready made interval training whichever direction I turned. It is not possible to head out for a nice easy 20 mile ride, so every time I went out on the bike I would be subjected to periods of extremely high intensity as I toiled up the hills, and periods of low intensity as I descended them. There was no need for me to involve stopwatches or power meters. I decided I had been doing my own interval training without even realising it.

14

I saw a post on Facebook advertising Total Immersion swimming lessons at a pool about 45 minutes away. I sent the lady a text and she offered me a one hour lesson the following week. I turned up at the outdoor pool, full of confidence at the progress I had been making. Having watched every YouTube video available, and spent several hours in the pool refining my stroke, I was fairly satisfied with how my Total Immersion training had been going. All it needed was some fine tuning.

'Right, well there's still obviously a lot to work on,' said the teacher, as I completed my first length while she observed from the sides.

'Is it almost there, though?' I asked.

'Well... er... no. Not really. You're still sort of doing some of it wrong. Actually, pretty much all of it wrong. But don't worry, we'll get there. Do you have your phone with you?'

'Yes, it's over there in my bag. Why?'

'Is it ok if I film you? Then you can watch it back and see how you improve as the lessons go on?'

'Yes, of course.'

Who does she think she is? I'll show her. I'm prepared to admit that my stroke does need a couple of tweaks, but it is pretty damn good. I've been practising for hours. And what does she mean by lessons? Surely one lesson will be enough to polish it off.

'Ah, I see what you mean,' I said, after watching back a video of one of my lengths, where I looked nothing like how I imagined I was swimming. 'I look a bit... shit, don't I?'

'A little. Yes.'

The next hour was one of the more humiliating of my life. Total Immersion is taught in stages. All of the different

113

elements of the stroke are taught and practised until they become second nature, and then they are gradually all combined. Despite looking like normal front crawl, most of the elements differ greatly to how front crawl is traditionally taught and so it takes a lot of work to override bad habits.

To begin with, I was asked to do the *'superman glide'* – pushing off gently from the side, with my arms relaxed and shoulder width apart, rather than with hands joined together. This was supposedly the easy bit, but I couldn't even glide in a straight line. I drifted off to one side, as though my rudder was lopsided. Actually that sounds a little dodgy. Ignore that sentence.

I then had to swim along on my side, with one arm continuously stretched out ahead of me. This was excruciatingly slow and painful for my back.

The hardest part came halfway through the lesson. One of the key elements of Total Immersion is the low and relaxed hand position during the reach stage of the stroke. Rather than having quite a high arc through the air, as traditionally taught, the finger tips are supposed to lightly skim the water as they come past your head. The idea behind it is that it promotes a relaxed arm movement, because unnecessary energy is expended by lifting your arm too high.

This all made sense to me in theory, but the training drill was too much for me. To encourage the fingers to be as close to the water as possible, the teacher asked me to bring my hand back from my waist to the reach position THROUGH THE WATER. So, after completing each paddle with the hand (the pull phase of the stroke), I then had to push my hand back through the water the way it has just come. You should try it sometime. I felt like it was the first time I had ever encountered water, let alone tried to swim in it. The two lifeguards who had been quietly chatting on the poolside had both readied themselves and were poised to throw me a lifebelt.

It honestly felt like I had never swum a length in my life. Everything that had started to feel natural over the previous few weeks had become redundant and I was a complete beginner once again. I was right back in Stroke Development 1.

'That's looking a little better,' she said, towards the end of the lesson. 'But you're not using your core.'

Oh here we go again, I thought. *Just when I thought that things couldn't possibly get any worse, she goes and mentions the damn C word.*

'Ok, how do I use my core?' I confessed.

'You just have to use your core to drive your hips down and then power your arms forwards.'

'Riiiight.'

It still didn't make any sense to me.

'Swimming is all about using your core,' she said.

So everyone keeps telling me. How can it be? I thought to myself. *Your core doesn't do anything. You can't kick it, or paddle it. It's surely the least useful part of a person's body. I can do more with my ears than I can with my core. At least I know what and where my ears are.*

'Ok, let's see if you can put all those things I've taught you together and try a couple of lengths for me,' she said, as the clock ticked towards the hour mark.

'You mean my simulated drowning?' I muttered.

'What was that?'

'I said I'd do my best.'

I swam a couple of lengths, trying my hardest to remember all the different elements we had practiced. I was halfway down the pool when I realised I hadn't breathed once.

'Sorry, I forgot to breathe,' I said, as I reached the end.

'Don't worry about breathing. We can work on that next time.'

Next time? I thought to myself.

'What made you decide to learn Total Immersion?' she asked as I climbed out of the pool.

'I've stupidly signed up to do an Ironman,' I said.

'When is that? Next year?'

'It's in five weeks.'

'Right. Ok. And how far is the swim in an Ironman. Is it a mile?'

'2.4 miles,' I said.

She didn't respond. She just stared at me, with wide eyes and a sort of sympathetic smile that said, *You're going to drown, boy.*

'I know, I know, I've got a long way to go, but I'll get there.'

'Would you like me to book you in for another lesson next week? I mean, normally it would take months to get somebody of – no offence – your ability, up to that of a long distance swimmer, but I'm sure we can improve you a bit.'

'Thank you. I'll check my diary for next week and let you know, if that's ok?'

'Of course.'

I knew full well that my diary was empty. I didn't have anything on at the moment. I didn't even own a diary. But at this point I didn't know if Total Immersion was for me. I knew that if I stuck at it for several weeks, then it probably would be of great benefit. But I didn't have several weeks. I also couldn't afford to pay for many more private lessons, and the 90 minute round trip was not ideal.

I drove home from the lesson feeling completely deflated. An hour beforehand I had felt like I was almost there. I thought I had nearly mastered swimming. But the lesson was a massive wakeup call for me, and a reminder of the brutal fact that I was far from ready.

'How did your lesson go?' asked Rachel, as I walked in the door.

'Terrible,' I said, throwing my goggles onto the side. 'It turns out I'm even worse at swimming than I thought.'

'I'm sure you're not. Are you going to have any more lessons?'

'No, I think I've left it a bit late for that. I'm going to watch some more YouTube videos instead.'

'YouTube videos? How is that going to help?'

'Videos of swimming lessons.'

'Oh, I thought you meant cats playing the piano and stuff.'

'No. Things haven't got that bad just yet.'

15

The Dartmoor Way is a 95 mile signposted route around the circumference of the moorland that forms Dartmoor National Park. The route follows minor roads and cycle paths the entire way. I had cycled the route previously with my mum and dad a couple of years ago, taking two full days to complete the trip. It was brilliant fun but not without its problems. We cycled the route at the end of October when the daylight hours were limited and the tail end of a hurricane was sweeping over the south of England. I also got two punctures in the first ten miles, and we had to make a costly and time-consuming detour to a bike shop where I bought two new tyres and several new inner tubes to get my bike (the Dawes Street Motion) back to somewhere near a roadworthy condition.

During the ride, I did wonder to myself if – given a summer's day, more hours of daylight, and a decent bike – it would be possible for me to cycle the entire thing in a single day. There was only one way to find out.

On July 10th, I parked the car just off the A38, a couple of miles outside the village of Bittaford on the southern edge of Dartmoor. I had assumed I was much closer to Bittaford, but by the time I realised my error, my bike was already off the car and I couldn't be bothered to rack it back up. It would mean an additional few miles to my total, but covering a big mileage was what the day was all about.

The weather was expected to reach the high twenties, but at 6.30am it was brutally cold. I had no panniers but had managed to squeeze a small jacket into my saddlebag of my cyclocross bike which I swiftly put on.

At Bittaford I met the first signpost to the Dartmoor Way, and I remembered the hill the moment I saw it. It hadn't got any flatter since last climbing it, and once I reached the top I frantically stuffed my jacket back into the saddlebag and it stayed there for the rest of the day.

It was a beautiful morning and the sun was soon rising to my right as the route passed by the town of South Brent and skirted along the edge of the River Avon crossing the river at Shipley Bridge. I cycled through the towns of Buckfastleigh and Ashburton, which was where I had spent several hours in a bike shop on the previous trip. Things were already progressing much better than before.

I was in Bovey Tracey by 8am, just as a bakery on the high street opened its doors.

'Good morning,' said the smiling lady behind the counter. 'What can I get for you, dear?'

'Good morning. What would you recommend for breakfast?' I asked.

'Well the cheese and bacon pastries are popular for breakfast. They've just come out of the oven.'

'Sounds perfect. I'll have one of those please, and a custard doughnut. And would you mind filling my water bottles up for me please?'

'Yes, of course. Have you come far? Or are you just heading out?'

'I've come from just outside Bittaford,' I said.

'Blimey. You must have left early. That's about 20 miles away.'

'25 miles. I took the scenic route.'

'Wow. And have you got much further to go? Where are you heading to?'

'Back to Bittaford, but via Okehampton and Tavistock. I've still got about 75 miles to go.'

'That's incredible. Good luck, dear.'

'Thank you.'

I sat in a nearby park and ate the pastry which was greasy and salty and better than I could have imagined. A German Shepherd walked up to me and started sniffing at the paper bag and trying to lick the crumbs from my hand. It was a dog, I should point out, not an actual weirdo shepherd from Germany.

'Come here, Bruno,' called a lady who walked along a few paces behind, taking a swig from a can of Special Brew. 'Mornin'. Nice day for it.'

'Beautiful.'

'You didn't get that from the bakery on the high street did you?' she asked, gesturing to the pastry I was eating.

'Yes, why?'

'Disgusting stuff.'

'It tastes delicious. Just what I needed.'

'I wouldn't even feed it to my dog,' she said, without a hint of irony, as Bruno continued to nuzzle his face into the paper bag on the bench.

'Well, he seems pretty keen on it.'

'Rather you than me. Come on, Bruno,' she said, pulling him by the collar and walking off.

I finished my pastry and then my donut and set off through the park. I had only travelled 20 metres when a small terrier started barking angrily at me, blocking my way. I tried to push my bike around it, but it just kept yapping at my ankles.

Its owner, a man in his early forties, was walking briskly over from the other side of the park.

'I'm so sorry,' he said.

'That's ok. He doesn't seem to like me much.'

'It's not you. Charlie hates helmets. He has this weird thing about them.'

'Helmets?'

'Yes, well all types of hat really, but mostly bike helmets.'

I took my helmet off, and Charlie stopped his barking instantly. I went to put it back on my head and he went ballistic again.

'Wow, he sure does hate helmets.'

'Yes, I'm really sorry about that. I didn't think we'd see any cyclists at this time of day.'

I pushed my bike, with my helmet in my spare hand, until I reached the end of the park, then I put on my helmet and mounted my bike. I turned to see Charlie racing towards me, growling angrily like a dog possessed. I pushed my foot down hard on the pedal and got the hell out of Bovey. The town sure had some weird dogs and dog walkers.

The Dartmoor Way followed a beautiful stretch of old railway line through the woods under a canopy of trees. There were several dog walkers about but I thought it best not to stop to speak to any of them after my previous encounters. The route left the trail and joined a small road, ascending up a gruelling hill and down to meet the busy A382.

I faced a dilemma. At this point the Dartmoor Way crossed the main road and climbed up a long and particularly arduous hill. The official Dartmoor Way website even states *walking advised* for this section. However, Moretonhampstead – the next town I would pass through – was just a few miles down the nice, smooth, fairly flat main road that I was currently standing at the junction of. The last time I had cycled this route with my parents we had opted for the more direct route because we were quickly running out of daylight hours to get to Okehampton where we had rooms booked for the night. I wasn't able to use this excuse, but it still seemed masochistic to add on a particularly hilly section, just to avoid a stretch of road that really wasn't that busy. I could be in Moretonhampstead in no time if I just turned left.

But I was there to cycle the Dartmoor Way, and the Dartmoor Way said I should cross the road and head uphill. So I did.

It was long and horrible, but I refused to walk, shunning the advice of the Dartmoor Way website. I did have to stop many times, but I stayed astride my bike. That counts, right?

The road eventually levelled out and crossed a pretty reservoir that was sucked almost completely dry due to the recent spell of hot weather. I then followed a section of bridleway before an exhilarating descent into Moretonhampstead. Halfway down, I remembered that this had been one of the toughest climbs during the Dartmoor Classic; it was the one described as an 'absolute bastard' and was far more fun to cycle down than up.

Moretonhampstead is a pretty little town on the north-eastern edge of Dartmoor. Due to its location, it's a popular place for cyclists and walkers to pass through and the town has a lovely feel to it. There is a small cobbled square in the centre in which sit two huge wooden benches, complete with footrests for weary cyclists and ramblers. I bought another pastry and doughnut from a bakery and sat on one of these benches with my feet up, enjoying my mid-morning snack.

From Moreton (that's what the locals call it and as this was my third visit I felt I could join them) I followed yet more steep and narrow roads. These, I found, are the only type of road on Dartmoor. I passed through the pleasant small town of Chagford, which despite being in the middle of nowhere, was bustling. I foolishly didn't stop to fill up my water bottles and drank the last of my supply shortly after leaving the town. I didn't pass any civilisation for several miles. The sun was beating down, there was not a breath of wind, and the hills were really taking it out of me.

I reached the village of Throwleigh and parked up outside the village hall. I searched the perimeter of the building for an outside tap, and eventually located one under the fire escape at the back of the building. I turned it but no water came out. I was forced to struggle onwards and eventually reached Okehampton just after 11am, my mouth dry and my head pounding. I stopped at a bakery on the edge of town, filled up my bottles and bought a steak pasty, donut, crisps and a can of Dr Pepper. I sat at a bench opposite to eat my early lunch and celebrated the fact that I had cycled over 50 miles around the entire east side of Dartmoor, on extremely hilly minor roads, and had reached the northern most point well before midday.

The afternoon promised to be much easier.

After a steep climb up to the old Okehampton train station, I met the incredible Granite Way which I followed towards Lydford. There was more of a headwind than I had hoped but I felt like I was making reasonable progress. That was until an old man on a crap looking bike whizzed past me. It was very unlikely he had already cycled over 50 miles, but it didn't even look like he was trying and he overtook me with ease. I caught up with him a few miles later and he kindly held a gate open for me. I thanked him and pedalled hard to try and put some distance between us so that he wouldn't catch me. Minutes later he cruised by me again. What chance of completing an Ironman did I have if I couldn't even out-cycle an old man on a rubbish bike?

Again, I passed him a mile further on as he sat on a bench nonchalantly munching an apple, almost as thought he was mocking me. This was it. I wasn't going to let him catch me again, and I came out of my saddle and pedalled aggressively to try and leave him behind.

Eventually I sat back down and took a swig from my water bottle, fairly confident that I wouldn't see the old man again. But I soon heard a faint humming which grew slightly louder, but still little more than a murmur. I turned around to see the old man approaching again, and it was at this point I realised that he was riding an electric bike. The cheating bastard! I hadn't noticed before because the strong headwind had disguised the whirr of the motor, and it was not like any electric bike I had ever seen before. But it was certainly doing the job.

'Have a good day,' I said, laughing to myself.

'You too,' he smiled smugly.

I decided to let him have this victory. I wasn't going to put up a chase this time.

I reached Lydford in good time and was in Tavistock by 1.30pm, where I parked my bike in the cobbled market square and ate an immense double ice cream (one scoop of honeycomb and another of rum and raisin, in case you are interested). I couldn't handle a fourth pasty of the day. I had a quick wander up and down the high street in Tavistock, simply because I had cycled 72 miles and wasn't ready to get back on my bike, but I eventually did and followed the Dartmoor Way signs through Tavistock and back out into the countryside.

I met the Drake's Trail – another converted railway line – which I followed to Yelverton, before the route cut back onto the moor.

I still get scared cycling through tunnels on my own. I speed up and try to get through them as quickly as possible. The Grenofen Tunnel was built in 1859 by Isambard Kingdom Brunel, but lay unused since 1962 when the railway line closed, before being bought for £1 by Devon County Council in 2011. I built up some speed as I approached the tunnel but as I entered everything went black. I was still wearing my sunglasses. With one hand I frantically snatched at the glasses on my face, pulling them free just as the edge of my handlebars caught the wall of the tunnel and I fell forwards landing with my bollocks on the crossbar. After writhing in pain for a few seconds, I realised I had snapped one of the arms off my sunglasses in my haste. There was no point looking for it in the dark, and even if I found it I had no means to repair them. I was still able to balance them on my face, and providing I didn't move my head too much, they would hopefully last the rest of the day.

At the village of Cornwood I had to wrestle with my conscience again about not taking the easy option of dropping down to the main road. The marked route went further up onto the moor, so I reluctantly followed the signs and the tough climbs were rewarded with spectacular views and the added satisfaction that I had stuck rigidly to the Dartmoor Way. An enjoyable long descent off the moor came out on the outskirts of Ivybridge and I followed the main road up past my official start and back to my car. I had covered 97.9 miles in a little over 9 hours cycling time, plus some additional stops for pasties and ice-creams. My average speed was a fairly pathetic 10.7mph, but considering the elevation gain of 9,100 feet, and the often uneven surface, I was very pleased with my achievement. To make the day even better, I was home in time to catch the end of Andy Murray verses Roger Federer in the Wimbledon semi final.

I received no medal, goody bag or accolades. I left the house early in the morning before my family were awake, cycled almost 100 miles, and was home soon after they had returned from school. It was my longest ever bike ride, by a considerable distance, and it was also by far my toughest. But there was no fanfare and no congratulatory messages from friends and family. Rachel was the only person that even knew I was going to do it. There was something immensely satisfying about my unplanned, understated adventure.

I do understand the irony that I have spent several pages writing about it in a book.

16

'Is everything ok?' I asked Rachel, as we sat on the sofa the following evening.

'Yes why?'

'You seem quiet.'

'Oh.'

'What's wrong?'

'Nothing.'

'Do we have to do this every time? Please just tell me. I know something is the matter.'

'I found your hospital letter from a few months ago,' she said.

'What hospital letter?'

'The one that says about your 'suspected cancer'.'

'Ah. Where did you find that?'

'It was in your bedside drawer. I was looking for a tape measure. Why didn't you tell me about that?'

'I didn't want to worry you. I phoned the doctor straight away and he told me he didn't think it was necessarily anything to be concerned about.'

'I wish you had told me.'

'I know, I'm sorry. I didn't want you to get upset about something that might not be anything at all.'

'But it must have been a horrible feeling for you.'

'Well, it wasn't the best. But thankfully it all turned out ok.'

'Yes, it did. And we should be very grateful of that.'

'Definitely.'

'I was thinking, though… are you sure you should continue with the Ironman?'

'What do you mean?'

'I mean, perhaps it's not such a great idea after all. You've been very lucky to have made such an amazing recovery, but it would be awful if you did yourself some serious harm in the Ironman or during the training.'

'But you encouraged me to enter in the first place.'

'I know I did, but I don't think I had thought about it properly then. I'm really worried about you.'

'Have you been talking to my mum?'

'No.'

'Have you?'

'Well, we might have had a couple of chats about it.'

'When did you speak to her?'

'Yesterday. She phoned when you were cycling the Dartmoor Way. She couldn't believe it when I told her you were cycling it all in one day.'

'But it's not even the equivalent distance of the Ironman bike ride.'

'I know. That's why she is so worried.'

'What did she say?'

'She's just really worried about you. She thinks you're going to push yourself too hard and really hurt yourself.'

'I haven't done anything that the physiotherapist said I couldn't. Apart from catch that rabbit. But that was your fault.'

'Yes, sorry about that. I feel a bit hypocritical about that now. But I think maybe your mum is right. Maybe this is all a bit too much for you to be taking on so soon after your operation?'

I had a long chat with my mum the following morning, and did my best to reassure her that I wasn't overdoing it. I explained that, if anything, my back felt better when swimming and cycling than it did when I was just standing or sitting around doing nothing, and that it was getting easier all the time. I reassured her that I had only signed up for the Ironman as an incentive to get fit, and I would only line up on that start line in Vichy if I truly felt like I was ready. I promised not to do anything that would compromise my health. Because, as she kept reminding me, I had a young family to help look after.

By the end of the conversation, she seemed to feel much happier about the situation. Although still not completely in favour of the Ironman, she trusted me to be sensible, and I think deep down she knew there was a strong chance that I wouldn't go ahead with it anyway. Once my mum was happy then so was Rachel, and Operation Ironman was back on.

17

As you may have noticed, my running had been completely neglected so far in Operation Ironman. It was the last on the list of exercises that the hospital physiotherapist advised me to undertake, so I assumed, by basic logic, that it meant it was the most likely to aggravate my back. I also knew from past experience that running was the thing most likely to cause me an injury. I've never sustained a serious cycling injury (other than the gash to my hand), or injured myself whilst swimming, but running has always caused me problems of various sorts.

I wanted to minimise my risk of getting injured so had taken the decision to do the minimum amount of run training. The minimum amount turned out to be absolutely none.

But I couldn't delay it any longer. The time had come for me to pull on a pair of trainers and go for a run. Nothing long or strenuous, but a short run just to see how it felt.

It was worse than I expected. I managed little more than half a mile before I had to walk. My back felt extremely uncomfortable and my running felt slow and laboured. My running has always felt a bit like that, to be fair, but this was much worse. Something needed to change.

Christopher McDougall argues in *Born to Run* that the development of the cushion-soled running shoe in the 1960s has contributed to an increase in sports injuries. On the face of it – and as the manufacturers claim – cushioned running shoes should provide added protection to the body, reducing impact and softening the blow. But, as McDougall argues – and many others have also claimed – it actually does the opposite.

The human body is designed to run. We have a complex respiratory system and sweat glands to help cool us down, and, even though it might not feel like it when we are panting up a hill, when compared to other animals, our bodies are particularly adept at running over long distances.

Humans are naturally barefoot runners. For thousands of years we didn't wear footwear. The naturally soft midsole of the foot and its flex provide a readymade shock absorber. A cushioned heel on a pair of trainers doesn't allow the wearer to land with the forefoot first. The raised heel strikes the ground first, and the bodyweight is transferred through the heel of the trainer with multiplied force, up the leg and into the spine. No amount of cushioning in the sole can stop this. The weight of the human body, and the force placed with each stride, means that the heel will compact down any amount of cushioning until it has formed itself a solid surface from which to push off from.

As well as the damage that all this can do to your body, running with a heel-strike stride is also far less efficient. Each time the heel hits the ground, the impact is breaking the momentum of the stride, and you are, in a sense, stopping yourself from moving forward with each step.

Running with the front part of your foot, however, and leaning forward slightly, allows gravity to do a lot of the work for you. The weight of your upper body causes you to almost fall forwards, and the legs move underneath you, keeping you upright, and not having to work as hard as when pushing. It all made perfect sense to me. It was time for me to become a barefoot runner.

Only, I like running in trainers. I don't like stepping on broken glass. Or dog poo. Or in icy puddles. And anyway, barefoot running is prohibited at Ironman Vichy. But barefoot running doesn't just mean running with no shoes. It refers to the style of running of using your forefoot rather than your heel.

'I'm going out to buy some new trainers,' I said to Rachel.

'Ok. What's wrong with the trainers that you've got?'

'They are too cushioned in the heel.'

'And that's a bad thing?'

'Yes. I'm going to become a forefoot runner.'

'Really? Why's that then?'

'Well, it turns out that I've been....'

'Let me guess,' she interrupted. 'You've been running wrong all your life?'

'Exactly. How did you know?'

'Just a guess. Next you'll be telling me you've been walking and breathing wrong all this time too.'

'Well, it's funny you should mention that. I was reading this book that said...'

'Not again!'

Running shoe manufacturers have caught on to the current trend of barefoot running, and have launched various ranges of 'barefoot' shoes trying to cash in. You can even buy shoes that have individual 'fingers' for each toe. They are basically a glove for your foot and they make you look like a proper dick.

I steered well clear of everything that was aimed specifically at barefoot runners. I wanted something minimalist; a simple, lightweight shoe that would purely be a layer of protection between my foot and the road.

The cheapest pair of trainers in the entire sports shop fitted the bill perfectly. They were a pair of Hi Tec *Haraka*. Bright blue in colour and so light they practically floated off the shelf (that's not true). My first ever proper trainers as a child were a pair of the legendary Hi Tec *Silver Shadow*. These were like a modern, bluer, less retro version of the *Silver Shadow*. After years of running in various gel soled, extreme cushion, extra air, added bounce trainers, I had gone full circle and was back where I began.

My first run in the new trainers was harder and far more uncomfortable than I thought it would be. I had secretly hoped that running would feel effortless. My legs would glide across the tarmac like I was born to run. It didn't quite go to plan. Christopher McDougall had lied to me.

My posture was still all wrong; my body still unconsciously trying to protect itself from the recent invasion of the surgeon's knife, and my joints and muscles screamed from lack of use. My calf muscles, in particular, were burning in a way they never had before. I had read that this is a common feeling for people trying 'barefoot' running for the first time. The legs use muscles in a slightly different way, and so it takes a while for the body to condition.

I stuck at it; building up my mileage very gradually. At the end of the first week I was able to run four miles without stopping and without too much pain or discomfort. My running style was already feeling lighter and more natural. Leaning my shoulders forwards slightly, I was letting gravity do its job, providing the natural momentum to move onwards. With my knees slightly bent on impact to reduce the shock, I concentrated on trying to make my footfall as silent as possible. It's a good technique to use to practice making your stride as easy as possible. The quieter the stride, the less impact it is having on your body.

Another key tip that I read was to look ahead when running. It sounds obvious, but plenty of runners (including me) look down at their feet when they are running. Head hung low, body slumped as we trudge out the miles. Lifting your head up has two profound effects. Firstly, it encourages the body to naturally open up the chest, giving the lungs more space to expand. The more space the lungs have, the more oxygen your body can take on. The more oxygen in your body, the better your muscles perform. The other effect is on the posture. Lifting your head a few inches transforms you from a slumped trudger to a purposeful runner. Next time you go out for a run, give it a try. Look ahead of you for a few strides and then look down at your feet. You will notice the difference simply by the change in volume as your feet hit the road.

Whilst my running began to improve, my swimming was still causing plenty of problems. Watching more swimming videos on YouTube complicated things further. I discovered another extremely popular teaching method called Swim Smooth. Swim Smooth differs greatly to Total Immersion, and instead focuses on the speed of the arms, almost replicating the cadence of pedalling a bicycle. But I hadn't allowed myself enough time to start from scratch with Swim Smooth either.

Instead, I spent a few hours making notes of the key elements of the main front crawl techniques in various different tuition videos, and looked for any overlap (do I know how to party, or what?). Thankfully there were quite a few similarities.

For those of you who are interested – and to save you from having to watch as many videos as I did – these are the common elements that seem to be widely established as being essential for an efficient front crawl stroke, whatever specific variation you chose. All I had to do was focus on these key elements and I stood a chance of being able to swim.

The first was the body position. Except when breathing, the head should remain still in the water, with the eyes towards the bottom. Raising the head, even slightly, results in the back and legs lowering in the water, adding drag and resistance.

Whilst on the subject of breathing, when turning the head to breathe, it's ideal for only half of the face to exit the water. This also means that only half your mouth exits the water. Unless you have a particularly lopsided face, that is. Breathing through half a mouth takes practise, but not over rotating to breathe keeps the body nice and streamlined in the water.

Bilateral breathing – breathing on both sides, usually every three strokes – is the favoured technique, especially for endurance swimming. Most Olympic swimmers will breathe every two strokes, but their speed requires a more regular supply of oxygen to the body.

The benefits of bilateral breathing are that it encourages an even stroke, and also, if swimming in open water with waves to one side, you have the ability to breathe away from the wave, having experience of breathing either side.

Breathing out whilst the face is in the water is also vitally important. Not only does it allow the lungs to be emptied in time to inhale – which is particularly important if you are only breathing in through half a mouth – but also because if you hold your breath, you are keeping the CO_2 in your system, which is what creates the desire to breathe.

Rules of hydrodynamics apply to all methods of swimming, too. As with making yourself aerodynamic when cycling, it is a scientific fact that the lower the resistance you cause in the water, the easier you can propel yourself through it. To make yourself as hydrodynamic as possible, you have to make yourself as long and thin as possible. Rotating the body at the waist allows for an extended arm reach, and makes the body narrower, cutting through the water. Finding that natural rhythm where your hips rotate from one side to the other is key – streamline right, streamline left.

The legs are a contentious issue. There is no doubt that kicking the legs will make you go faster, and some swim coaches will argue that if you don't kick your legs, you are only doing half a stroke, and the added propulsion from your legs gives you more momentum, creating less resistance. Others will point out that the energy required to kick your legs is not efficient – especially for long distance swimming, when conserving energy is hugely important.

The other commonly used argument by triathletes is that the legs should be used very little as they need to be preserved for the bike and run stages.

The final element was hard for me to admit. I almost didn't write it down and just discarded it as an urban myth. But I swallowed my pride and I reluctantly added it to my list. The core. The elusive fucking core. It seems widely agreed – by everyone but me – that using your core is a key component to a successful front crawl stroke. All I needed to do was find out what the hell it was and how the hell to use it.

A few hours in front of the computer with a notepad and pen and I felt like a swimming expert. I now knew everything there was to know about front crawl. All I needed to do was put that into practice. I had a Bachelor's in Bilateral Breathing, an HND in Hydrodynamics, and a PhD in Pool Position. I just needed to become a Professor of the Core.

So over the next couple of weeks I spent quite a few more hours in the pool. Not once did I do a set. Not once did I try to swim a certain number of lengths without stopping. Not once did I use a float, or a pull-buoy. I focussed solely on my stroke. I wasn't concerned with the speed I was swimming at, or the distance I had covered, I simply kept trying to adapt my stroke until it felt easier. Until it felt natural. Until it felt right.

And eventually it sort of did.

18

I had continued to run a couple of times a week and was feeling happy with my new technique. But I still hadn't managed more than five miles in one go, so I signed up for an organised 10k in our local town at the end of July. It's a gruelling, hilly course that feels much tougher than a 10k should. It would be the furthest I had run since the same race the year before. On that occasion, I struggled around the course, still in denial that my back pain was anything more than something minor that would get better in time.

You will notice that I alternate regularly between metric and imperial measurements in this book. This is not a deliberate ploy to be annoying or confusing. The UK is the only country in Europe that still defines speed limits in miles per hour, and uses miles as the unit of measurement for road signs. America does too, but the rest of the world (even Liberia and Burma, which, until recently had been the only other two countries in the world to still use the imperial system) has adopted metric, using kilometres as the unit of measurement for long distances. In the UK, as well as in America, kilometres are popular when it comes to long distance events (especially running), with 5k and 10k being extremely popular, so I will use a mixture of the two. Sorry.

Rachel signed up for the race too, and a friend of ours who lives on the 10k route kindly agreed to look after the children for us. To avoid any marital disharmony, we agreed to run together.

We ran the first half kilometre at a nice steady pace. Then we hit the first hill and I thought we would continue to take it steady. Rachel had other ideas. As soon as she felt the incline under her feet she accelerated away up the hill. I gave chase, having to dodge in and out of the other runners, who, like me, were taking it easy. I assumed that she would ease up halfway, but if anything she sped up the closer we got to the top. People were doing double-takes as we passed them.

'What the hell are these loons doing?' they said with their eyes.

As we reached the top, Rachel reduced her pace by half and all of the people we had overtaken up the hill slowly caught us up.

'What was that all about?' I panted.

'What.... do.... you... mean?' she wheezed.

'Why did you sprint up that hill?'

'That's... that's.... how... I run... up hills.'

'Ok,' I said, not wanting to cause a domestic in the first mile.

A brief section of downhill followed, before another tough climb up to the church. Again, the moment the gradient changed, Rachel's stride lengthened and she began sprinting up the hill. I only just managed to keep up with her, my lungs gasping for air as I reached the top.

'Why do you... why do you speed up on the hills?' I asked.

'Stop criticising my running,' gasped Rachel between breaths.

'I'm not criticising. It just seems unnecessary if you then have to slow down once you reach the top.'

'Well that's what I do, ok?'

She was still wheezing by the 3km marker after a nice long stretch of flat.

'I'm finding this really tough today,' she admitted. 'I don't normally have trouble breathing like this.'

'Er... I'm finding it really tough too. Maybe it's because you sprinted up the hills.'

'That's what I always do!'

We spotted Layla, Leo and Kitty sitting on chairs at the side of the road cheering us on. As we got closer, amongst all the cheering, we could hear Kitty shouting 'Loser' repeatedly. At the time we assumed that this was a special bit of ridicule that she saved just for Rachel and me. We later discovered that she had shouted 'winner' to the first person who passed her and then proceeded to shout 'loser' to everyone that followed. All of the other children had laughed which only encouraged her, so she kept it up for the duration of the event. We will make alternative arrangements for her next year.

'I don't normally talk this much when I run,' said Rachel as we went through the halfway point.

'Yes you do. You always get back from runs with your friends and tell me how you have been chatting for hours.'

'That's different.'

'Why?'

'I'm not racing when I run with them.'

'But this isn't a race though. It's a fun run.'

'It IS a race. And it's certainly not fun.'

'It might be more fun if you didn't sprint up the hills. Who are you racing against, anyway?'

'Oh please be quiet,' she said.

But I knew she meant me.

Although not directly competing against me, this was a show of determination on her part to prove how far she had come.

The one and only time Rachel and I had ever run together previously was a year earlier when we took part in an event called The Great British Relay. It was a record attempt for the world's longest relay – a continuous running event around the perimeter of the UK. The route was split into roughly 10k sections and people could sign up for a stage, being given a date and an estimated start time, which, because it was non-stop, could be any time of the day or night.

An article appeared in our local paper a few weeks before the relay was due to pass through town, stating that one of the stages – a 3am stage, typically – still needed filling. This was the first I had heard of The Great British Relay and I thought it sounded like a great idea (and secretly I've always wanted to be a world record holder), so I signed us up.

The relay had travelled several thousand miles around the UK coastline, anti-clockwise from Southend, and had stuck pretty much to its timings – give or take a couple of hours. Whenever the relay dropped behind schedule, a faster runner would put in a good shift to help bring it back on time. Runners carried a GPS baton in the form of a black plastic lunch box. This lunch box also contained a small camera taking photographs every minute to create a time-lapse montage of the trip, and provide evidence to Guinness World Records that the baton was in continuous motion.

There was a nice community spirit to the relay, and runners were often asked to fill in at short notice due to others pulling out with injury or illness. Occasionally, runners were forced to put in a double shift when they reached their pre-arranged meeting point only to find the next runner absent.

Things ran very smoothly until the relay reached the south west. Many of the routes followed the South West Coastal Path, which is a notoriously undulating and difficult footpath. The average speed dropped considerably and the relay lapsed severely behind – occasionally by up to nine hours – which then caused a logistical nightmare for the organisers, as runners who had committed to a certain time had other commitments nine hours later.

With some tweaks to the route to save time, and with runners stepping in to fill gaps, the relay somehow clawed its way back to within a few hours of its target time.

Rachel and I got to our meeting point just before 3am. It was a clear night and the sea lapped at the shore on the beach next to us. We were wearing head-torches, having anticipated running at night, but by the time the runners of the stage before us reached the handover point at 5.30am, the sky was beginning to lighten. I had been dreading the handover for days, waking up sweating in the night after dreaming of fumbling and dropping the baton, causing hundreds of dedicated runners, and months of organisation to go to waste. Others had had the same fears as me, and on internet forums people posted advice about their favoured techniques for carrying the baton, and, more specifically, the dreaded handover. People also invested in special gloves to wear whilst holding it, believing that sweat on bare fingers could lead to that catastrophic failure. I didn't wear gloves, but I did spend several seconds blowing every speck of moisture from my hands as the runners approached.

The handover went smoothly and once I was holding the lunch box shaped device – or Casey, as it had been nicknamed (it was a case, see) – I realised there was a handy strap to put over my wrist for added security.

Running with Rachel for the first time was a strange experience. She didn't like me to talk to her. I tried filling the silence with idle chat, offering witty observations on the countryside and its inhabitants as we passed.

'Be quiet, David Attenborough,' she said.

So I tried talking her through the route we were taking.

'So we follow this route up to the end and then turn left up the steep hill. We then turn right at the top and follow that road....'

'Oh please shut up, Sat Nav,' she said.

It's fair to say that running together was not the best thing for our relationship.

We made it to the handover and successfully passed the baton on to the next runner, happy that it was no longer our responsibility. The relay continued over the following weeks along the south coast and then around Kent before finishing in Southend, bang on schedule. It was a remarkable achievement; 7000km and more than 600 runners over the course of several weeks. And all of us would be world record holders.

Well, we would have been if some moron hadn't put the relay baton down. When checking through the photos taken by the baton, the event organiser found two frames back to back with long grass obscuring the front of the lens, which meant that the baton had been put down on the ground for more than two minutes. The record attempt had failed. The organiser quite rightly didn't name and shame the eejit who dropped the baton, and the runners unanimously rallied together and agreed to repeat the attempt the following year.

Rachel and I signed up to repeat our leg this year, but due to various logistical reasons, the event was postponed at the last minute until 2016, so our chance at being world record holders will have to wait.

Where was I? So Rachel and I are not the most compatible running partners. I like running with her, but she hates running with me.

We reached the top of the longest downhill on the course. It's a downhill that's so long and steep that it's almost as tiring as running uphill; the knees and ankles jolting at every impact with the ground.

As we approached the top, I noticed the runner up ahead of us was exactly the same runner who had been ahead of me at the same point in the race the year before. I don't have a habit of remembering other runners, but this man was unique. I have never seen anyone run downhill at the speed he does. He was a big guy, well over 6 foot tall and quite stocky, but he used his long legs to their full advantage and just let gravity carry him down the hill at an obscene speed.

Like last year, by the time we had started our descent, he had disappeared out of sight, around the corner at the bottom of the hill. I almost caught him up a couple of kilometres later last year, once the road had levelled out, but he had gained too much of an advantage and he beat me by 14 seconds.

This year we started reeling him in again once the road levelled out, and with less than a kilometre to go, we overtook him. I kept glancing back during the final few hundred metres, but this year the victory was ours. Rachel and I crossed the line together, 20 seconds ahead of our big gangly nemesis, with Rachel knocking three minutes off her previous year's time, and possibly a few years off her lifetime.

19

Operation Ironman had always been about doing all I could to enable me to line up at the start in Vichy. If I was able to get that far, I would then do everything I could to get round the course inside the 17 hour cut-off. It didn't matter to me how long it took, providing I could beat that looming 17 hour deadline.

'It says here that the cut-off for Ironman Vichy is 16 hours,' said Rachel one evening.

'No. The Ironman cut-off is 17 hours. Trust me, I've read enough about Ironman.'

'Well, I'm on the official Ironman Vichy website, and it says here: *'Cut-off for the complete race is 16 hours (11.30pm) for IRONMAN Vichy'.*'

'Let me have a look. It must be a typo.'

But it wasn't a typo.

Further investigation uncovered that although the worldwide Ironman cut-off time is 17 hours, some countries – most noticeably France and Germany – impose a stricter 16 hour cut-off, and, in Germany's case, 15 hours.

My confidence was knocked. I had the various time allowances for each leg of the Ironman sorted in my head, and now I had to somehow make up an hour somewhere.

When you swim a couple of times a week, you start to notice familiar faces. There's the middle-aged lady who swims backstroke with her arms flailing out at right angles, and if you swim in her lane you are guaranteed to be smacked in the face on every length. There's the annoying man who waits at the end and lets you through, only to start swimming his length straight away and be scratching at your feet the entire way. Then there is the lady who alternates her swim sets between using flippers so that she is twice the speed of everyone else in her lane, to using no flippers and a float so that she is half the speed.

There was one guy that I saw regularly who looked like an experienced swimmer. He swam length upon length of crawl, making it look easy. He was usually in the pool before I got in, and still there when I left. On this occasion, I was swimming alongside him in an adjacent lane and I realised I was matching him for pace. But even more significantly, I was swimming with almost half the number of strokes that he was. I felt elated that all of my hard work was paying off, and I had developed, what it seemed, was an efficient, effective swimming stroke.

My moment of elation lasted just two lengths. At the end of the second length my arms were so tired that I was forced to pause for breath, whereas the man in the adjacent lane carried on with ease.

I had upped my personal best to three lengths (that's 75 metres) of front crawl without stopping or doing breaststroke. Layla, my now 8 year old daughter, could swim four (I could kick her arse at breaststroke, though). My stroke was improving but I had a long way to go to improve my endurance and stamina.

20

All of my cycle training so far had been on my cyclocross bike. I was happy with my choice and enjoyed riding it, but it was never going to be the bike that I used for the Ironman.

My dad owns a road bike. It was not the same one that I loved as an 11 year-old, but a newer one. Only slightly newer, though. It was a Specialised Allez; quite a few years old, a little rusty in places and had certainly seen better days. But it was more than adequate for my needs and he kindly agreed to let me borrow it for the Ironman.

He brought it over one morning in late July so that I could get a chance to ride it a few times before taking it to France.

'There's a bit of a knack to changing gear,' he said.

'Ok.'

'If you want it to drop to the lower ring, you'll find it just keeps making this annoying clicking sound and it won't go into gear.'

'So what do you have to do?'

'You have to count back four gears on the back ring, and then change the front ring, then move the other one back four again. You'll work it out.'

'Ok. Thanks.'

'Oh, and the front tyre was flat when I got it out of the shed. I pumped it up, so hopefully it will be ok.'

When I checked the tyre later in the day it was already flat. I replaced the inner tube and took it out for a quick spin around the block. By the time I made it home, the front tyre was soft again. I checked the tyre thoroughly for any thorns, and although I couldn't find any, I did notice many small holes in the tyre where the rubber had perished. Both tyres felt incredibly thin, and sure enough, on a short ride the following day I got my third puncture in two days.

Just to be on the safe side, I bought two new tyres and even squirted some oil on the chain, because I've heard that's what cyclists do.

I tried to raise the saddle slightly as it felt a little too low. The nut was seized, and as I tried to force it with my Allen key, it rounded the head off and I had to accept that the saddle would remain at its current height forever.

It is recommended to have a bike professionally 'fitted'. Many cyclists and triathletes spend hundreds of pounds having an expert adjust every bit of the bike's anatomy to maximise comfort and efficiency. I now had to ride a bike that couldn't even have the saddle adjusted. Thankfully my dad and I are a similar size (not that he ever had the bike professionally fitted either), and it's better to have a saddle fixed at an almost acceptable height, than one that slides down if you apply any weight to it like my fold-up bike did.

Incidentally, I managed to sell the fold-up bike on eBay for almost what I paid for it. I even included a free bag with the sale to ease my conscience about the self-adjusting saddle.

The Ironman was a little over a month away and I had never worn a pair of cycling shoes before. Cycling shoes have mechanisms on the soles called cleats that attach to special pedals. They make cycling more energy efficient, as you are able to transfer power to the bike as the legs pull up as well as when pushing down. I had completed my Dartmoor Way bike ride in a pair of trainers and didn't find it too problematic, but during the Dartmoor Classic sportive I witnessed that every other cyclist taking part was wearing cycling shoes. I figured that maybe they were onto something and I should give them a try. Thankfully my dad has the same size feet as me, and was able to lend me his cycling shoes too.

I soon got the hang of attaching and detaching the cleats to the pedals. You have to twist your foot to release them, so that they don't accidentally come off whilst cycling, and it takes a bit of getting used to.

It's a well known rule amongst cyclists that at some point during the first few rides wearing cleats you will have a fall. It's inevitable. The instinct when reaching a junction, or a set of traffic lights, is to put your foot down onto the ground, and when first using cleats, it's extremely common to forget to unclip until you find you are lying prostrate on the tarmac.

I returned from a test ride of about four miles without any incident and managed to stay upright the entire time. I couldn't understand what all the fuss was about. *Idiot cyclists,* I thought. *It's a piece of cake.*

And then a few days later I went out on my second ride. All went well for the first half an hour, until I followed a car down a narrow, high-banked lane. I was a safe-distance behind the car, and as we came round a corner we met an SUV coming the other way. I slowed down, unclipped and came to a stop behind the car. The approaching SUV had pulled into a passing space and flashed to let us through. The car in front of me pulled off and continued onwards, but as I clipped in and went to cycle after it, the waiting SUV decided not to wait for me as well, and pulled out. I slammed on my brakes as there wasn't room to cycle safely by, but on this occasion I forgot to unclip and I collapsed sideways into the hedge, the bike bouncing up into the air, still attached to both feet. As the SUV passed, the driver looked over at me, and I registered his amused smirk.

I thought that would be my one and only fall. I had learned my lesson and it wouldn't happen again. But the following day it did.

I was approaching a t-junction at the top of an incline. I unclipped my right pedal with the intention of pausing at the junction to let a car past and use my right leg to balance on. But as I came to a stop, because of the incline, my bike leaned slightly to the left and I wasn't able to unclip from my left pedal in time. I toppled in slow-motion and then splatted down onto the road in spectacular fashion, my bike still attached to my left foot. The car drove by, and this time the driver – an elderly lady – offered a sympathetic and slightly bewildered expression.

The experience wasn't as painful as I feared. My knee and elbow were both badly scraped, but I hadn't broken anything and the bike was absolutely fine. It could have been a lot worse. I had passed my first cycling initiation test. I had taken two falls with my cleats and survived. There would no doubt be many more, but I was on my way to becoming a proper cyclist.

21

I couldn't put it off any longer. It was time for me to venture into the open water. Rachel had bought me a swimming wetsuit for my birthday back in May, but I was yet to test it out. I don't have a great relationship with wetsuits – I'm not sure anyone does – but I was hoping that would all change in time for the Ironman.

A few years ago I was gorge walking during a friend's stag do in Wales. Gorge walking involves putting on a wetsuit, lifejacket and helmet, and following the course of a river by wading, climbing and swimming along it. We had just jumped off a waterfall into the pool below, and were all sitting around on some rocks at the bottom waiting for everyone to complete the jump. When the last of the group hauled themselves out of the water the instructor announced that it was just a short walk through the woods back to the minibus.

'WHAT?' shouted my friend Damo, 'I thought we were getting back in the water?'

'No. This is the end,' I said.

'But I've just done a piss in my wetsuit.'

'What, when you were in the water? So what? Everyone does that.'

'No. Just now. While we've been sitting here on the rocks.'

'Why did you do that?'

'I was cold and I thought it would warm me up. And I thought we were getting back in the water.'

We all mocked him about this the whole way back to the minibus (and about his claim that his grandma had invented Banoffee pie). We were to then get changed into our normal clothes, before being dropped at a pub in Chester for the start of a night out. Damo was first to take his wetsuit off, keen to rid himself of the foul stench of urine. He tossed his soggy wetsuit into the back of the van as we removed our own. I then went to retrieve my jeans, and discovered them wet and stinking underneath his wetsuit in the back of the minibus.

With no other clothes to wear, I was forced to wear the jeans and suffer from wafts of someone else's stale piss from my trousers for the rest of the evening. I have been suspicious of wetsuits ever since.

My sister and her family were holidaying down in Devon for the week so I asked my brother-in-law Guy if he would be happy to kayak with me whilst I did my first open-water swim. He agreed, so we met at the river estuary, and both carried my kayak down to the water's edge.

'Thanks for coming along,' I said.

'Thanks for inviting me. This is my first proper activity of the holiday. I'm looking forward to it.'

I waded slowly into the water and was relieved to feel that the wetsuit did its job.

We set off at high-tide so there was very little movement of the water. I wanted to be able to concentrate on my stroke, rather than worry about being swept out to sea. I followed Guy out into the middle of the estuary, sticking closely to the end of the kayak. It felt reassuring him being there, not only to help me with my sighting, but because of the reassurance that I could reach out and grab it if it all got too much.

We dodged in and out of the moored boats, and into the depths of the river.

'Right, I'm just going to see how far up the river I can get before the tide turns,' he said, and before I had a chance to protest, he was off. Minutes later he was just a speck on the horizon, and I was alone in the middle of an almighty river.

I looked back to the shore where Rachel, my sister and the kids were crab fishing and I considered swimming straight back to them. But I had told myself I wanted to be in the water for about an hour. Plus there was nothing really to be afraid of. I could swim. And I had a wetsuit so wasn't going to suffer from hypothermia. It was just my own irrational fear and that was something that could only be overcome by confronting it.

I began swimming up-river, in the direction Guy had paddled. The tide would begin to turn soon and so I wouldn't have to fight against it for my return journey.

The buoyancy of the wetsuit was incredible. My legs seemed to float effortlessly behind me and it felt like I was slipping through the water like a seal.

As well as my first proper open water swimming session, this was also my first experience at spotting or sighting – the process of looking ahead to check your location. It took a little practice but I soon got into the habit of lifting my head to the front every eight strokes to check I was heading in the right direction. Only I didn't really know where the right direction was, or what I was supposed to be heading towards, so I mindlessly zigzagged up the river aiming for various boats and distant trees on the river bank.

Jellyfish were my biggest fear. I am terrified by the thought and the sight of jellyfish. I don't see them very often in the sea in Devon, but often enough to know that they are there.

Last year, I was kayaking in deeper water off the coast near to where I was now swimming. It was a perfectly calm day and the water was crystal clear and it enabled me to see into the depths. There were jellyfish of all shapes and sizes in every direction I looked. From the safety of a kayak they looked almost serene and magical, but for a swimmer, they are anything but. The situation is not helped by the British press and its annual sensationalised headlines:

KILLER JELLYFISH SET TO INVADE BRITISH SHORES THIS SUMMER

JELLYFISH THE SIZE OF DOUBLE DECKER BUS SPOTTED OFF CORNISH COAST

I have never been stung by a jellyfish, and that is part of my fear. I react badly to insect bites and stings and the affected body part swells to gigantic proportions. I was once stung on the arm by a wasp at school. It swelled to twice its size and I was known as Michelin Man for a couple of days. On another occasion I was bitten on the ear lobe by a mosquito and half of my face swelled up. This time the comedians at school called me Elephant Man. Fortunately – or perhaps disappointingly – I have never been stung on the penis.

Most jelly fish stings are supposedly little more than a nettle sting, but I was worried about suffering from some form of anaphylactic shock out in the middle of the river. The water was dark and murky and I couldn't see any further than my outstretched arm, but sometimes as I pulled my hand through the water it created a large air bubble that resembled a jellyfish and made me panic on each occasion, causing me to flail about erratically before I realised – for the hundredth time – that it was just a bubble.

I felt like I had been swimming for about half an hour and I could feel the increasing power of the tide pushing against me, making it harder for me to swim up river. There was no sign of Guy, so I turned and headed back towards the shore and soon found myself in a comfortable rhythm. It all seemed to be coming together. I could feel my hips driving down each time I extended my arm. My breathing was regular and controlled, and my legs – aided by my wetsuit – were tagging along effortlessly for the ride. But it was more than that. It was more than just the coming together of the different elements that I had been practising in the pool. Something felt different. And then it hit me. I don't know how it happened, but it suddenly all made sense. I was using my core.

It is quite hard to describe how to use your core when swimming. That's presumably why my two swimming coaches were so vague about it. I have heard people say that you should imagine you are trying to hold a 50 pence coin between your butt cheeks. In America they use the example of a quarter. Personally, I don't think it makes any difference what coin you are imagining. My experience of carrying coins between my butt cheeks is non-existent, but I don't think my technique would vary considerably if I was to, say, hold a 10p instead of a 50p. But perhaps there's more to it than I think. I'll take the experts' words for it.

So, imagine you have a 50p or a quarter between your butt cheeks and you are gently tensing your cheeks together to squeeze it. Not too tightly now. You don't want to suck that bad boy right up inside you.

Squeezing your butt encourages the upper legs and the lower torso to become more rigid and streamlined, making your body more buoyant, and allowing it to work together as a whole, rather than your arms and legs working independently.

'I'm using my core!' I shouted to myself. But my face was underwater at the time, so it came out very differently.

As I got into shore, my sister was chatting to someone she had bumped into whom she coincidently knew from London.

'This is my brother, George,' she said. 'He's training for an Ironman.'

'Impressive,' said the lady, 'I thought you looked like a proper swimmer when we passed you in the boat earlier.'

'Ha, thanks. That's the first time anyone has ever said that,' I said, sitting down in the shallow water because of an extreme bout of dizziness. Not because of what the lady said, but because of swimming in cold water for an hour.

'No really. You have a really nice natural stroke. Good luck with the Ironman.'

'Thanks. That means a lot.'

'You did look really good out there,' said my sister after her friend had left. 'I think perhaps you're ready for Dolphins after all.'

22

When I first heard the term 'brick session' used in discussion about triathlon training I ignored it. I assumed it meant running, cycling or swimming while weighted down with bricks; presumably to build up endurance and strength. Some people do actually train with bricks (the weirdoes), but that's not what brick sessions are about.

A brick session is combining two or more triathlon disciplines one after the other. For example a swim followed by a bike ride, or a bike ride followed by a run. The idea being that you need to train your body to get used to a sudden change in physical exercise and the use of different muscle groups.

My extremely limited triathlon experience – a sprint distance triathlon in 2012 – taught me just how difficult it is to go from one to the other when you are not used to it. Climbing out of the pool following a short 400 metre breaststroke swim, I ran to the transition area and it felt like I was on one of those moving walkways that you find at airports. I had been in the water for only 15 minutes, but back on dry land, my body and mind still felt like it was in the water. This sensation continued for the first few miles of the bike ride.

Then, after the bike ride, I imagined that the 5km run would be a doddle. It's only 5km. How hard can it be? Bloody hard, it transpired. I had been on the bike for less than an hour, but it was enough for my legs to reject my encouragements to make them function normally. The pain was excruciating and they refused to move in any sort of fluid motion. They jerked forwards at odd angles and for most of the run I looked like I was roller-skating. I started to feel pains in parts of my legs where I didn't even know it was possible to feel pain. And all of this was during a sprint triathlon. Imagine the shock to the body during an Ironman. As much as I wanted to eschew traditional training techniques, a few brick sessions seemed like an essential thing to do.

My first session was a swim followed by a cycle. It started off well and I got on the bike – which I had left outside the leisure centre – feeling fresh and energised (the leisurely shower and slow change in the leisure centre changing room probably helped), and my legs felt pretty good. Then, two miles in, I began to feel uncontrollably hungry. I had neglected to realise how much energy I had used up in the pool, and was now feeling the effects. I slowed down to a crawl, and at the first cafe that I came to I stopped for a coffee and a large piece of cake, and by the time I finished, I felt so lethargic that I just cycled home.

My bike-to-run sessions were just as unsuccessful. After a ride of about 20 miles, I returned home, swapped my cycling shoes for a pair of trainers, inhaled an energy gel, had a swig of water, and set off on a four mile run. My legs didn't feel too bad, but half a mile in I got an awful stitch. I don't think I'd had a stitch since school. To be honest, I thought stitches went out of fashion in the 90s. It turns out they are still lurking around and this one hit me so painfully that I had to walk.

It happened again the following week. This time I had planned to follow my bike ride with a slightly longer 10k run. The stitch was so painful that I ended up walking most of the way. It was a real concern, as there would be no way I could complete an Ironman marathon with a stitch like that.

23

Feeling inspired by my first open water swimming session, and being told that I looked like a proper swimmer, I met up with my dad at another nearby estuary and brought along my kayak for him to be my guide. He promised he wouldn't go off and leave me alone like my brother-in-law had done. I had been in the water for an hour on the previous occasion, but had no idea what distance I had covered. This stretch of water, however, is situated adjacent to a road so I was able to measure it in the car beforehand. It was half a mile from the bridge to the end of the creek, which meant if I swam the length of the creek and back to the bridge I would have covered a mile (just in case you weren't able to work that out for yourself). Timing myself over the distance would give me a better indication of my progress.

Things started well and it was reassuring having the tail of the kayak within reaching distance as I swam steadily down the creek. The trees hung low on the shore and a pair of egrets stood and questioned what the hell I was doing in their river. I didn't have an adequate answer for them.

I reached the end of the creek and turned and started heading back towards the bridge. I had set off at high tide, and the water should have been on its way out by the time I turned homewards, giving me the benefit of the current, but it felt far from easy. The river was so shallow at this point that I kept catching my hands or knees on the bottom. I regularly swam into patches of seaweed, which made me thrash about hysterically, rapidly speeding up my breathing, and breaking my momentum. My goggles had also fogged so much that I couldn't even see the kayak in front of me, and I had to stop every couple of minutes to rinse them out.

I felt like I was fighting the tide the entire way back, and when I eventually pulled myself onto dry land and lay slumped on the harbour wall, demoralised and exhausted, I didn't think there was any chance of me completing the 2.4 mile swim required in the Ironman.

The mile had taken me 55 minutes. Based on that speed, even if I were to be able to maintain it for the entire 2.4 miles, it would take me 2 hours 12 minutes. The swim cut-off at Vichy was 2 hours 10.

I kept trying to remind myself that this was just a blip. I had felt really good during my previous open-water swim, when I had found my rhythm, found my composure, and found my core. The weed, the goggles, the tide, and the shallow water had all conspired against me this time. It was time to forget about this swim session and move on. Strike this one from the memory. I had a much bigger test coming up that would prove, once and for all, whether I was capable or not of completing the Ironman swim.

24

I had taken part in a sportive. I had cycled almost 100 miles around Dartmoor. I had ridden a road bike for the first time. I had worn cycling shoes. I had taken a couple of falls. There was no denying the fact that I was on my way to becoming a proper cyclist. But I wasn't quite there yet. I couldn't put it off any longer. The time had come for me to buy some Lycra.

I didn't know exactly what benefits Lyrca (or 'spandex' for readers across the pond) had, but there must be plenty, otherwise surely all those cyclists wouldn't put themselves through it.

I had left it a little late as I was catching a train to London the following day to take part in the RideLondon-Surrey 100 bike ride. I ordered a pair of budget padded cycling shorts on the internet and the cheapest cycling top I could find. They arrived the next day, just in time for me to board a train to London. I did have time to try them on quickly beforehand, and although they did look revolting – the shorts and shirt colours clashing violently – they did feel strangely alluring.

The RideLondon-Surrey 100 bike ride is a mass-participation cycle event that has been going since 2013. It was created as a legacy event for the London Olympics of 2012. Keen to maintain Britain's enthusiasm for cycling during the Olympics, RideLondon allows cyclists the unique opportunity to cycle from the Queen Elizabeth Olympic Park, along closed roads through central London, before looping through the leafy Surrey countryside and then eventually returning to London and ending on The Mall in front of Buckingham Palace, with the queen waving a flag and blowing a hooter from her bedroom window. Possibly.

The event has been a phenomenal success, and vast over-subscription means that the 25,000 places are allocated via a ballot. I applied for the first two years and was unsuccessful both times. In February 2015, a couple of months before I had my back surgery, I received notification that I had a place this year.

At the time I didn't think there was any possibility of taking part. I was still awaiting the results of a brain scan, and there was no indication of when my surgery would be.

After surgery, I realised that there was a slim chance that I would be able to take part, so set my sights on being there at the start line at the beginning of August, even if I had not been able to get fit enough to take part in the Ironman.

I booked my train a few weeks in advance and then found out that riders were required to register in person during the three days prior to the event, to pick up their race numbers and timing chips. My train didn't arrive in London until after the registration closed on the day before the race.

Riders were allowed to assign a friend or relative to pick up the documents on their behalf, providing they had a signed document and a letter authorising permission. A couple of weeks before the event I rang my good friend Ben who lives in London. Ben was my companion for my Land's End to John O'Groats bike ride.

'So you want me to go all the way to the bloody Excel Centre just to register you?' he sighed. 'You realise how far away from anywhere the Excel Centre is?'

'Yes, I'm really sorry. Do you mind?'

'Of course I don't, Porge. I'm only joking. It's not a problem at all.'

'Thank you, that's brilliant. It's really important for me to get the race numbers and timing chip. I won't be allowed to start the race without them. Are you sure you won't forget?'

'Porge, have I ever let you down?'

'No. Thank you. I really appreciate it.'

'How will I get the stuff to you before the race? Do you want me to meet you somewhere on that morning?'

'Ah, yes, I knew I had something else to ask you. Is it ok if I come and stay at yours the night before?'

'Of course it is. That would be awesome. We'll go out for a few beers.'

'Maybe just one beer. Remember, I've got to cycle 100 miles.'

'Yeah, yeah, ok. Just the one then.'

As I was sitting on the train to London I looked at my phone and noticed that I had five missed calls from Ben. I called him back immediately.

'Hi, Ben. Everything ok?'

'Er, yeah it is now, Porge. What a day though!'

'What happened?'

'Er... well... I have a slight confession to make.'

'Go on.'

'I sort of forgot you were coming to London this weekend.'

'Oh. Have you made plans?'

'No... well... yes I had, but it's all sorted now. I had agreed to drive up to Yorkshire to help my mum decorate her new house and I was just packing my things when I noticed the envelope you sent me with the letter for RideLondon, just poking out from under a pile of crap on my desk.'

'You mean you haven't registered me?'

'No, don't worry. It's all sorted now. I was like FUCK SHIT FUCK, so I got in the car and caned it over to the Excel Centre cos I didn't have time to bike there or get the tube. I got there and the parking costs like £15 so I was like fuck that shit. I pulled into a space near the entrance and legged it in there just as they were closing the desk. I handed over all your documents, they gave me your timing chip and all that crap, and this old bloke was trying to go through all the terms and conditions with me and the rules of the race, and I had to just rudely run off mid-conversation.'

'Did you get a parking ticket?'

'No, thank fuck for that.'

'Ha ha, you are such a dick. So are you still going up to Yorkshire?'

'Nope, I've told my mum I'll go tomorrow instead. It's all cool. Really looking forward to seeing you, Porge.'

'I hope I haven't messed up your weekend too much.'

'Not at all. I nearly truly fucked up your weekend though, mate. Sorry about that. You would have got to London and I'd have been up in Yorkshire. Not only would you have had nowhere to stay, but you wouldn't even have been able to do the bike ride either.'

'Well I guess I should be thanking you for saving the day then?'

'Damn right! See you soon, buddy. Looking forward to it.'

I arrived at Paddington Station feeling relieved that despite Ben's incompetence he had come good. After almost leaving my dad's bike on the train, I tried to navigate my way across London to meet up with Ben.

The first section was easy, as I skirted through Hyde Park, dodging in and out of roller-bladers, couples enjoying romantic walks, joggers, children, and fellow cyclists. I passed under the Wellington Arch, and then planned to cycle along Constitution Hill, but it was already fenced off as this was the finishing straight of RideLondon the following day. I followed the perimeter fence, hoping to find a way through, and then started to hear cheering. As I moved further along I could see cyclists whizzing past. But they didn't look like normal cyclists. They were all riding fold up bicycles. Similar to the one I had

163

used in Edinburgh. But less shit. I had been impressed with the speed I travelled at, but these guys were showing how it should be done. And what was even more remarkable was that they were all wearing formal clothing; most were in tweed suits complete with shirts and ties.

'What's going on?' I asked a lady who was also peering through the fence.

'It's the Brompton World Championships?' she said.

'Really? Wow, I didn't even know that was an actual thing.'

'Neither did I. It's very funny. They all start in a line, on foot, and then when the gun goes they have to run to their bike and assemble it, before climbing on and doing several laps.'

'Amazing. And what's with the tweed?'

'It's one of the requirements.'

I stood and watched as they raced lap after lap at ridiculous speeds. When the winner crossed the line, I realised I would have still been trying to unfold my bike in the time it had taken him to complete the entire race. The Brompton World Championships does not always take place in London. It happens all over the world, and this year it was London's turn, so they combined it with the RideLondon weekend. I hope to compete in the Brompton World Championships one day. It's a new addition to my bucket list.

Ben met me on his bike near St Paul's Cathedral, and we agreed to go and have one beer before heading back to his flat in Whitechapel.

Ben is a very competent London cyclist and cycles across London every day to work in his recording studio. I am not a competent city cyclist, but I hoped my Ironman training would have at least allowed me to keep up with Ben.

I was not prepared for the speed at which he navigated London. I pedalled crazily behind, trying desperately to follow his lead. I had absolutely no idea where we were going, my phone battery had died, and I had no desire to be lost on the streets of London without him.

'I'm impressed,' said Ben, looking back. 'Good following.'

'Do you mean you are trying to lose me?'

'Of course not. I just didn't think you would be able to keep up this pace.'

'I didn't have much choice.'

We turned a corner into a housing estate and faced a car that was taking up too much of the road. Ben swerved to avoid it and I did the same. The driver was already hanging half out the window, mouthing off at Ben.

'Get your bike out of the fucking road, you piece of shit,' shouted the driver.

'Sorry,' I said, raising a hand as a matter of habit.

Ben had raised his arm too, but not as means of an apology. Instead, his middle finger was raised at the driver and a big smile across his face.

'I'm gonna get you, you prick,' shouted the driver, slamming the car into reverse and following us up the street.

'Oh shit. Quick, down this way,' said Ben, cutting across the street and into the car park of a block of flats.

The car had screeched around the corner, and then turned around so that it was now facing us.

'Isn't this a dead end?' I said.

'This way,' said Ben, following the car park around to the back.

We could hear the car engine getting louder behind us. This wasn't quite how I had hoped my nice weekend in London was going to be.

We hastily cycled alongside the wire fence at the back of the flats, all the time expecting the car to come screaming around the corner. Eventually, a gap appeared and a footpath led away from the block of flats further into the housing estate. We hopped our bikes up the kerb, dodging around shards of broken glass, and pedalled frantically down the pathway, into a cul-de-sac, onto another pathway before eventually meeting the sanctuary of a main road.

'Oops, sorry about that,' said Ben.

'You idiot. What did you do that for? Did you want to get us both killed?'

'No, I don't know what came over me. Sorry.'

'Couldn't you just have waved like I did?'

'He was in the middle of the road. The knob.'

'Yes, but we did turn that corner pretty quickly.'

'Well, that's not the point.'

'Is this like a regular day in London for you?'

'Not at all. I would never normally stick my finger up at a driver like that.'

'Yeah right.'

'Honestly, I wouldn't. I think cos you're here I felt added security.'

'Great, thanks. It's a privilege to be your bodyguard. Anyway, where are we?'

'I'm not really sure. I think there's a great pub overlooking the river just down this way. Let's go and have a pint.'

It is always great to see Ben. Living 250 miles apart means we don't see a huge amount of each other, but when we do it is always easy and he never fails to make me laugh. He gave me the rundown on his latest dating escapades and one pint predictably turned into another.

An hour later, we cycled back to Ben's flat, dropped off our bikes and my bag, and headed out again for some dinner.

'What do you fancy?' asked Ben. 'Are you supposed to be carb loading or something for the bike ride?'

'Probably, but I can't be bothered with that. I'll eat anything.'

'Great. There's a burger place up here. Best burger you've ever tasted.'

'Perfect.'

Dirty Burger was a lively atmospheric restaurant, with no sign outside (like all cool places in films), with long wooden tables with people squashed onto benches. Tables could not be reserved, so we were faced with a 20 minute wait.

'Can I tempt you with a cocktail while you wait?' asked the pretty waitress, who I am fairly certain was the main reason Ben frequents Dirty Burger so often.

'Porge? Up to you, buddy. You're the one cycling 100 miles tomorrow.'

'Oh go on then. Just the one though.'

We were onto our second cocktail by the time we sat down to eat, and had moved back to beer by the time our burgers arrived. You can't eat a burger with a cocktail. Those are the rules.

The burgers were immense. Smaller than I imagined, but perfectly formed and as dirty as the name suggested; served simply, wrapped in paper with a side of fries and coleslaw. What made the restaurant so appealing to my eyes was its simplicity. The menu had a choice of just three main courses: burger, bacon burger or vegetarian burger (the *Cop Out*). Nothing annoys me more than restaurants with extensive menus. It should be made illegal for a restaurant to serve more than five dishes. Life is complicated enough as it is.

We moved on from Dirty Burger and it took all of two seconds for me to be persuaded to have one last beer at a nearby pub. Yes, I had come to London to cycle 100 miles, but I had also come to see Ben, and an early night would have been very boring. We sat at a table outside a pub on Mile End Road. It was a beautiful balmy evening in August, and I realised I was very, very drunk.

We eventually staggered back to Ben's flat via Tesco to stock up on doughnuts for pudding and tomorrow's breakfast.

'You can have my room,' said Ben, heaving a huge pile of clothes and papers off the bed and dumping them on the floor.

'Jesus. How do you sleep in that bed with all that crap on it?'

'I don't sleep in here. The room got too messy so I sleep in the spare room at the moment. But check this out,' he said, switching on a shiny white contraption that was plugged in on the bedside table.

'A TeasMade? Holy shit, do they still make those?'

'They sure do. It's the best thing ever. I'll set it up for you. What time have you got to get up?'

'Er... 4.30.'

'4.30? Seriously? What time is it now?'

'Midnight.'

'Fuck. That's like... er... not many hours sleep.'

He filled the machine with water, then placed a tea bag in a cup and added some milk. I know that adding milk before the water is verging on criminal, but I didn't want to offend him.

'I might see you when you get up, but if not then good luck with the bike ride,' he said, giving me a hug. 'Thanks so much for coming to stay.'

'Thanks so much for having me,' I said. 'It's been an awesome evening.'

I was just climbing into bed when I remembered that I still didn't have any of my race numbers or timing chip.

'Ben,' I whispered, knocking on his door. 'Whereabouts did you leave the stuff I need for the race?'

'Oh bollocks. It's all in my car. I'll run and get it for you.'

'It's ok. I can get it.'

'No, I'll go. The car is parked down the road a bit.'

He pulled on a pair of shoes and ran out of the front door in just his boxer shorts. He returned a few minutes later and handed me an envelope.

'Hopefully that should have everything you need.'

'Thanks mate. Good night.'

The instructions seemed overly complicated to my drunken brain. What seemed like an endless number of stickers and tags lay before me, and it took me nearly 15 minutes to plaster them on to what I hoped were the correct places on my bike, helmet, and race jersey. It was 12.30 by the time I climbed into bed, which meant that I would only get four hours sleep.

But even that proved optimistic. A group of girls in a neighbouring flat seemed to be celebrating a birthday or a hen do very loudly until about 2am. When the TeasMade started doing its thing at 4.30am, the idea of cycling 100 miles felt like the worst thing in the world.

My head was pounding and my mouth felt like something had died in it. Beers, cocktails, dirty burgers and a couple of hours sleep were not ideal preparation for my first ever century bike ride. But it was too late to do anything about that. It was my own stupid fault, and regardless of how the bike ride went, I'd had a damn good evening.

Ben emerged from his room just as I was wheeling my bike out through the hallway. It had just gone 5am, and he claimed that he was going to get in the car to drive up to Yorkshire to be at his mum's in time for breakfast, but I'm fairly certain I heard him climb back into bed as I walked out the front door.

It was a beautiful still morning; the calmest I had ever seen London. The sky was beginning to lighten as I pedalled through the quiet residential streets of Whitechapel.

I met Mile End Road, which I would follow all the way to the Olympic Park and was shocked to meet a steady stream of cyclists as far as I could see in either direction. What was eerie about the whole scene was that it was still deathly quiet. It was as though the cyclists had climbed from their beds onto their bikes, still half asleep, and started pedalling towards the start line. Which in most cases, they probably had.

As we approached the Olympic Park, signposts clearly directed us to our designated starting gates. I had just got off my bike when I heard a familiar voice in conversation behind me.

'Morning James,' I said.

'Hi George. What are the chances of that?'

James is a good friend of mine, and a RideLondon veteran, having taken part every year. We had agreed to phone each other when we arrived at the start to potentially meet up and say hi. There were 25,000 cyclists at Olympic Park, and we happened to be standing next to each other.

After a brief chat, we said goodbye and went to our respective starting pens. James is a proper cyclist who cycles in the Alps and Pyrenees for fun. The weirdo. Cycling RideLondon with him was never a consideration, but we arranged to meet for a beer in Green Park if he was still there when I finished.

'Nice Lycra, by the way,' he called as he cycled off.

'Thanks. I want to be just like you.'

I had been to a few events during the London Olympics but they were all at venues outside of the Olympic Park. Next to us sat the Olympic Stadium and the Aquatics Centre, both scenes of so many inspiring stories a few years ago. My hangover was wearing off, and despite the lack of sleep, I was feeling relatively spritely. It was impossible not to be taken in by the atmosphere.

It is not practical for 25,000 cyclists to all set off at the same time. Instead, cyclists start in waves a few minutes apart from six different starting areas that all merge into the same start chute. Times are recorded on a timing chip when you cross the start line, so those in earlier waves don't have any advantage.

Each starting wave was given a different song to begin their ride to; a rousing feel-good anthem to inspire and energise the cyclists, lift their spirits and fire them up, ensuring they got off to the best possible start.

Don't Stop Me Now by Queen and *Eye of the Tiger* by Survivor accompanied the start of two of the waves ahead of me. I was excited to hear what would be chosen for my start. It was a landmark event in my Ironman training, and the first 100 mile bike ride I had ever attempted. This momentous occasion would be marked by a song that would potentially become my fight song for years to come. I couldn't wait to hear what it would be.

The song that played as I crossed the start line was *Club Tropicana* by Wham.

A few ironic cheers went round our wave as we shuffled forwards on our bikes.

'What a load of shite,' laughed the man next to me.

Well, the drinks certainly were free. That's if you ignore the entry fee, and providing you are happy for the drinks to be either water or energy drinks. As for the fun and sunshine – enough for everyone – the weather forecast looked hopeful, but I wouldn't know about the fun element until later in the day.

My main concern about the start was clipping into my pedals too early and crashing sideways into a pack of stationary cyclists, causing 25,000 people to topple like dominoes. I made sure I was moving at a decent speed before clipping in.

It took me less than 100 metres before I started to love the event. After leaving the Olympic Park, the route joined the

A12 – a busy dual-carriageway that cuts through the heart of east London. Only today, it was only busy with cyclists. The entire 100 mile route is closed to traffic, which in itself is a phenomenal achievement for an event in central London. It was surreal cycling along a car-free dual-carriageway, through tunnels then over Holborn Viaduct, along Fleet Street and The Strand, ignoring all red lights and junctions. We continued on through Trafalgar Square, along Pall Mall and then Piccadilly.

I loved every minute of it. I was going at what I thought was a decent pace, but cyclists of all shapes and sizes were whizzing past me, and already people from the wave behind – identifiable by a code on their race number – had caught me up. It was slightly demoralising as I had hoped that getting on a proper road bike, with cycling shoes and the Lycra would have transformed me into a proper cyclist. But there I was, surrounded by proper cyclists, and they all seemed to be going much faster than me.

My dad's bike had a cycle computer strapped to its handlebars. But I discovered shortly after my first ride on it that it didn't work, so I had no idea what speed I was travelling, or what distance I had covered. I pulled my mobile phone out of my back pocket to check on my progress. I had been recording the route on Strava (other mapping apps are available) and was keen to see what speed I had been cycling.

My phone showed my average speed to be 20mph. We were 18 miles into the journey and I was averaging 20 MILES PER HOUR! You couldn't drive across central London at anywhere near that speed. My average speeds had all been around 12 mph in recent weeks. I averaged 10.7mph for the Dartmoor Way, so 20mph was completely new territory for me. I knew it wasn't sustainable though, and it was no wonder I was finding it such hard work already. I needed to ignore the cyclists overtaking me and settle into my own rhythm. I dropped into a lower gear and allowed my legs to spin a little quicker and more freely.

I no longer felt a fraud. I had the road bike. I had the Lycra. I had the cycling shoes. I even had some energy gels. I started to feel like I belonged.

We were soon into Richmond Park – a place I felt oddly familiar with, despite having never ventured through its gates (mostly because of the antics of a dog named Fenton). Richmond Park has become a cycling Mecca in recent years, with MAMILS frequenting its roads year-round. It also marked one of the first hills of the day, but what is considered a hill by London standards, felt little more than a slight incline compared to what Dartmoor had offered.

The route passed through Kingston upon Thames for the first time after 25 miles (it passed through again at about 85 miles), and the town had a fun street party feel to it, with hordes of spectators, cheering and clapping, music blaring and hooters squeaking.

Having passed the first feed station (or 'hub' as the organisers call them) at Hampton Court Palace without stopping, I needed a break just before the halfway point as there were a couple of big climbs to come. My feet were beginning to ache and I felt like a quick stint off my bike would do me good. Plus, I remembered the feed station in Princetown on the Dartmoor Classic and had visions of the trays of sandwiches and cakes. I could have murdered a piece of homity pie too.

There was no such luck at the RideLondon Hub. Catering for 25,000 people would be very problematic, so we had to settle for an all-you-can-eat banana buffet and some energy powder to add to our water bottles. After a quick toilet stop and a stretch of the legs I was back on the bike.

Leith Hill after 55 miles was the toughest hill of the day. Like the section during the Dartmoor Classic, Leith Hill also had a *King of the Mountains* competition. As before, I had no intention of competing beforehand, but again I couldn't resist once I passed the *Start* line. I was the 4,767th fastest up Leith Hill that day. But 10,336 people took part, which meant I was in the top half (just). I considered this progress.

The climb of Box Hill 15 miles further on gets all the attention, though. It's an iconic, National Trust owned summit surrounded by stunning Surrey countryside. The tarmac still bears the remnants of professional cycling races from recent years (most famously the Olympic 2012 road race). Messages such as *'Go Cav'*, *'Froome Dog'* and the National Trust's own branded graffiti such as *'I love cycling'*, *'I love tea and cake'* and *'I love boobies'* adorn the road's surface. That last one might not be the National Trust's.

As intimidating as it sounded, Box Hill was not nearly as tough as I had feared. It's a long old climb, but set over a series of switchbacks so the gradient isn't too strenuous.

As the route passed back through Kingston upon Thames and many other towns and suburbs, the crowds of supporters were phenomenal. I tried to acknowledge each cheer with a wave, which then caused an even louder cheer. Often people would lean over the barriers with their hands outstretched, encouraging you to dole out high-fives as you cycled past. I did this on a few occasions, but there's a fine art to it. Make too much contact and you risk knocking yourself off the bike, or snapping the spectator's arm off, which is never well received. But play it too cautiously and fail to make contact and you have to suffer the humiliation of a missed high-five. An air high-five is almost worse than breaking someone's arm.

My legs were tiring and my average speed was slowing considerably as the route made its way back into central London. I had consumed the last of my gels several miles ago and I was desperate to get off my bike.

The finish line at The Mall came into view and I put on a burst of speed to show willing. I raised both hands in the air and crossed the line, losing my balance slightly and almost clipping the barriers before grabbing for the handlebars just in time. Completing my 97 mile solo Dartmoor Way had been an amazing experience, and I loved the lack of fanfare and the understated nature of the journey. But there was also something about crossing the line in a mass participation event and having a huge chunky medal hung around my neck that was an impossible feeling to beat. RideLondon is a phenomenal event and having the opportunity to cycle 100 miles on closed roads around the nation's capital is a unique experience. It's an event that I will keep applying for again and again.

I completed the 100 miles in 5h 43m. I had hoped to finish in less than 7 hours, which would have been the equivalent speed to avoid the cut-off in the Ironman. I was in no state whatsoever to run a marathon, but I had cycled much quicker than I would during the Ironman, and I felt full of confidence that come the end of August, providing I survived the swim, I stood a good chance of completing the bike leg too.

I met up with my friend James who had been sitting in Green Park with a beer for a long while. The ride had taken him just 4.5 hours.

'How did you find it?' he asked, as I sat down on the grass and untied my cycling shoes.

'I loved it. It was an amazing experience. The last 30-40 miles were really painful though. My feet were in agony. Is that normal?'

'No, not really. You do realise you are wearing mountain bike shoes?'

'What does that mean?'

'Your cycling shoes are designed for mountain biking, not long road races.'

'Oh, what's the difference?'

'Here, look at mine,' he said, reaching for his shoes. 'The sole is rigid. It doesn't bend at all.'

I tried bending my own shoes and was almost able to fold them in half.

'I thought flexible shoes would be more comfortable,' I said.

'No, because your mountain bike cleats are much smaller than my SPD-SL cleats, so there is a smaller surface area and the sole of your foot bends around the pedal. That's why your feet are so sore.'

'Are your pedals bigger then?'

'Yes, much. It's a bigger surface area, and because the soles are rigid all of the pressure from your foot goes into the pedal, rather than around it. Imagine hammering a nail with a hammer, compared to hammering it with your foot.'

'Yeah, that makes sense. I think maybe I should invest in some road cycling shoes. I couldn't run a marathon with feet like this.'

'Why would you run a marathon after wearing cycling shoes?'

'Oh, did I not tell you? I've entered an Ironman.'

'An Ironman? When?'

'It's in four weeks.'

'Didn't you have back surgery recently?'

'Yes. Just over three months ago.'

'And how is your back?

'It still gets uncomfortable quite often, but the exercise doesn't seem to make it worse.'

176

'Well you're completely mad, but good luck,' he said. 'I hope it all goes well. I think road cycling shoes are definitely a good idea in that case.'

'I think so too.'

'Same time here next year?'

'I hope so,' I said.

I limped slowly back to Paddington Station, via McDonalds, and then sat and tried to keep myself awake for four hours as I had bought a cheap non-transferable ticket for an evening train back to Devon, assuming that I would have finished a lot later than I did. I slept the entire way home, and woke just as the train pulled into the station.

25

While in London with Ben we got talking about procrastination. As a fellow self-employed layabout, Ben and I have a lot in common. Having all this free time at your disposal should be an amazing thing, but it is never as good as it sounds. Ben forwarded me an article that he had read on the website *waitbutwhy.com*, written by Tim Urban. In it he talks about the *Dark Playground*.

'The Dark Playground is a place every procrastinator knows well. It's a place where leisure activities happen at times when leisure activities are not supposed to be happening. The fun you have in the Dark Playground isn't actually fun because it's completely unearned and the air is filled with guilt, anxiety, self-hatred, and dread.'

I realised that I spend a lot of my existence in the Dark Playground. Training for an Ironman could have been fun, but every bike ride, swim or run, was laced with guilt that I should be using my time more constructively. I shouldn't complain. People with 9 to 5 jobs who train for endurance challenges have to sacrifice far more than I had to. All of their training sessions have to be squeezed into the anti-social hours around work and other commitments. But that training time is at least earned. They deserve the right to spend their time doing a largely selfish leisure activity. I couldn't claim that luxury.

I tried to convince myself that my training was work. I would complete the Ironman and then write a book about it, therefore justifying all the hours I was 'wasting' on my leisure activities. But that didn't seem to work either. I couldn't even think about the possibility of writing a book until I had crossed that finish line.

Both before and after my surgery, I had been trying to write a book about my travels in America. Progress was slow and it had proved too painful to sit and work at my desk for any length of time. Yet it felt hypocritical to go out for a long bike ride instead. If I could cycle, surely I could sit at my desk? However, the more active I was, the more comfortable my back felt.

I talked it through with Rachel and she didn't seem to think there was a problem.

'If anything I think you should be training more.'

'Really?'

'Of course. I thought people who trained for Ironmans were out doing stuff all day every day. You have been for a few bike rides and been swimming once or twice a week. That's hardly overdoing it.'

'But I haven't earned it?'

'Why do you need to earn it? Forget the Ironman. You're getting fitter than you would have been if you hadn't entered it. You're making an amazing recovery from your operation. Wasn't that the whole point anyway?'

As usual, Rachel was right. I had become blinded by the Ironman and forgotten why I had signed up. It wasn't to get the medal. It wasn't to get the t-shirt (although they were both undoubtedly factors). It was to give me an incentive to get fitter, stronger and healthier following my surgery. That was more important than any medal, t-shirt or book I needed to write.

It was now the school holidays, and realistically I knew the chances of me getting any writing done at home were minimal. There was little point in trying to fight it. In September, things would be back to normal; the children would be back at school, the Ironman would be over and I could try and get some work done. Until then, it was time for me to get out of the Dark Playground. It was time for me to have some fun.

179

26

The only way for me to gain some self confidence about my ability to complete the Ironman swim was to actually attempt to swim the required distance. I could try swimming 2.4 miles in the pool, but the conditions would not be the same. I needed to attempt a long swim in open water.

I had searched for fresh water swimming lakes in or near Devon, but couldn't find anything suitable. I then came across the Plymouth Breakwater Swim – an annual charity swim in Plymouth Sound – held in the middle of August, two weeks before my Ironman. Swimmers are loaded into boats and ferried 2.2 miles out into the ocean towards France. They then jump into the sea, and swim back to shore. 2.2 miles was not quite the Ironman distance, but it was damn near close enough.

I went to the website to register, but it had sold out months before. So I sent the event organiser an email to have my name added to the waiting list, and had a reply straight back telling me he was in the process of replying to the email of another swimmer who had just pulled out. He offered me their place if I could fill in the forms and get my entry fee in the post that same day. So I did.

The thought of being in open water 2.2 miles out to sea terrified me. The thought of then having to swim back to the shore was pretty much my idea of hell. But I knew that it was a fear I needed to overcome. If I could do this, then there was every chance that I could complete at least the first part of the Ironman. And if I couldn't complete it? Well, I didn't really want to think about that, but it would put a massive question mark over the chances of me even starting the Ironman in Vichy.

In the event of bad weather, the swim would be postponed for two weeks, and the backup date was scheduled for the day I would be doing the Ironman. This was my only chance. The weather forecast had been bad all week, but I was greeted on the morning of the event with blue sky and almost no wind. The conditions were absolutely perfect.

After registering and collecting my hat and luggage tag, a volunteer wrote a number onto my arm and leg with a permanent marker.

'It's so they can identify the body,' she joked and laughed. I laughed too. And then there was a slightly awkward pause before she added: 'Actually, I think that really is the reason. But don't worry, you'll be absolutely fine.'

I still had an hour to wait before we got on the boat and nothing to do, so I lurked around on my own looking nervous.

'It doesn't look too bad,' I said to another guy standing next to me, as I gazed at what I assumed was the breakwater in the distance.

'What? That's not the breakwater. That's just the harbour wall. That's the breakwater,' he said, pointing to the horizon.

'You're joking,' I said. 'Jesus, it's miles away.'

'2.2 miles away. But it looks a lot further.'

'Have you done this before?' I asked.

'Once. A couple of years ago.'

'And you're back again, so it can't have been that bad.'

'I'm just a glutton for punishment. I assume this is your first time?'

'Yes. How did you guess?'

'You've got that look,' he said. 'Have you swum this sort of distance before?'

'No. I don't think I've ever swum further than a mile.'

'Oh, ok. You're obviously a glutton for punishment too. You'll be fine.'

Eavesdropping on the conversations of others didn't do much to calm my nerves.

'This is just a warm up for me for the River Dart 10K swim in September,' I heard one of them boasting.

'I've postponed my channel swim for a week so that I could take part in this,' said another.

At 1.30pm we were all asked to board the boats. I took a seat at the back next to two other men who looked equally nervous. It turned out neither of them had taken part before either. One had swum the equivalent distance in a pool before, and the other had a lot of open water experience but nothing at this level.

As the boat began its journey out towards the breakwater, Plymouth started looking smaller and smaller. Because that is how perspective works. But for some reason, the breakwater remained a thin line on the horizon. We would be swimming back to Tinside, which is a small cove below Plymouth Hoe. The Hoe is marked by a prominent red and white striped lighthouse. This lighthouse – known as Smeaton's Tower – was originally used to mark the notorious Eddystone Rocks between 1759 and 1877. These rocks lie nine miles off the coast of Cornwall, and are submerged at particularly high tides and extremely feared by sailors. So much so, that many ships used to hug the coastline to try and avoid them, and end up getting shipwrecked on other rocks nearby instead.

Smeaton's Tower was revolutionary in design, and paved the way for other lighthouses. It was eventually dismantled in 1877 and rebuilt – piece by piece – on Plymouth Hoe as a memorial to its designer John Smeaton. It's a landmark that dominates the Plymouth shoreline. It would be the landmark we were to aim for when swimming back to shore.

Although this monolith measures 72 feet tall and 26 feet wide, it appeared as just a speck on the horizon once we neared the breakwater. I was genuinely terrified. Looking back at the shore, it didn't seem possible that ANYBODY could swim that distance, let alone me. As the rest of the swimmers on the boat chatted casually to each other, as though this was just a normal Sunday swim for them, me and the other two Breakwater virgins just looked at each other and laughed at the ridiculousness of the situation. What the hell were we doing?

The boat came to a stop close to the breakwater, which was vast and imposing up close. It is a wall almost a mile long, and was first conceived in 1806 during the Napoleonic Wars as a means to protect Plymouth harbour from both the sea and the enemy. Four million tonnes of rock were used to create the breakwater during its construction in 1812, and it has undergone many transformations since.

We were told to jump into the water from the side of the boat and congregate between our boat and the other about 50 metres away. The water felt cool and refreshing, and far cleaner and clearer than I had expected the harbour of a big city to look. I wished my two friends good luck, and once we were in the water with our hats and goggles on I was unable to identify either of them again.

After my unsuccessful training swim with my dad in the kayak, I realised I needed to do something about my goggles to try and prevent them from fogging up so often. There are many suggested remedies including buying dedicated anti-fog sprays, or using a smear of olive oil or Vaseline inside the lenses. But the method most commonly recommended, and the one taught to me way back in Stroke Development 1, is the use of good old fashioned spit. Just put a bit of saliva in both goggles, smear it around a bit, give them a quick rinse and you're good to go. I'd forgotten how effective it is, but it works wonders.

We all treaded water for a few minutes before the event organiser told us to get ready. He then sounded an air horn and all hell broke loose. Two hundred swimmers were spread out over a width of 50 metres, and I had been towards the far end of the line so didn't expect the start to be too much of a scrum. The start line was only about three swimmers deep so there didn't seem much that could go wrong. Immediately after putting my face in the water, I was caught in the nose by the heel of the swimmer in front. As I came up for air, the swimmer behind then swam directly over me, forcing me underwater. I had heard of these things happening at mass swims, but for some reason I had expected this 'charity swim' to be a little more sedate.

By the time I composed myself and started swimming again, most of the swimmers that had been around me were powering ahead and I felt a surge of panic that I was completely out of my depth. Quite literally.

It isn't a race, I kept telling myself. *All I need to do is complete the distance, just to prove that I can, and it doesn't matter if I am the last person out of the water.*

I put my head down and tried to get into a rhythm. Right arm, left arm, right arm, breathe, left arm, right arm, left arm, breathe. My once concrete legs glided effortlessly behind me, and my body – and that all important core – was rotating and cutting through the water with ease. But each time I looked up to check my direction the swimmers in front of me had put even more of a gap between us. But if it wasn't a race, then why did I care?

And then I realised that it wasn't being last that I was concerned about. It was swimming alone in the middle of the frickin' ocean. Surrounded by other swimmers at the start I hadn't felt vulnerable as there were so many of us. And if there were any angry sea creatures beneath those waves, then hopefully they would eat one of the other poor swimmers instead. But left on my own, I was a sitting duck.

Just three months previously, a giant conger eel, measuring over 7 feet long and weighing 131 lbs, was caught in these very waters. Despite this being an extremely rare catch, and the fact that conger eels pose no danger to humans, it still got my heart racing quicker than it should have.

On the plus side, we had started our swim at low tide, which meant that after about 20 minutes the tide would have started to come in, reducing our chances of being swept out to France.

I eventually managed to control my breathing again and got back into some sort of rhythm. I was still alternating my front crawl with breaststroke because I didn't yet have the stamina to swim front crawl long distance.

I approached a yellow shipping buoy which, from a distance, had appeared the size of a football. Alongside it, it towered above me, threatening and intimidating, the water gently lapping against its sides causing it to lightly clang. I gave it an extremely wide berth and tried not to think about the size or state of the underwater chain that must be holding a device like that in place.

Plymouth Sound, despite being a relatively calm and sheltered bay because of the breakwater, is also a busy shipping lane. They had thankfully timed the event so that we didn't have to swim into the oncoming path of one of the scheduled Brittany Ferries. But Plymouth is also the location of the largest naval base in Western Europe, and there were plenty of other ships about. Although not close enough to be of any risk to the swimmers, the wake felt as the ships passed was considerable. I could feel the swell rushing under me, lifting me effortlessly with its raw power, before dropping me down into the bow of the wave, before rising again.

The rollers were so big that once in the bow, the horizon was completely out of sight, making it very disorientating. I have never suffered from seasickness, but trying to swim in the undulating current was making me feel dizzy and nauseous. I started treading water as there was no point trying to swim against these rollers. After a minute or two they flattened out as the frigate eventually passed the breakwater. I've no idea if it was actually a frigate. I just wanted to use the word as I like it and have never written it before. Frigate. There it is again.

The organisers had stated that, depending on tides, they would install a cut-off time of about two hours to complete the swim. Rather than just remove any swimmers still in the water at this point, they would pick up slower swimmers earlier in the course on paddleboards and kayaks, and move them closer to the shore. That way everyone, however slow, still got a chance to actually complete the swim, even if they hadn't covered the full distance.

I glanced at my watch. I had been in the water for 25 minutes. *Was this quick enough to avoid being picked up?* I had no idea. There were no distance markers and no way of being able to gauge how far we had come.

It was a supported event, which meant that there were kayaks and people on stand-up paddleboards dotted around. If we got into any trouble, we were told to roll onto our back and wave our hands in the air. Help would then soon be with us. This was comforting to know, but as the field spread out, so did the distance from the nearest support raft. In the bow of the waves from the passing ships I could not see any of the support crew. This also meant that they couldn't see me.

The field had spread out considerably and I could see swimmers far off in the distance ahead, nobody behind me and nobody to my right either. A girl in a kayak soon paddled towards me and I concluded that I must have been going far too slow and was surely going to be hoisted aboard.

'Am I going to miss the cut-off?' I asked, treading water alongside her.

'No, you're making great progress. You've just drifted very far to the right. The current is dragging you that way, so try and aim a bit further left.'

'So I'm not one of the last?'

'No way. You're somewhere in the middle. Everyone is just way over that way.'

I looked left, and could see in the distance, at least 100 yards away, plenty of flailing arms and kicking legs. They had been there all along. I had just drifted so far to the right that it felt like I was the only swimmer left.

I set off again with renewed energy... and a new bearing. After a few minutes I was amongst other swimmers once more and feeling a lot more comfortable.

We had been in the water for almost an hour when I was able to pick out the beach at Tinside. Tinside is a small enclosed bay in Plymouth that has been popular with swimmers for generations. It is relatively sheltered and there are purpose built steps and covered benches for changing that look like they have been there for almost as long as the breakwater. I was just able to make out a mass of people congregating by the water's edge, and could hear the faint cheering and clapping in the wind.

Rachel had offered to bring the children and come and watch me, but I had persuaded her not to. Open water swimming is a pretty rubbish spectator sport. Tiny red dots on the horizon (we all wore identical swimming hats) all get closer and closer to shore, where they eventually emerge from the

187

water clad in black neoprene and goggles, all still looking identical. I was still a long way from shore, but already I was wishing I had not discouraged them.

Despite my spells of breaststroke, I was still just about keeping up the pace of those around me. We swam past another couple of shipping buoys and I was relieved to see other swimmers giving them a wide berth, too.

For the final half an hour I began to tire considerably. My arms felt twice as heavy as they had at the start, and it was a real effort just to lift them from the water to keep my stroke going. I started to experience the most excruciating pain in my forehead, like an intense migraine. I think it was a combination of my head being face down in cold water for so long – something it certainly wasn't used to – and my goggles being too tight. I had to stop every couple of minutes to lift off my goggles to relieve the pressure and allow my head to defrost slightly.

I could make out the shapes of people on the shore now. There were hundreds of them. Many were the swimmers who had already reached the shore, and the rest were friends and family.

I now had land to my left and was inside the cove. The shore was only about 400 metres away. It wasn't until this point that I knew I was going to make it. Even if I swam doggy paddle the rest of the way I would be able to complete the distance.

The last few hundred metres seemed to take an eternity. My body was completely drained and I started trying to put my feet down way too early, which kept resulting in me disappearing awkwardly beneath the water and then resurfacing and trying to act like I meant to do it. Eventually, a few metres from the shore, my foot made contact with the loose rocks of the sea floor. I rose to my feet and a couple of race volunteers took hold of an arm each to help me out of the water.

'Fantastic, well done,' said one of them as he hung a medal around my neck. 'How do you feel?'

'Glad to be on dry land,' I said.

'Go and sit down and take it easy for a few minutes. There's chicken soup and coffee up at the cafe whenever you're ready.'

The crowd were all cheering and whooping. Not just at me, but at all those that were still making their final few strokes to the shore. Then I heard a couple of familiar voices.

'Daddy!'

I looked around excitedly, assuming it was just a voice similar to one of my children's, but Layla, Leo and Kitty all emerged in the crowd, dodging in and out of spectators and tired swimmers as they made their way over to me.

'What a lovely surprise. I didn't know you were coming.'

'We had to keep it a secret from you,' said Leo.

I spotted Rachel standing a little further down the beach, and I staggered towards her with three children clinging to my legs.

'Urgh, you're all soggy,' said Kitty.

'Well done, Daddy. We knew you'd make it,' said Layla, holding up a hand-drawn sign she had made, that said *'Go Daddy'* and then, weirdly, underneath she had written *'Go George Mahood.'*

'Thanks so much for coming. This is very sweet of you all,' I said to Rachel.

'We weren't going to miss this. Well done, we're so proud of you. You were so quick too.'

'When did you decide to come?'

'As soon as you said you were doing it.'

'And the children kept it a secret all this time?'

'As if! I only told them this morning after you had left.'

'Well it's so good to see you all here. I was secretly hoping that you might be.'

'How do you feel?'

'Dreadful,' I said, lowering myself onto the pebble beach. 'I feel like I might be sick, and my head is spinning.'

'Would you like anything to eat? We've got all sorts of sweets and snacks here.'

'No thanks. I just need a few minutes.'

I sat there on the pebble beach with my head between my knees, trying to stop the world from turning. I had mixed emotions. I had successfully completed one of the hardest, most intimidating things I had ever attempted. It was a distance almost equal to the Ironman swim so I felt more confident about my chances of finishing that. But another part of me was wondering how on earth I could then get on a bike and cycle 112 miles, and follow that up with a marathon. I could barely even walk, let alone cycle.

I hoped a lot of what I was feeling was because of the cold water. I had felt dizzy after my other attempts at open-water swimming, and then later read that this is caused by cold water getting into the inner-ear and interfering with your body's balance sensors. It's probably not called a balance sensor. I'm sure there's a medical term for it, as that sounds like something you're more likely to find in a car, but you get the point.

The other factor was the current and the waves. My Ironman swim would take place in a lake. Hopefully a nice, calm, warm, flat lake. I could but dream.

After ten minutes I was able to get to my feet and I staggered slowly up the concrete steps to the cafe where they were handing out cups of chicken soup with bread and cups of coffee. On the way home I joined Rachel and the kids for a celebratory burger and chips and I devoured my bodyweight in greasy junk food.

I began to feel a bit more human, and wondered about the practicalities of arranging to have hot soup, coffee, a burger and chips waiting for me in the transition area at the Ironman. It seemed unlikely.

I had just completed a 2.2 mile sea swim. It was something that before my surgery – just four months previously – I would never have dreamed possible for me to achieve. Even a few days ago I had very much doubted my ability to cover the distance. Yet here I was with a medal proudly hanging around my neck, and a feeling that maybe, just maybe, I might now have what it takes to complete the Ironman swim.

27

I received a message later that evening from a good friend of mine named Emily.

Emily is a florist from Northampton, and during my years working as a wedding photographer we used to see each other regularly at wedding venues. She would be there early in the morning to set up the flowers for the wedding breakfast and the ceremony rooms, and I would be taking photos of the venue before the bride arrived to get ready.

We used to play a childish game with some of the other wedding suppliers to keep us amused. The game involved replacing the word *'love'* from song titles with the word *'knob'*. It is surprisingly fun and would entertain us for many hours.

Some of my favourites were:

Knob Me Tender – Elvis Presley
Knob Is All Around – Wet Wet Wet
I'm Just a Killer for Your Knob – Blur
You Can't Hurry Knob – Phil Collins
I Will Always Knob You – Whitney Houston/Dolly Parton
Knob Me Do – The Beatles
I'd Do Anything for Knob (But I Won't Do That) – Meatloaf

Once the bride arrived, I got rid of my immaturity and became a focussed professional for the rest of the day. That was until the first dance started and the happy couple had chosen a song such as Elton John's *Can You Feel The Love Tonight* and I had to spend four minutes with my face squashed up against my camera to hide my tears of laughter.

Emily had major knee surgery at a young age. She was told she wouldn't ever be able to run again. 15 marathons later, she has never looked back. Emily then entered the Frankfurt Ironman in 2014 having never competed in a triathlon before and being unable to swim at the time of entering. She spent six months having intensive swimming lessons and then found out a few weeks before the Ironman that she was a few months pregnant. She still took part, completing the swim inside the cut-off, and being the last female out of the water. She then cycled about 70 miles of the 112 mile bike course in ridiculously hot conditions, getting two punctures in the process and was eventually pulled up by marshals who decided she would miss the strict German 15 hour cut-off time.

Undeterred, she knew she would complete an Ironman one day. She had her baby and recently began training for a second attempt at Ironman Frankfurt in 2016. When she found out I had signed up for Ironman Vichy in 2015 she sent me a message telling me she thought I was completely mad but that it was exactly the sort of thing she would have done in my situation. I replied, only half jokingly, telling her that there were still spaces available for Vichy and why was she waiting until next year? She replied saying 'don't tempt me.' So I obviously tried to tempt her.

It turned out that Emily was going to be holidaying in France with her husband and daughter at the time of the Ironman anyway. They would be staying about 300 miles from Vichy, but still, it was in the same country at least.

Emily had been trying to persuade her husband Pete that it would be a good idea to drive a few hundred miles during the middle of their holiday for her to take on the Ironman, and then drive back a few hundred miles to finish the rest of their holiday before tackling the long drive back to the UK.

In the evening after the Breakwater Swim, Emily's message told me that Pete had finally relented. She was in.

It was reassuring to know that there would be a familiar face amongst the crowds when I lined up for the start in two weeks' time.

28

The following morning I returned to Plymouth Hoe. This time with my bike. I planned to tackle my toughest ride yet. The Devon Coast to Coast.

Sustrans Route 27 is a marked cycle route that stretches from Plymouth on the south coast all the way up the western edge of Dartmoor to Ilfracombe on the north coast of Devon. It is a distance of about 101 miles, and on mostly traffic-free routes.

I planned to attempt the coast to coast at a decent speed, with far fewer stops than I had done on my Dartmoor Way ride. I had a bed booked for the night in Ilfracombe, and if all went to plan, I hoped to cycle back to Plymouth the following day.

Having completed the Plymouth Breakwater swim only hours before, it would also be good practice for my body going from one endurance event to another in a relatively short space of time. If only I would have the luxury of a couple of meals and a seven hour sleep between my swim and bike in the Ironman.

It was 7am and I had lucked out with the weather once again. There was not a cloud in the sky, and not a breath of wind. It was forecast to be a hot one, so I was anxious to get a good chunk of the distance completed before the temperature rose too high.

From below Smeaton's Tower (the red and white striped lighthouse) I looked out towards the Breakwater. It was now high tide so even less of it was showing in the distance. It was surreal to think that only yesterday I had been in that water, swimming that incredible distance.

Following my friend James's advice after RideLondon, I bought a pair of road cycling shoes, and some new pedals. This was to be the very first time I had used them. What better way to test out a new pair of cycling shoes, than by cycling over 100 miles in them? Walking around on the pavement in them was a strange sensation. It was like wearing a pair of clogs. Not that I've ever worn clogs. They were comfortable though, and once on the bike, they clicked into the pedals far more effortlessly than the mountain bike shoes I'd worn previously.

I was back on my cyclocross bike for this ride. The majority of the coast to coast is fairly well-surfaced, but I knew from experience that there were a few sections of rough gravelled path and a couple of short stints of tough rocky track that were unsuitable for a road bike. I had also bought and fitted a rear pannier rack to hold a change of clothes for my overnight stay in Ilfracombe.

The blue Route 27 sign directed me down the hill into Plymouth Barbican. The Barbican is the original harbour area of Plymouth, and it was one of only a few parts of the city to miraculously escape the bombings in the Second World War. It's a beautiful area full of old buildings and cobbled streets. Once the site of the main fish market, it is now a centre for bars, cafes and galleries. It also, more importantly, has a public toilet, which I had to wait outside until it automatically opened at 7.30am.

I didn't have a map with me. Or any form of directions. I wanted to see if I could cycle coast to coast relying solely on the trusty blue signposts.

I love maps. I'm a bit of a geek when it comes to maps, and will happily sit and look at an Ordnance Survey map for hours, just for the simple pleasure of looking at it. This obsession – inherited from my dad – is not just confined to proper maps used for navigation. Even at a theme park, or family attraction, I will make sure the free map and guide is always in my hand. It's not because of a fear of getting lost, but a desire to make sure I've seen everything there is to see.

My mapless coast to coast was going to be hard, but I hoped it would be therapeutic. Like an addict trying to rid the habit of a lifetime, I would be going cold turkey. I didn't have an emergency map in my pannier in case I couldn't hack it any longer. I didn't have the route saved into my phone. I didn't have a get out clause. I was being thrown in at the deep end, and I found it strangely exhilarating.

The route crosses the harbour at the Barbican via a footbridge.

The bridge was closed.

My route was blocked before I had even covered half a mile. I cycled along the cobbled streets around the perimeter of the Barbican, trying to keep the other side of the bridge in my sights, hoping to rejoin the route there. Another section of the harbour was being redeveloped so I had to detour around a building and by the time I emerged I had lost sight of the bridge.

'Excuse me, how do I get to the other end of the footbridge that crosses the Barbican?' I asked a smartly dressed lady presumably on her way to work.

'Which bridge is that, dear?'

'It's a white one that goes across the harbour from one side to the other.'

'I'm not really sure, I'm afraid. Where are you trying to get to?'

'The bridge that goes over the harbour. It's closed so I am trying to get to the other side of it.'

'Yes, but where do you want to go from there. I might be able to give you directions to get to your destination?'

'I don't really know where I am going after that. I am following blue signs and I'm hoping that I will meet another one there.'

'Oh, ok,' she said, looking at me as though I was a lunatic. 'If you follow this road, then turn left, past the aquarium then I think the bridge you are talking about pops out the other side somewhere.'

'Fantastic, thank you.'

'You're welcome. I hope you find your next signpost. Where are you hoping it will lead you eventually?'

'Ilfracombe.'

She laughed.

'Really? But that's in north Devon. How many days will that take you?'

'I'm hoping to be there by the end of today.'

She looked at me as though I told her I was hoping to fly to the moon.

'Well good luck. You'd better get cracking.'

I followed her directions, and sure enough, there was a trusty blue sign at the other end of the bridge.

The Devon Coast to Coast has been a project many years in the making. Graham Cornish – a National Cycle Network Project Manager at Devon County Council – had the vision of a mostly traffic-free route linking the coastal town of Ilfracombe in north Devon with the city of Plymouth on the south coast. Initially in partnership with SUSTRANS (a UK charity devoted to sustainable transport), he spent many years assembling the route using predominantly old railway lines and sourcing funding to link all of the various sections together. Old bridges and viaducts were restored, tunnels reopened, and an infrastructure put in place to make it all possible. The result is one of the most beautiful and accessible long distance cycle routes in the UK.

I followed the route along the coast, through the Cattedown suburb of Plymouth with views over the mouth of the River Plym. The route then turned inland and joined the Plym Valley trail at the National Trust-owned Saltram. The Plym Valley trail follows the wooded route of the old Plym Valley railway for a little over ten miles. The route gradually climbs onto the moor, but the gradient is fairly gentle making this an extremely popular spot for families. At 8am on a Monday, however, I had the place to myself.

I was making good progress, and, as I followed the Drake's Trail to Tavistock, then Lydford and onto the Granite Way, it was refreshing to cycle through areas I felt familiar with, having cycled them twice on my previous two Dartmoor Way trips. But this time I was tackling it in reverse. I mean south to north. I wasn't cycling backwards.

I reached Okehampton by lunchtime and stopped at the same bakery I had stopped at during my Dartmoor Way ride for yet another pasty and to refill my water bottles.

Diet and nutrition play a huge part in many people's preparation for an endurance event. Hundreds of books have been written on the subject and the internet is full of blogs and nutrition guides extolling the virtues of particular diets such as *paleo, vegan, ketogenic, carb-backloading* and their benefits to endurance sport.

I have nothing at all against these diets, and I'm sure they each have their benefits for different types of people. But not for me. Any positive effect that such a strict diet or eating regime might have on my performance or well-being, would be counteracted by the added hassle caused, and the disappointment of missing out on eating the foods I love. I hadn't altered my diet at all during my Ironman training. I had continued to try and eat a balanced diet and had not abstained from anything. I had just eaten more of EVERYTHING. As a compromise, and to show willing, I planned to eat a big bowl of pasta the night before the Ironman. It seemed like the right thing to do. That was as far as planning my diet extended.

If I had been taking part in an Ironman in Wales or Bolton, I might have considered avoiding alcohol for a few days before the race. But we were going to be on holiday in FRANCE. What sort of a holiday would it be if I abstained from beer and wine for the duration? It would be an insult to the people of France, and incredibly disrespectful. My night out in London with Ben hadn't done too much to sabotage my performance or enjoyment of RideLondon, but I realised that might have been a fluke. I was prepared to make a small sacrifice for the possible greater good. I would drink beer and wine in moderation all week on our French holiday, but abstain from alcohol on the evening before the Ironman.

The stretch north of Okehampton was unfamiliar to me. I followed quiet country roads through the market town of Hatherleigh and on towards the brilliantly named village of Sheepwash.

I can picture the scene back in 1166 when the first use of the name is documented.

'Hey, Edward, we should probably give this darn settlement of ours a name, don't you think?'

'I agree, John. What shall we call it?'

'I don't know,' said John, while washing a sheep. 'How about Sheepwash?'

'Perfect.'

It was not long after leaving Sheepwash that I realised I was lost. I hadn't seen a route 27 sign in over half an hour, and instead had been aimlessly following signs for a different cycle route hoping that it would rejoin the coast to coast further on.

But the other route's signs had disappeared too, and I was becoming more and more convinced that I was cycling way off route.

I stopped to ask a lady for directions, but because I didn't know where the coast to coast was supposed to pass through, and because she hadn't ridden a bike in 40 years, we didn't make much progress. She pointed in the direction that she thought was Ilfracombe, which was vaguely in the direction I was headed, and filled me with a tiny fraction of hope.

My mileage for the day was going to be in excess of 100 miles and I didn't want to add any unnecessary diversions to increase this. I could use Google Maps to pinpoint where I was, and then see if any of the towns or villages nearby sounded familiar. Would that be breaking my no map rule? Yes, but I was lost, and it was a fairly stupid rule anyway. Even the Sustrans website had recommended taking a map. They even sell a guidebook for the route, which implies that it does require a bit of navigating.

I reluctantly pulled my phone from my pocket.

There was no signal.

I laughed at myself and was left with no choice but to just trust my instincts and hope I was heading in roughly the right direction.

To my relief, a mile or so later, I met the end of the Tarka Trail, which forms part of the Devon Coast to Coast. The Tarka Trail is a series of cycle paths and footpaths, covering 180 miles in a figure-of-eight around Barnstaple. The coast to coast follows a beautiful 30 mile – mostly tarmacked – section of it all the way to Braunton, just north of Barnstaple.

The section between Bideford and Banstaple was the busiest section of cycle path I have ever cycled on. It was the school holidays and lots of families were out enjoying the rare section of flat, traffic-free land in Devon. My speed slowed considerably as I had to weave in and out of other cyclists, but it felt great to see so many people enjoying being out on a bike.

Lots of bikes were towing trailers, and I just assumed that these were for young children. As I approached one of them, I heard some angry snarling coming from the trailer. I guessed it must be a petulant child, but as I passed I saw it was a small Yorkshire terrier sitting snugly in the trailer and it yapped and growled at me as I went by.

'He doesn't seem very happy,' I said to the lady towing him.

'Oh he loves it back there. He just doesn't like other cyclists.'

'Oh I see.'

I thought it was a bit odd seeing a dog in a trailer, but then I started to take a closer look at all of the other trailers, and almost all of those that I passed contained dogs. Pugs, Terriers, Dalmatians, Alsatians, Labradoodles, dogs of all shapes and sizes, all going for 'walks' in trailers. I had never seen anything like it. I had thought Bovey Tracey dog walkers were weird, but Bideford had just raised the bar.

The final few miles between Barnstaple and Ilfracombe were the hardest of the day. This was partly because these two towns are either side of an enormous hill, but mostly because the coast to coast had just about broken me.

I averaged 12.4 mph for the day, which doesn't sound particularly fast (it would not be anywhere near quick enough to make the bike cut-off time for the Ironman), but I had been on a cyclocross bike, heavily laden with panniers, covering a distance of over 100 miles with over 6,000 feet of climbing on often unsurfaced tracks. It was no wonder I felt so wrecked.

Despite my suffering, it had been an amazing day; probably my best ever day on a bike. The weather and scenery had been wonderful, but, more importantly, I had experienced an immense feeling of fun. During a leisure activity. On a work day. I was well and truly out of the Dark Playground.

I had booked a hostel in Ilfracombe for the night, with the intention of cycling back to Plymouth the following day. I now knew the cycle home wasn't going to happen. I laboured up the final hill before the descent into Ilfracombe, my bike seemingly getting heavier and heavier the closer I got to the finish. As I freewheeled down the long, steep hill into town, I felt a huge sense of relief and satisfaction. Not only had I completed the Devon Coast to Coast in a day, but my Ironman cycle training was now over. I had completed three rides of around 100 miles – two of them on terrain that would be far tougher than the terrain in France – and I truly felt like I was ready.

'Where have you come from?' asked the young man at the reception of the Ocean Backpackers hostel in Ilfracombe.

'Plymouth,' I said.

'Ah, you did the coast to coast?'

'I sure did.'

'Nice one. When did you leave?'

'About 9 hours ago.'

'You did it in one day?'

'Yes.'

'That's impressive. We don't get many people in here that do it in one day. Most do it over two or three days.'

'That sounds far more sensible.'

'I've always wanted to cycle it.'

'You should definitely do it. Are you a cyclist?'

'Not really, well, yeah... I mean I do quite a lot of cycling.'

'I was going to cycle back to Plymouth tomorrow, but it's broken me. I've decided to get the train instead.'

'You should definitely cycle back. Don't get the train.'

'But it's a very long way, and I'm knackered.'

'You'll feel better in the morning.'

'I know, but I'm going to quit while I'm ahead and get the train.'

'It's cheating taking a bike on a train. Everyone knows that.'

'Do they?'

'Yes, it's frowned upon,' he smiled.

'Well, if anyone frowns I will tell them I cycled 101 miles today.'

'But it's mostly flat isn't it?'

'No, it really isn't. I thought it would be but it's not. Can you get a train from Ilfracombe directly to Plymouth?'

'No.'

'Where can you get to from Ilfracombe?'

'Nowhere.'

'Why?'

'The train station closed about 50 years ago.'

'Oh. Where is the nearest train station?'

'Barnstaple. But to get to Plymouth you have to go from Barnstaple to Exeter and then get another train to Plymouth. So you might as well cycle straight to Exeter instead.'

'How far is that?'

'Not far. Only about 50 miles or so.'

'50 MILES? No chance! I'll just get the train from Barnstaple. Could you possibly book me a taxi for about 9am tomorrow please?'

'No, putting a bike on a train is bad, but putting a bike in a taxi is pretty much criminal. I can't let you do that.'

'How far is Barnstaple train station from here?'

'Not far. Maybe 11 miles.'

'Is it a nice 11 miles?'

'Yes, if you follow the old Barnstaple road it's lovely. It's straight the whole way.'

'Ok, fine,' I conceded. 'I'll cycle to Barnstaple.'

As annoying as he sounded, I did sort of agree with him. It did feel a bit wrong getting the train back to Plymouth. And paying for a taxi to transport me 11 miles would be a crime. I conceded that I would cycle to the train station, but I was not going to feel guilty about not cycling back to Plymouth. In less than two weeks I would be taking part in an Ironman (in case you hadn't got that message). I had completed an extremely long and tough training ride, and, if I pushed myself, yes, I probably could make it back to Plymouth, but I wouldn't have gained anything.

I wheeled my bike around to the back of the hostel and put it into the storage room amongst some drying washing and a couple of surfboards. My room on the top floor was nice and simple with a bunk bed and a chair, and a bathroom just across the hall. I had a quick shower, put on my glad rags (a clean t-shirt, shorts and flip flops) and hit the town. It was 6pm and Ilfracombe was bustling with families enjoying the gorgeous summer weather.

I sat at a table outside one of the waterfront pubs and had a beer overlooking the harbour. It's incredible how much nicer beer tastes after a hard day's exercise. I finished that beer and then had another, before realising that two beers after that amount of exertion had made me feel a little tipsy.

There was a long line of people queuing outside one of the fish and chips shops, which I assumed meant it must be good. The other similar-looking fish and chip shop a few doors down had no queue. It's possible that everyone in line had the same mentality as me, and that on a different night, the crowd could be at the other, but in typical British fashion, I joined the queue.

The fish and chips were particularly good. But again, food always tastes better after you have earned it. And I had certainly earned it.

It was a beautiful evening and I sat on the harbour wall, next to the imposing figure of Verity, with her pregnant belly and lofty arm wielding a sword above her head. Verity is a statue, I should add, and not just some crazy local.

The artist Damien Hirst donated Verity to the town of Ilfracombe in 2012. Made of stainless steel and bronze, she stands 66 feet tall, staring out into the Bristol Channel, and, at the time of installation, was the tallest statue in the UK. Verity has done wonders for Ilfracombe's tourist industry. She is meant to symbolise truth and justice, or something like that. There was certainly something incredibly empowering about her. It took me a little while to warm to her, but by the time I had finished my fish and chips, it was difficult to imagine Ilfracombe's harbour without Verity.

I spent an hour or so wandering around the town. Up the steep high street, then along the promenade past Capstone Hill – which is a large grassy outcrop of rock with a spectacular vantage point looking out to sea. I didn't actually make it to the top to look at the view, as my legs didn't take too kindly to the gradient, but judging by the gathering of people sitting atop watching the sunset, it was a spectacular spot. I continued along to Runnymede Gardens and the Landmark Theatre, before buying an ice-cream from a kiosk just as it was closing, and sitting on the harbour wall to watch the sun set. It was a beautiful end to a brilliant day, and the thought that I didn't have to cycle back in the morning made it all the more enjoyable.

I retreated back to the hostel, and fell asleep fully clothed on the bed.

I was on the road by 8am the following morning. Ilfracombe was still asleep so I pedalled out of town and asked directions to the old Barnstaple Road. The man from the hostel had lied about it being a nice easy ride. To get out of Ilfracombe, you have to scale a ridiculous hill that stretches for miles. My legs were in a state of agony after yesterday's ride and I was not expecting to be pushing my bike up a hill by 8.30am.

The road eventually levelled out and the cycling became more pleasant. The early morning light cast a shadow of my bike onto the hedgerow and we rode along together for several miles. At one point, another shadow sped past me and then disappeared. And then another, and another. I looked up and realised I was cycling alongside a giant wind turbine; its huge sails ghosting through the air. On both sides of the road, acres of turbines sat majestically spinning away.

The final few miles into Barnstaple were downhill and I arrived in town soon after 9am. At a coffee shop near to the train station I saw a mobility scooter parked up outside. It was a mobility scooter that I had seen a couple of times before, and not one that you could forget in a hurry. Attached to the scooter was a large silver trailer. It was like a Winnebago that had been shrunk in the wash, and barely bigger than a shopping trolley. This was the third time I had seen it, yet I had still not had a chance to meet its owner.

The first time was 18 months previously. I had been driving to the beach on a narrow lane near to our home and had pulled over to let this mobility scooter pass. The driver gave a cheery wave, and I clocked the stickers on his trailer that mentioned his *'Around Britain on a Mobility Scooter'* challenge. I later Googled him and discovered that Mark Newton was a former tank driver in the army, injured in combat in 1991, and he was driving around the entire perimeter of Great Britain, raising money for various charities that had helped him. I followed his progress via his website and social media, and he successfully completed his mission around Great Britain.

A year later I was shopping at our local Tesco (other supermarkets are available) when I noticed the familiar trailer parked outside. I walked over to it but there was no sign of Mark or his scooter. The side of the trailer was propped open and inside were two cats, fast asleep. A Tesco employee walked over to me and we got chatting. Mark was off visiting local war memorials for the day, and Tesco had allowed him to leave his trailer there whilst he was out. The employee had promised to keep checking on his cats for him.

'So he sleeps in this capsule, with the cats?' I asked, not quite getting my head around it.

'Yes, it must be quite a squeeze, but the cats seem happy enough.'

I called back to Tesco later that day, hoping to meet up with Mark, but he had already packed up and left. I later learned he was undertaking a new challenge – to visit all of the war memorials in the UK.

Seeing his trailer parked up in Barnstaple, I couldn't let this opportunity slip by. I parked up my bike, stroked the two cats that were both sleeping soundly in his trailer, and went and found Mark sitting by the window in the coffee shop with a cup of tea and his laptop.

We chatted for ten minutes and I discovered he was a fascinating and inspiring man. What began as a challenge had now turned into his whole life and existence. He survived on his pension – which was enough to feed him and his cats – and he was also well looked after by the people of Great Britain, often being given free meals and allowed to charge his scooter at many local businesses. I offered to buy him a cup of tea and breakfast, but he declined as he had already eaten.

'It must be tough when the weather gets colder and wetter,' I said.

'It is, but the winter has its benefits too. Most of the places I have been going to for the last two years are on the coast so

208

they are often very touristy. In the winter I have the roads to myself.'

'How much longer will you be on the road for?'

'I'm not entirely sure. Probably about ten more years, I would guess.'

It was extraordinary to think that although he had already been on the road for more than two years his journey was still in its early stages. I have no doubt that I will bump into Mark again at some point during his travels. If you do (he's impossible to miss) go and say hello to him and his cats. He's a remarkable man.

I said goodbye to Mark and cycled to the train station and arrived in time for the earlier train. A considerable crowd of people were already waiting to board, amongst them another cyclist, also heavily laden with panniers. I doubted whether the small train would have room for both of us, and as she was there first she would take priority.

After everyone had boarded, I caught the attention of the train guard.

'Is there any chance I could squeeze my bike on too, please?' I asked.

'Yes, but you'll have to stay with your bike. There's nowhere to secure it, and it's a bit of a bumpy line between here and Exeter.'

I propped my bike against the train window, and perched on one of the fold down seats opposite, next to the owner of the other bike.

'Is it ok to sit here?' I asked.

'Yes, of course. Have you come far?' she asked.

'Only Ilfracombe today.'

'Ilfracombe? Already? It's not even 10am.'

'It's only about 12 miles away,' I said.

'Yes, but it's just one big hill isn't it?'

'Yes, if I'd known that I would have probably got a taxi.'

'Where are you heading to?'

'Home. Exeter and then on to Plymouth. I cycled the coast to coast yesterday.'

'In one day? That's incredible. I've done most of it over the years, in various stages, but I'm not a fast cyclist. I like to just potter along. I carry my own tent and sleeping bag and all the camping stuff. I don't need too much.'

The lady's name was Jenny and she was in her mid 60s. Despite bad arthritis in her fingers, she was still exploring all corners of Great Britain on her bicycle. She was heading back to John O'Groats to complete the part of a Scottish bike tour that had to be cut short due to a family commitment.

'I just love cycling and heading off on adventures,' she said. 'I read loads of cycling travelogues, too.'

'Really?' I said, my eyes lighting up at the mention.

My first, and most successful book, is a cycling travelogue. But in the three years since it was published, I have never met anyone who has read it. Apart from people that know me, of course. Surely this was my moment.

'Which cycling travelogues have you read?' I asked tentatively.

'I've read them all. You name it then I've read it. I can't get enough of them.'

She then reeled off a list of books that she had read recently, many of which I had read too, and others that I was familiar with. Having finished her list, I coyly told her:

'I've published a cycling travelogue.'

'Have you really? No! You're not... did you write the book I'm reading at the moment?'

'I don't know,' I said excitedly. 'What is it called?'

This was my moment. How should I play it? Should I leap up and hug her and tell her she was my first ever fan, or should I just play it cool and say, *'yep, that was me'*?

'I can't remember what it's called, but it's about this man cycling from Mongolia. Is that you?'

'Ah, no. That's not mine.'

'What is your book about?'

'It's about a Land's End to John O'Groats trip, but with a difference. We set off without any bikes, money, clothes...'

'NO!' she shouted. 'It's not you, is it?'

I smiled and raised my eyebrows, in a way that said, *'Yes, it sure is'*.

'You are... oh... wait... what's your name again?'

'Geor...' I started.

'THE NAKED RAMBLER! That's it! You're The Naked Rambler! That guy in the news that keeps getting arrested!'

My heart sank.

'No, no, that's not me either. Isn't he about 50?'

'Yes, he doesn't look much like you, come to think of it. So what is your name and what's your book called?'

'My name is George Mahood, and my book is called *Free Country*.'

'*Free Country?*' she paused. 'No, sorry, I've not heard of that one.'

Jenny tracked me down on Facebook a few weeks later. She told me her local library didn't stock my book, which was why she hadn't heard of it. So I sent her a free copy in the post, and I am awaiting her verdict.

29

To take part in any endurance events in France you are required to have a doctor's certificate to prove that you are medically sound to compete. I didn't realise this until a few days before we were due to leave for France.

I had a routine follow up appointment booked with Mr H, my neurosurgeon, four months after my surgery, which happened to be scheduled during the week before our holiday.

'Well, you're doing really well. I don't think I will need to see you again,' he said at the end of the brief consultation.

'That's fantastic. Er… I don't mean fantastic about not seeing you again. No offence.'

'None taken. You will have to have an annual MRI scan for the next five years, just to check that the tumour hasn't grown back, but I would be gobsmacked if anything shows up again. We got the entire thing out.'

'That's really great news. Thank you so much. So, am I back to normal now? Is there anything that I should still abstain from?'

'No, not really. Your back muscles are fully healed and we didn't make any structural changes to your spine so you're as good as new.'

'That's brilliant. I was wondering if you could sign this for me then please?'

'Sure, what is it?'

'It's a medical form.'

'What for?'

'An Ironman.'

He laughed.

'No, really, what's it for?'

'An Ironman. It's next week.'

'You must be joking, surely?'

'No. I have been training for it, within the guidelines that the physiotherapist set me, of course.'

'But still, it's an Ironman.'

'I know, but you did just say that there was nothing that I couldn't do.'

'Yes, but I didn't mean an Ironman. I think that's probably a little ambitious at this stage.'

'But you said I'm fixed.'

'Yes, you are. But I still think it would be a little irresponsible of me to sign you off anyway.'

'But...'

'I'm sorry,' he said. 'I'm not saying that you couldn't or shouldn't do it. I just don't want to be the person that says that it's ok.'

'Oh well, it was worth a try. I completely understand and I'm sorry for putting you in that position. Thanks again for everything you've done. You really have turned things around for me. You've made me feel young again.'

'You're very welcome. Good luck with the Ironman,' he smiled.

A few days later I booked an appointment with my GP. We had a similar conversation.

'I can't sign you off for an Ironman, I'm afraid,' he said. 'It would be irresponsible.'

'I thought you might say that.'

But then I played what I thought was my trump card.

'I cycled the Devon Coast to Coast last week,' I said.

'Well done. I've done that too,' he said.

'I know. I saw the article about you in the local paper. It's a tough ride isn't it?'

'Very tough.'

'How long did it take you?'

'About 12 hours, I think.'

'I did it in 9,' I said smugly.

'That's very impressive.'

'So does that mean that you'll sign my form for me?'

'I'm sorry, I can't.'

'But what about the coast to coast? You did that too.'

'Yes, but I wouldn't even sign myself off as medically fit for an Ironman.'

'But...'

'I'm really sorry,' he said.

'Ok. Thanks anyway.'

I did some Googling to see what others had done. Surely I can't have been the most unfit person to ever take on an Ironman in France. Surely less fit people than me must have had medical certificates signed by doctors.

A lot of people suggested in the forums that the forms should just be forged. Nobody is actually going to check that it's a real doctor. The organisers just want a signature to cover their own arses. I did consider this, but didn't want my Ironman challenge to be jeopardised by a French fraud investigation.

A couple of days before we were due to leave for France I was put in contact with a friend's doctor who agreed to carry out a basic assessment of me and complete my 'certificat médical' (that's French for 'medical certificate', in case you were confused). I passed with flying colours, and decided to gloss over my recent spinal surgery. I now had my signed form and was eligible to take part in Ironman Vichy.

30

Lying in that hospital bed when I first had the pipe dream about the Ironman, I could not have imagined the training going as well as it had. It had been tough. Really tough. And there were many, many moments when I felt like I had bitten off way more than I could chew. But I had survived, and somehow overcome all of the obstacles along the way. I still didn't know how I would fare in the race itself, but to be packing the car for France knowing that I would be lining up at the start of an Ironman in a week's time, after everything I had been through, was an incredible feeling.

My training was complete. I had done all I could to prepare. I knew I could swim the distance. I knew I could cycle the distance. I knew I had previously run the distance. All I needed to do was try and put it all together.

We filled every inch of space in the boot of our Xsara Picasso with camping equipment, clothes, accessories for the Ironman, and four bikes (Rachel wasn't taking hers) – three strapped to a bike rack, and another on the roof alongside an overstuffed roof box. We were ready for our first family holiday abroad.

We boarded a ferry from Plymouth to Roscoff on the Sunday morning, one week before the Ironman. We all took a stroll out to the back deck and watched Plymouth shrink into the distance. I glanced to my right and noticed that we were passing the end of the breakwater.

'Look, kids,' I said, 'this is where I started my swim from last week.'

'What swim?' asked Leo.

'The one when you all came to surprise me.'

'But that was near a beach,' he said.

'Yes, I finished at the beach, but I started my swim from here.'

'No you didn't, Daddy. You're just tricking.'

Kitty just laughed at me.

'You trickster,' she said, punching me quite hard in the leg.

'Did you really start from here?' asked Layla, looking at me suspiciously and then up towards Plymouth in the distance.

'Yes, I promise. Look, there's the breakwater.'

'Woah. That's amazing,' she said. 'How could somebody swim that far?'

'But you can still swim more lengths of front crawl without stopping than me, though,' I said.

'Yeah, that's true. Loser,' she said.

Rachel put her arm around me.

'It really does seem even more incredible when you look at it from out here,' she said. 'You're going to rock that Ironman.'

I took a photo from the back of the ferry to show how far away it looked. I needed to remind myself how a few weeks ago there was no way I could have swam that distance. Even now, it still didn't seem possible. But I had the medal to prove it. It made me have more faith in myself for the Ironman, and I knew that if I could just keep moving, putting one arm (or leg) in front of the other, then eventually I would cover the distance. Any distance.

We arrived in France a few hours later, and by the time we had shepherded the children down the stairwell to the car deck, some of the lines had already disembarked. Our car was parked at the front of our row, and we hurried across the deck, followed by the glare of the angry motorists parked behind us. Quickly strapping the children into the car, I offered an apologetic wave to the cars behind before disembarking.

Driving on the other side of the road is always terrifying for the first few minutes. You feel like there's no chance you will ever get your head around the road layout and that the entire holiday will be spent trying to exit a bloody roundabout near the ferry terminal. To make matters worse, ferry ports are full of drivers equally panicked and uncertain.

'BE QUIET!' I shouted at the children. 'I'm trying to concentrate.'

'Do you know where we are going?' asked Rachel.

'No. Could you sort out the sat nav please?'

'Have you got the address?'

'Yes, it's on that bit of paper, but you'll need to change the sat nav to France first.'

'Ok.'

'Tournez a gauche,' said an irritating sounding lady a few minutes later.

'What have you done?' I said, as I circled a roundabout for the fourth time.

'Changed it to France, like you said.'

'No, you've changed it to FRENCH. I still need the directions in English.'

'I thought that was the same thing.'

'You have to change the country to FRANCE, because we are now in FRANCE. You have just changed the language to FRENCH. Look, it's still trying to navigate me across the channel back to Plymouth, but in French.'

'Tournez a gauche,' the lady barked again, this time with more venom.

'SHUT UP, MADAM!' I shouted.

'Who is Madam?' asked Kitty.

'The French lady on the sat nav,' I said.

'Are we lost, Daddy?' asked Leo.

'No, we're not lost,' I said, trying to keep cool. 'We just don't know where we are going yet.'

'So we are lost.'

'We are not lost. Mummy is going to get the Sat Nav sorted and stop it speaking in French to us.'

'Er... I think you'll have to pull over and try and sort it out. I can't work out how to change it back to English, because all the menu instructions are now in French.'

Vichy is approximately 500 miles from the ferry terminal in Roscoff. We planned to drive as far as we could, find a hotel for the night, and complete the journey the following day. The CD player had broken in our car so we were forced to listen to French radio for seven hours. Who knew *Hotel California* by The Eagles is still so popular in France? We heard it three times during this journey alone.

Just before midnight, we checked into our two rooms at a Formule 1 hotel on the outskirts of the city of Bourges. We used to have occasional overnight stays in Formule 1 hotels on family holidays when I was a child. Camping in southern France, we would have a stopover on the way down at what we thought at the time were the most futuristic hotels in the world. It turns out 'futuristic' meant 'budget', but our stays in budget French hotels always proved to be one of the highlights of the entire holiday.

This was mostly because of the bathrooms. The bathrooms were nothing special on first inspection but they had many hidden secrets. The first was the close proximity of everything. The shower, toilet and sink were all in the same cubicle. You could, if you wanted, have a shower, shit and shave, all at the same time. We then discovered the bathroom's trump card. They were self cleaning. After each use, blue bathroom cleaner would spray from the ceiling over the entire room. It would then be rinsed off by jets of water, ready for the next visitor.

The bathroom would obviously not clean itself if the cubicle was occupied, but we discovered that if you held the door shut from the outside, with someone on the inside, and held the lock with a coin so that they couldn't lock the door, and waited patiently for a couple of minutes while the occupant struggled frantically to break free, they would get sprayed with blue bleach. My sister and I used to play this 'game' with each other frequently. Ah, those were the days.

My other lasting memory of French hotels as a child is our one and only family visit to Paris. We were staying in a big hotel in the city centre with some friends. All five of the children, aged between 7 and 11, had been allowed down to reception to pick up some leaflets. Returning to our room, we knocked on the door so that our mum and dad could let us in. But a man answered the door and he wasn't Dad. He was speaking to us in French and was joined at the door by his French wife and children. We tried, in broken French, to tell him that he was in our room, but he insisted it was his and closed the door. So we went to the room of our friends' parents a little further down the corridor. A French lady opened the door. She too insisted it was her room.

We were all really shaken up by this point. Where had our parents gone? Who were these French people who had taken our rooms? We knew we had gone to the correct rooms because our parents had written the numbers on our hands so we couldn't possibly get lost.

We returned to the hotel reception in floods of tears, trying to explain to the confused French receptionist that our parents had been abducted and we were alone in Paris with nobody to look after us. We gave them our name and they looked through their booking system but there was no record of any guests under our name.

Eventually, after half an hour of sobbing – by which point the hotel staff were on the verge of calling the police to report the incident – both sets of parents burst through the hotel entrance doors, huge relief on their faces.

'What are you doing here?' they asked.

'You said we could go down to the reception,' we said.

'Yes, of OUR hotel.'

'But this is our hotel.'

'No it's not. It's the one next door. Why did you go outside?'

'We didn't go outside. We just went down the stairs.'

After lengthy discussions between our parents and the hotel staff, we discovered that the two hotels had an interconnecting door on one of the stairwells, used by service staff. We had inadvertently walked through it and into the identical-looking sister hotel next door.

Ever since, I have been extremely wary of unmarked doors in hotels, worried they might transport me to a parallel universe, where my family become French.

We arrived at our campsite in Vichy just after noon the following day. It was a smaller and less glamorous site than I expected, and we were directed to a patch of gravel surrounded by mobile homes.

'Are you sure this is a campsite for tents?' asked Rachel, as we pulled up alongside our pitch.

'Of course it is! I'm hardly going to book us a spot in a caravan site if we don't have a caravan,' I said, trying to hide the fact that I seemed to have booked us a spot on a caravan site despite not having a caravan.

'But there are only caravans and mobile homes here. And it's a patch of gravel.'

'Maybe the French aren't into tents. And maybe the gravel is to stop it getting too muddy.'

She didn't look convinced.

When we went camping as a child my mum would always get very anxious and slightly miserable for the first few hours after arriving at a campsite. She recognised her change of mood and referred to it as 'New Campsite Syndrome' as though it was a known medical condition. For many years I truly believed it was. She would sit there rocking backwards and forwards for a few hours muttering to herself, as my dad tried to reassure her, whilst secretly suffering with his own case of NCS.

As a child, I couldn't understand New Campsite Syndrome. Children are thankfully immune to it. What was there to be anxious about? Everything was new and exciting. As children we had no expectations of what it would be like, and we didn't know what the brochure had claimed. We were free to explore our thrilling new surroundings, and, to us, arriving at a new campsite was the best feeling ever.

Now, as adults and parents, Rachel and I were hit with our first bouts of New Campsite Syndrome. And it hit us hard. As we sat in the car, staring at our patch of gravel, all of the people on the neighbouring pitches gawped at us suspiciously, with our heavily laden car and our three noisy, excited children.

There was no escaping the fact that we were the new kids on the block. It felt like everybody else knew each other and knew everything there was to know about the campsite and its surroundings, which of course they didn't; many of them probably having only been there a matter of hours.

'Well, we're here now. Let's make the most of it,' I said, pulling on the handbrake, putting on a brave face, and getting out of the car.

Within an hour there were signs of a recovery from New Campsite Syndrome and after two hours, all symptoms had disappeared completely. The campsite was absolutely perfect. It had a great swimming pool, fun water slide, games room, bar and a small takeaway. It was small enough for us to allow Layla and Leo to do circuits on their bikes unaccompanied, and, having never been afforded such freedom before, they really seemed to relish it.

Pitching a tent on the gravel was not an easy task, though. Despite the curious looks from the Italian family in the mobile home opposite, I eventually managed to get it up using a heavy rock and a total of about four pegs.

I had naively assumed that the campsite would be dominated by French families – none of whom would be taking part in the Ironman. Ironmen don't do camping, surely? They would all be occupying the hotels and villas in Vichy. But as the day went on and we had a wander around the site, I started to notice more and more abnormally bulging calf muscles, cycling shorts hanging from the washing lines, and posh looking road bikes being tinkered with. Ironmen were everywhere.

Layla soon made friends with a Welsh girl the same age, and we later met her parents whilst washing up after dinner. Simon was an experienced Ironman having completed four previously, plus several half-Ironmans. He was aiming to finish Vichy in close to 11 hours. Simon was a font of all knowledge with regards to Ironman and triathlons in general, and I learned a huge amount from him during the week. You could be sure that he would be hanging around outside the toilet blocks chatting to someone about something to do with swim, bike, or run. Every visit to the toilet ended up taking upwards of an hour.

'Where have you been? I thought you were just going to the loo?' Rachel would ask, when I returned to the tent an hour after I left.

'I was. I bumped into Simon.'

'Ahhhh.'

The campsite was situated on the banks of the River Allier. In 1963 a dam was built at Vichy, a couple of miles down the river from the campsite, and an area of the river known as Lake Allier was formed. A large sports centre and sports pitches were also built on the banks, and this addition of 'Le Centre Omnisports' helped turn Vichy into a haven for sports enthusiasts. It was here by Lake Allier that the Ironman would be centred.

It became a game to try and spot the Ironmen. Sometimes it was obvious; people walking around a campsite in compression socks, or the telltale sign of an Ironman 'M-dot' logo on the back of a leg. As the week went on, the game became less of a challenge as almost every single person on the campsite was either taking part in the full Ironman on the Sunday, or the half Ironman (often referred to as *70.3*, after the total mileage covered) on the Saturday.

Being surrounded by Ironmen all week was fairly intimidating. I had no plans to do any training whatsoever during the week. I felt like I had done all of my preparation and I wanted to relax and enjoy the holiday. You are supposed to taper your training the week before a big race, and 'taper' is Latin for 'do absolutely nothing'. Probably.

The rest of the campsite had other ideas. Despite the extreme heat-wave that central France was experiencing, most of the other Ironmen were constantly on training rides, runs, or swims. We had all received an email from Ironman stating that swimming in Lake Allier before the event was strictly forbidden. I took this as the perfect excuse to not go for a practice swim session. Others took this as an incentive to swim earlier in the morning to avoid detection.

As I was coming back from the toilet at 7am one morning, I saw a group of half a dozen men and women with wetsuits pulled down to their waists, swimming hats and goggles on, walking stealthily towards the water. They passed me an hour later while I was enjoying a coffee and croissant in the early morning sun. Simon was amongst them.

'Good swim?' I asked.

'Not too bad. We didn't go far. Only 1.5 miles or so.'

'1.5 miles? Yeah, just a warm up really,' I laughed.

'The current was much stronger than I was expecting, though' said Simon.

'Current? What current? I thought it was supposed to be a lake?'

'Yeah, me too. It's a dammed river so there is still a noticeable current when you're swimming upstream.'

'Oh great. Just what I wanted to hear.'

Later that day Simon asked if I would like to join him and some Dutch athletes on a short practice ride of the bike course. The bike course was two circuits of a 56 mile loop, so I didn't see how it was possible to do a short practice of it. I politely declined as I already had a commitment. I was playing crazy golf with my family.

Incidentally, during the aforementioned crazy golf game, I was leading Rachel by four shots going onto the 18th, and six shots ahead of Layla. I had really shown my family who was boss. The 18th had the hole precariously perched on a hump, sloping down in every direction. It took me ten shots to sink my putt. If it took me that many, imagine how long it would take the rest of my inferior loser family? It took Layla four shots, making her temporarily tied with me for first place. Rachel holed hers in one, winning the match by five shots. I laughed it off, but inside it was the worst thing that had ever happened to me.

I saw Simon after his bike ride and he looked completely exhausted, slumped on a sun lounger by the pool. The group had added a little more to their short practice ride, and ended up cycling over 70 miles in the scorching midday sun, just four days before the Ironman.

'We were just taking it at a nice steady pace, though,' he said, when I shook my head in disbelief. 'Well, apart from the hills when a bit of bravado kicked in and we all tried to race each other up them.'

'Is that it for training this week then?' I asked.

'That's the last big ride, yeah. I'll probably just do a couple of shorter rides and then just do running and swimming. What about you?'

'Er… Rachel beat me at crazy golf today. I'm hoping to get revenge by the end of the week.'

I did go for a 4.5 mile run/walk one morning. The Ironman run, if I got that far, was going to be such a significant part of my year that I wanted to prepare myself for it in some way. Seeing that I had done so little in the way of run training, becoming a little more familiar with the route seemed like some consolation.

As I said, Vichy is based alongside Lake Allier and there is a wide cycle/pedestrian path the entire way round. Crossing one bridge over the river/lake, down the side, over another bridge and back up the other side to where I started totalled about 4.5 miles. The Ironman run route incorporated this lap of the lake, plus a few detours into the cobbled streets of Vichy, making a total lap distance of 6.5 miles. Four laps of this would form the marathon.

The temperature had been in the high 30s all week and I had no desire to be out running in the heat, so set off for a leisurely lap early one morning. If you have to run 26.2 miles at the end of a tough day's swimming and cycling, then Vichy is a pretty damn perfect setting to do it. It's perfectly flat and the lake, bordered by long beds of stunning flowers, lay calm and peaceful in the morning light.

And then I saw the Ironman marker buoys floating in the distance and I had a desire to spew my guts out into the water. The lake sure was beautiful to run around, but I had forgotten the minor detail that I would have to swim 2.4 miles in it beforehand, and then go for a little bike ride.

The huge yellow inflatable buoy that appeared to mark the furthest point from the swim start seemed like an insurmountable distance away. It took me many minutes to run to it. Imagine what it would take me to swim it. And that was theoretically less than a quarter of the way through the swim. We would have to swim up to it, around it and back to the start, out of the water – in what is known as an Australian exit – and then into the water again to complete a slightly longer second loop. The longer I looked at the water and the buoys the worse I felt. I put my head down and kept running.

Most swimmers choose to wear a wetsuit for the Ironman swim. It increases buoyancy and wetsuit swim times tend to be faster than non-wetsuit swims – particularly for men who seem to benefit more from wetsuits than women do. If, however, the water temperature exceeds 24.5 °C on the morning of the race, then wetsuits are prohibited, as it is considered a health and safety risk.

I had assumed that as Lake Allier was fed by a river, the water temperature would never rise high enough for it to be a concern. But just ten days before the Ironman, the temperature had exceeded this limit significantly, and only cooled down a couple of days later due to the rainwater following a huge storm.

During our week in France, there were constant rumours going around about the water temperature. The general feeling seemed to be that it was on the rise, and it was looking likely that wetsuits would be prohibited. Some even suggested that, due to the extreme heat, they had heard Ironman staff stating that the decision had already been made.

The thought of swimming 2.4 miles without the help of a wetsuit filled me with dread. But it was something that was beyond my control. I couldn't influence the water temperature, so I just had to hope for the best, and accept whatever reading the race officials took on the morning of the event.

I took a quick shower after my run, and on the way out bumped into Simon, as usual.

'George, this is my friend Andy from home. Andy, this is George.'

Andy was from the same triathlon club as Simon in Wales. He arrived in Vichy just two days before the Ironman, having been elsewhere in France on a dedicated triathlon training camp. Like Simon, Andy was taking part in his fifth Ironman.

'I've never run a marathon,' he said, after we had all been chatting for what felt like several hours, me still wrapped in a towel after my shower.

'What do you mean? You've done four Ironmans.'

'Yes, but I've never actually run a proper marathon. Only during an Ironman.'

'Really? How come?'

'I'm not sure I could do it.'

'Of course you could do it. If you can do it having swum and cycled that far, then you can definitely do it without.'

'Yes, but there's too much training involved.'

I laughed at the absurdity of what he was saying, but I sort of understood what he meant. The expectations of an Ironman marathon are very different to a standalone marathon. There's no way to predict how your body will cope during the run part of an Ironman, so it's just a case of adapting and trying your best to get through it. A marathon on its own carries with it a different set of expectations.

Other than a handful of short runs and the 10km run with Rachel, I had done very little in the way of run training. I had completed marathons in the past, but nothing more than 10km for almost two years. I had been concerned about the possibility of injuring myself and I knew that however much run training I did, I couldn't really prepare myself for the Ironman run.

The Ironman marathon is unlike a normal marathon. It doesn't matter how experienced at running you are, you cannot do any training that will simulate how your legs will feel after swimming and cycling such extreme distances. Many experienced runners crash out of the Ironman during the run, because they naively assume that, as their strongest discipline, they will be able to cruise it.

A Mexican runner named German Silva found this out the hard way. Silva won the New York marathon twice and had a PB of 2 hours 8 minutes, which ranked him as one of the fastest runners in the world. He entered an Ironman as a bet a few years after retirement and smashed both the swim and the bike with very respectable times. He left himself almost 10 hours to complete the run. An athlete such as Silva could crawl a marathon in 10 hours. He managed just 800 metres and then pulled out because the sensation was so unfamiliar to him. The Ironman marathon is not like a normal marathon.

When those on the campsite weren't cycling, running or swimming, they were tinkering with their bikes obsessively for several hours a day. There was an Italian in a mobile home next to us, who reminded me of a serial killer. Not that I have ever met a serial killer. At least, not that I'm aware of. He was meticulous in everything he did, from hanging out his washing, to laying the table, to the way he did the washing up. Everything was done quietly and methodically. But his bike tinkering was like nothing I had ever seen before. Two days before the Ironman, he pulled out a bike toolbox from his mobile home which was the same size as my suitcase. He then dismantled his bike completely before rebuilding it piece by piece. He did the same to his wife's bike, and she wasn't even competing. I was tempted to offer him my dad's bike to rebuild too, but seeing as I wasn't even able to adjust the saddle, I didn't think he would have much luck.

'Ah, back from a training ride I see,' said Lars, a Danish triathlete from a plot near to ours as I climbed off my bike one evening. 'I knew you wouldn't be able to resist. How far did you go? Did you do the full bike loop?'

'Er... no. I just cycled to Lidl to get us some dinner.'

'Ah, ok then.'

Lidl was less than half a mile from the campsite, and my brief cycle there wearing my flip-flops was the only time I touched my bike between taking it off the car, and checking it in the day before the Ironman.

In a campsite full of Ironmen all competing with each other to see who could cram the most amount of training and bike tinkering into the days before the event, Martin from Kent was a breath of fresh air. Like me, Martin from Kent had no desire to get involved with any of it. A softly spoken man in his early 50s, Martin from Kent had completed a couple of Ironmans before, and was staying in France for the week with his partner Sue (also from Kent, I presume). The thing I liked most about

Martin from Kent was that he looked even less of an Ironman than me. A little on the short side and perhaps a tiny bit biggishly built, Martin from Kent was on holiday and quite rightly had no intention of exerting himself in the days leading up to the Ironman. Martin from Kent, his partner Sue and I would stand next to each other at the sink, each with a bowl full of dirty dishes, and chat about our day and how little we had done.

Whenever I told other Ironmen that I had never taken part in a 70.3, or an Olympic distance triathlon, they would take a sharp intake of breath as though I was breaking the first rule of Ironman. Martin from Kent showed no such concern. He was so calm and relaxed about everything that he made the Ironman seem like nothing at all.

Kitty celebrated her fourth birthday while we were in France. We marked the day by hiring a weird quadracycle contraption called 'la Rosalie' that seated all five of us. It was a four-wheeled, human powered car, with two sets of pedals and two steering wheels (only one of which was connected to the wheels). We completed one lap of the lake, which took us an hour and was far more exhausting than we had predicted.

'Can I have a go at driving, Daddy?' asked Layla.

'Of course you can,' I said.

'Really, George?' asked Rachel. 'Are you sure that's a good idea?'

'Yeah, why not. They will be fine. It's a nice straight cycle path. What could go wrong?'

'I'm going next then,' said Leo.

'Then me,' said Kitty.

Rachel narrowed her eyebrows to make it clear she didn't approve.

'How on earth are you going to be able to cycle and run in this heat on Sunday?' said Rachel, as we pedalled down the final section to return our quadracycle.

'I'll be fine. I'll make sure to drink lots of water.'

'But I'm drinking lots of water today and I'm still burning up and absolutely exhausted. And you're the one doing most of the pedalling.'

'I think it will feel different when I'm moving along on the bike or running. The air should help cool us down.'

'It was horribly hot when I went for a run yesterday,' she said, 'and that was at 8am. The forecast says it's going to be 38°C on Sunday. I'm really worried about you.'

'I'll be fine.'

'I know you've done lots of training but you couldn't prepare for this type of weather.'

'No, it's not ideal, but it will be the same for everyone.'

'Please, please promise me you'll be sensible, and if it gets too bad then just pull out. There's no shame in that.'

At this point I had to dive across three seats and frantically grab the steering wheel. Layla and Leo had began an argument about whose turn it was to drive, both leaving the wheel unattended, as we veered towards the edge of the path that would drop directly into the lake.

'I promise I'll be sensible,' I said, swerving La Rosalie back into a straight line. 'I'm driving from now on.'

'Ohhh,' shouted Leo. 'That's SO unfair.'

Rachel's rage that I had witnessed during her Edinburgh marathon made a dramatic return that night as the campsite's French Elvis impersonator continued his set until well past midnight. I lay there in the sweltering tent smiling as the dulcet tones of *Blue Suede Shoes* sung with a French accent filled the air, and Rachel lay beside me sighing heavily and getting increasingly agitated. I was certain that she was going to climb out of the tent at one point and go and knock him down, step in his face, and then slander his name all over the place.

The Ironman was to take place on Sunday. On the Friday, I went down to le Centre Omnisports to register, hand in my certificat médical (medical certificate, remember?) and pick up my transition bags.

'George!' called a voice as I stood aimlessly at the end of a queue that snaked its way around the registration tent several times. It was Emily, my florist friend from Northampton.

'Emily! How are you?' I said, walking over to her near the front of the queue and giving her a hug.

'Terrified,' she laughed. 'I can't believe you made me enter this.'

'I know. Sorry about that. Although it didn't take too much persuading.'

'I can't believe I am doing another Ironman. This is ridiculous! And what about you? You've only recently had back surgery. What on earth are we doing?'

'Ha, I keep asking myself that same question. What did your friends say when you told them you had entered?'

'I haven't told any of them.'

'What about your parents and your sister? They must think you're completely crazy.'

'I haven't told them either.'

'What? You haven't even told your family that you're doing an Ironman in two days?'

'No. You're the only person who knows I'm doing it. Apart from Pete, of course. Everyone else just thinks I'm on holiday in France.'

'Ha, that's amazing. When are you going to tell them?'

'Once I've crossed the finish line. Hopefully I'll be able to send Mum a message saying *I AM AN IRONMAN*.'

'Brilliant.'

'And if I don't finish it, then I might never tell them I even entered,' she laughed.

'You will definitely finish it. There's no doubt about that, and you'll be sending your mum a text on Sunday night, I guarantee it.'

We chatted for a while and then it was Emily's turn to go and sign her forms with a race official.

'Well, I'm sure we'll see each other before the start, but if not, good luck and I'll see you at the finish.'

'Where are you going?'

'To the back of the queue where I was.'

'Don't be ridiculous. I was standing in that bloody queue for two hours. You're here now. Look, it'll be your turn next.'

'Ok,' I said, awkwardly. 'Thanks.'

31

Back in April when I signed up for Ironman Vichy I received an email advertising IronKids. IronKids is an initiative organised by Ironman for children as young as six. For the younger children it consists of a run-cycle-run format of varying distances, depending on their age. After checking the small print, I discovered that although Leo was only 5, he was eligible due to the fact he would turn six before the end of the year.

I didn't want to be an annoying dad pressuring them into something that they didn't want to do, but I also didn't want the event to sell out and for it not to be an option if they did want to do it. Registration was only 10 Euros and included a medal and t-shirt for all finishers, so I signed them both up and would let them decide nearer the time if they wanted to do it.

'We get a MEDAL?' asked Layla.

'Yes,' I said.

'And a T-SHIRT?' asked Leo.

'Yes. What do you think? You don't have to do it.'

'I'm definitely doing it. I've never won a medal for anything in my life,' said Layla.

'Me too. I'm going to be an IRONKID,' shouted Leo.

'Ok, if you're sure. Leo, you will be one of the youngest in your group, but you'll do just fine.'

'I don't mind.'

I was delighted that they seemed to be following in their father's footsteps of entering races purely for the mementos.

They talked about little else in the weeks before we went to France. Layla would tell everybody we met that she was going to be doing IronKids. She also made a point of telling everyone that it only cost 10 Euros. I've no idea where she gets her cheapskate attitude.

During the week at the campsite, Layla and Leo created their own training camp; cycling and running laps of the campsite with Simon's daughter who was also taking part in Layla's age group.

IronKids took place at Le Centre Omnisports on the day before the Ironman. We loaded Leo and Layla's bikes onto the car ready to head down to the start.

'Layla, Leo, where are your helmets?' I asked.

'I dunno,' they both said.

There was just 40 minutes until the start of the race, and our campsite was a 20 minute drive away. We searched the tent, inside and out, searched the car, the roof box, the surrounding bushes. Rachel checked the playground to see if they had been discarded there, I checked the swimming pool and asked at reception to see if they had been handed in.

'We'll just have to do it without our helmets,' shouted Layla. 'Come on, we're going to be LATE!'

'They won't let you start the race without your helmet,' I said.

'Why not? I won't fall off.'

'It's one of the rules. They won't make an exception.'

She burst out crying and then Leo began crying too. We searched the campsite again but the helmets were gone.

'Any ideas?' asked Rachel, trying to remain calm.

'If we are quick we could stop at Decathlon on the way. They probably sell cycling helmets.'

After a quick detour to Decathlon where I bought two new cycling helmets (for a very reasonable 9 Euros each), we parked up at the Ironman centre and made a dash for the start. The Ironman 70.3 was still going on, with the tail-enders just completing the course. The area was packed with athletes and spectators and we had to ask several people before anyone knew where the start of the IronKids race was. Located on the far side of the arena, we lugged the bikes and children to the start line where the Mini Mites (Leo's group) were just assembling. He was ushered to go and leave his bike and helmet in the transition area and then gather round for a race briefing. A marshal began shouting instructions in French at the assembled children. Leo stood there looking traumatised. There were about 50 children; Leo being one of the smallest.

'What did the man say?' he asked, walking over to me at the barrier.

'I'm not really sure. I don't think it was important. Just follow the other children. You'll be fine. Good luck, pal!'

They were guided over to the start line. The gun sounded and the pack of children all ran off down the path that followed the edge of the lake. It was all too much for a couple of the children, and when the gun fired they turned and ran the opposite way in floods of tears.

After 100 metres they went round a cone and then back to the transition area where they put on their helmets and jumped on their bikes. Leo rides a small BMX, as I assumed all five year olds did. Not IronKids, though. A high proportion of them were on proper road bikes, at the age of five and six. Leo managed a brief smile as he set off on the 1km bike loop. After returning back to transition, they then had another 200 metre run to complete. Leo finished somewhere in the middle of the pack and crossed the line looking slightly stunned.

'Well done, pal. Did you enjoy it?' I asked.

'Yes!' he shouted. 'It was BRILLIANT! When can I do another one?'

Layla found her event much tougher. Her age-group – made up of 8-9 year olds – had some seriously fast and competitive children in it. Her group had to complete two laps of the 1km bike course. The speed at which some of the children completed the cycling leg – many of them finishing their second 1km lap before Layla had finished her first – was quite astonishing. They would dismount their bikes whilst still travelling at full speed and then run with their bike to the transition area, like seasoned triathletes. I later learned that Lance Armstrong was an IronKid winner in his youth. Maybe he added something special to his Weetabix even back then.

Layla finished her race in last place and broke down in tears as she crossed the line. Not because she finished last, but because she had found it so difficult and the occasion so overwhelming.

'That's my first and last ever medal,' she said defiantly.

'I promise it won't seem so bad tomorrow,' I said.

'It will. I never want to do anything like that EVER again.'

'I think maybe you shouldn't have entered them,' Rachel said to me later that evening.

'Why?'

'You saw how emotional Layla got. I don't think it was good for her.'

'She'll be fine. She really wanted to do it. She just didn't realise that it would be so hard, and that other eight year olds could be so good. Neither did I. I'm sure she will feel really proud of herself for finishing it.'

'I hope so.'

Layla wore her medal continuously for several weeks, and proudly told everyone she met she was an IronKid. The experience didn't seem anywhere near as bad the following day. She even mentioned the possibility of doing it again one day.

I returned to Le Centre Omnisports later that day with my bike and two large drawstring bags; one labelled *Bike*, the other labelled *Run*. I had filled each of these with everything I would need during the two transitions (known as *T1* and *T2*). The bags were handed to a member of staff who then went and hung them on the corresponding pegs which were in numerical order (2000 bags in random order would be a little cruel – although it would add a fun new element to the Ironman).

Each bike had to be racked in a designated spot in a sprawling fenced off section of the transition area. Simon had advised me to let some air out of my bike tyres to avoid the possibility of them exploding in the evening sun. It would mean bringing a pump with me to inflate them before the swim, but that was certainly preferable to changing a flat.

My friend Damo (the wetsuit pisser) had a place in the RideLondon-Surrey 100 in its first year in 2013. He bought an expensive bike and added a pair of expensive aero bars to help him look the part. Aero bars are attachments that you fasten to the handlebars that stretch out a short way over the front wheel. They allow the rider to tuck themselves into a lower and more aerodynamic position. Shortly after buying his new equipment, Damo discovered that the use of aero bars was forbidden in RideLondon. Many sportives ban them as they prevent easy access to the brakes and are therefore considered dangerous. Due to the fact cyclists in an Ironman are not allowed to cycle in close proximity to each other (and very rarely use their brakes), aero bars are allowed, and most competitors use them. Damo's set had sat in his garage, unused and gathering dust since he bought them, and he kindly allowed me to borrow them for the Ironman.

I mounted them to my handlebars and then, because everyone else was, I gave both the wheels a spin, and gave the derailleur a prod. It seemed like the thing to do.

I had been nervous all week about the prospect of the Ironman but Rachel, Layla, Leo and Kitty had helped keep me distracted with swimming pools, water slides, crazy golf, quadracycles, meals out, a birthday party, great food and lots of other family activities. The beer and wine had also helped ease my anxiety. It was impossible to ignore the looming Ironman all week, but I had managed to enjoy the holiday and block it from my mind as much as possible.

Although the Ironman had always been the ultimate goal at the end of my challenge, there were so many potential things that could have gone wrong in the build up to prevent me from taking part. It had never really seemed real until I racked my bike and realised that in about 12 hours I would be back there, getting ready to commence one of the biggest days of my life.

Everyone around me looked fitter, taller, leaner and more experienced than me. They all had faster, lighter and more expensive bikes. But in that moment I felt like one of them. I was no longer a fraud. I had trained hard and prepared well (admittedly over a short period of time), but I was ready.

Whilst looking through the food cupboard a couple of days before we left for France, I found a carton of beetroot juice hidden away at the back. Rachel went through a phase of drinking lots of beetroot juice. I can't remember why. A few weeks previously I had been reading about Ironman Vichy on the internet and found a blog post by a man who had taken part in Ironman Vichy's predecessor – Challenge Vichy – in 2013. In his race report, he gave a special mention to a bottle of beetroot juice. He had used it throughout his training because it supposedly helps with oxygen intake or something, but he forgot to take a supply with him to France. So, the day before the race, he searched all of the supermarchés in Vichy, then all of the smaller marchés, then spread his search further afield to the neighbouring villages, but could not locate a single bottle of his precious nectar. Eventually, after hours of searching, his determination was rewarded when he found a single bottle for sale in a small health food shop on the outskirts of town.

He obviously thought it of great importance, so despite having never drunk beetroot juice before, I wasn't going to let this opportunity pass so I slipped the carton into my bag. The night before the Ironman I drank the entire carton.

With my bike and bags checked in and my swimming bag prepared and ready for the morning, I had nothing else to do. We ate pasta for dinner – as my strict diet plan had stated – and I managed to resist a glass of wine, before we all had an early night. Thankfully the campsite's evening entertainment was Bingo. If French Elvis had been there I'm sure he would have been lynched by dozens of tired and angry Ironmen.

32

My alarm was set for 4.45am, but Kitty had other ideas. Having slept through every other night of the holiday without so much as a murmur, she woke at 3.15am on the morning of the Ironman screaming hysterically. Rachel crawled through into their section of the tent and tried to settle her back to sleep. Kitty was adamant that she was positioned the wrong way and should be lying horizontally, across the legs of her brother and sister. After five minutes of uncontrollable screaming, she eventually calmed down. So did Kitty. But I was now wide awake and agitated. I lay there in the sticky tent trying and failing to get back to sleep.

At 4.30am, just as I was drifting off again, the most horrendous screeching noise filled the air. This time it wasn't one of our children. A car engine was revving loudly outside, accompanied by the most deafening sound of something being scraped along the road surface. The smell of burnt rubber wafted through the tent's air vent and as the noise disappeared into the distance, I decided that this signified the time to admit defeat and get up. I forced down a bowl of cold pasta, a banana, and a cup of coffee.

As I walked to the toilet block, a black tyre mark stretched the entire length of the campsite. An early morning caravan owner had apparently checked out of the campsite and decided to make things more challenging by leaving the caravan's brake on.

The toilet block was crawling with the walking corpses of other irritated looking Ironmen, pissed off at missing out on those precious minutes of sleep on the morning of the big day.

'Bloody annoying caravanners,' said a Dutch guy in perfect English.

I was secretly relieved that the bloody annoying caravanners had taken the attention away from my bloody annoying daughter.

'Good luck,' said Rachel, sitting up in her sleeping bag and throwing her arms around me. 'We'll be thinking of you all day.'

'Thank you. I can't wait to see you all this afternoon.'

'Have you got everything you need?'

'I hope so.'

'Good luck, Daddy,' called Layla, from the other end of the tent, where the other two were fast asleep.

'Thank you, sweetie. Have a good day. I'll see you later.'

'See you later.'

'I love you,' said Rachel. 'Please be sensible.'

'I will. I promise. I love you.'

I had offered to give Simon and Andy a lift to the start, and both were ready and waiting by the campsite exit. Simon was looking bleary eyed and had been up most of the night with a high temperature. He was seemingly suffering from the symptoms of sunstroke (try saying that ten times). He felt considerably better than he had done during the night, though, so decided to give the Ironman a go.

We arrived at the start just before 6am. The race wouldn't begin for the elite athletes until 6.50am, and my swim start was not until 7.30am, so I had a lot of time to sit around and feel anxious.

The swim start was located inside the bike enclosure, and competitors had to pass through a series of security points to get in; showing race numbers and arm bands on each occasion in order to be allowed access into an area in which a couple of thousand bikes – most costing several thousand pounds – were racked and ready.

It was still dark, and there was an eerie calm to the transition area as people carried out last minute checks to their bikes. The faces of family members were squashed up to the wire fence, hoping to catch a glimpse of their loved ones pumping up their bike tyres, or eating a last minute energy gel. The lake was calmer than it had been all week, and the lights of Vichy city centre on the other side shimmered on its crude oil-like surface.

I checked my bike's tyres and was relieved that they hadn't exploded in the heat. I inflated them fully, and then managed to reset my dad's cycle computer using some instructions that I downloaded on my phone. I hoped that it would now provide me with a valuable average speed reading during the bike leg.

I felt sick with nerves. The lack of sleep hadn't helped, but it was the thought of the long day ahead that made my stomach churn. I would have done anything to be curled up asleep in the tent still.

A nearby cheer broke the silence.

A small huddle of athletes gathered around a handwritten note attached to a post. It was the official water temperature, which would determine whether wetsuits were allowed or not.

T°C EAU
23.6°C

The wetsuit cut-off was 24.5°C. Less than one degree was all that saved us from a much more challenging swim. I breathed a sigh of relief and felt a rush of adrenaline course through my veins. I was convinced that wetsuits were not going to be allowed, and had still planned to give it my all. Having the added benefit of a wetsuit now made me even more certain that I was going to complete the swim. No, forget that, I was going to complete the entire Ironman.

At this exact moment, a familiar acoustic guitar track began playing from some speakers seemingly positioned out in the middle of the lake. The sound then escalated into a wail, almost like an air raid siren, before the bass kicked it. It was a deep, pulsating, electronic rumble that I could actually feel vibrating in my ribs. My initial thought was: *What must the locals think? 6.30am on a Sunday and they get woken to this?* And then I stopped caring about the locals, and realised how amazing the music made me feel. The silence of the bike transition area had been ethereal, but now it was a thriving mass of energy.

The song was *Radioactive* by Imagine Dragons.

'I'm waking up, I feel it in my bones, enough to make my system grow. Welcome to the new age....'

The song's video features a bizarre fighting ring in a secluded log cabin deep in the woods, where cuddly toys fight to the death. The 'Champion' – an ugly, evil, purple cuddly toy – is pitted against various 'Challengers', and in turn defeats them all, ripping off their stuffed limbs and tearing them apart. Then a mysterious lady arrives with a box and enters her small pink teddy bear into a bout. Initially the teddy bear is predictably battered by the purple brute, but then something changes inside of him. He unleashes his inner powers and destroys the purple beast. At that moment, standing on the shores of Lake Allier in Vichy, France, I was that pink teddy bear. Stay with me on this. Always the underdog, fragile, vulnerable and a little frayed at the edges, that pink teddy and I had a lot in common. And that ugly purple beast? He was the Ironman. Today was the day that I would summon my inner powers and kick the shit out of my nemesis.

With a spring in my step, I went to the transition bag area. We were not allowed access to our bike and run bags before the race, but could hand any last minute items to a group of marshals who would then add them to our bags for us. I wanted to add a tea towel to my T1 bag. But it was not just any old tea towel. A good friend of mine, James (the same friend I met at RideLondon who persuaded me to buy cycling shoes), got married last year, and his wedding invitation was sent to us in the form of a tea towel – the date, venue and contact details all printed directly onto it. It was the first of its kind that I had seen, and it quickly became our favourite tea towel. Although there wasn't a great deal of competition, to be fair.

It was the only tea towel we took to France, and I decided I could put it to further use as a means to dry my bollocks after the swim before putting on my cycling shorts. It's what James would have wanted. A marshal took the tea towel from me, made a mental note of the race number on my arm, and went to deposit it in the corresponding bag.

Over 2000 men and women were taking part in the Ironman, and all were killing time waiting for their designated start. Some were lying on the floor. Others were sat in meditative positions, legs crossed, eyes closed. Many sat with headphones on, presumably listening to their chosen fight song. Where was *Club Tropicana* when I needed it most? Whilst others, like me, aimlessly paced around the place, not quite knowing what to do. People were already getting into their wetsuits, but with over half an hour before I needed to be in the water, I didn't want to be sitting around sweating in my wetsuit for too long beforehand.

Instead, I just sat down and watched other people. Very few people were talking to each other. Despite the thousands of combined hours of training we had all been through, we were now very much on our own.

With ten minutes to go before I was due in the water, I casually emptied out my swimming bag, ready to get changed into my kit. Wetsuit – check. Goggles – check. Swim hat – check, Speedos – check. Timing chip – ch... what?... WHERE THE FUCK IS MY TIMING CHIP?

The timing chip was the single most important item in my bag.

And it wasn't there.

Without it, there would be no record of me even starting the Ironman, let alone finishing it. Where had it gone? I had checked my bag almost hourly since packing it the night before and it had always been there. I checked it before putting it in the car at the campsite and it was definitely there. How the hell had I lost it between the car park and the transition area? I bundled everything back into the bag and frantically started running for the exit and back towards the car, hoping that it had somehow fallen out in the car boot.

I started to panic that I wouldn't make it to the car and back in time for the start of the race, even if I did find it. Then I remembered something in the briefing notes about replacement timing chips being picked up after the swim section, in the event that they were lost. Presumably this was for instances when the timings chips accidentally came off in the water. Not for idiots who lost theirs before the start of the race. I ran over to a marshal who was standing nearby.

'Pardon madam. J'ai...' – *what's the verb for lost, dammit...?* 'J'ai... lost mon timing chip.' I said, pointing to my ankle, where the chip should be strapped and shaking my head with a sorry expression on my face.

'You don't have your timing chip?' she asked in English.

'Non. Je suis désolé. J'ai lost it.'

'We don't have it,' she said.

'Is it possible to get another one?'

'No, we don't have any. Sorry.'

246

I rushed to the bag drop off and spoke to a man there who gave me the same apologetic response. I then found another marshal and pleaded with her.

'You need a new timing chip?' she asked.

'Oui madam.'

'Go to the penalty tent. You can get another one there.'

'Merci madam,' I panted, as I rushed to the penalty tent. The penalty tent is a gazebo under which competitors have to wait for a period of between three and ten minutes to serve any time penalties they are awarded during the race for infringements of the rules. There are also penalty tents at intervals on both the bike and run courses. If a marshal spots you breaking the rules, such as drafting behind another cyclist (taking advantage of wind resistance), a card is shown and the competitor is forced to stop at the next penalty tent to serve their time.

I knew that it was my responsibility to ensure that I had my timing chip on me throughout the race. By losing it before the race, was I now going to have to serve a time penalty before the race had even started? I had visions of having to wait for ten minutes under the gazebo whilst the rest of my swim wave began their race, then having to make the walk of shame to the water's edge on my own, with ten minutes shaved off an already challenging cut-off time. But if it meant the difference between being able to compete and not, then it was a punishment I was happy to accept.

I explained the situation to the smiley lady in the penalty tent and she seemed amused by my terrible French. To my surprise she handed me a new timing chip and made a note of both my race number and the number on the new chip, so that the amendments could be made, and wished me 'bonne chance'.

Back in the hall, I slipped out of my clothes and into my swimming trunks. I then took four fingers of Vaseline and rubbed them shamelessly over the areas of my body prone to chafing with the wetsuit: my neck, shoulders, wrists, ankles, and, of course my more intimate areas. I considered trying to find somewhere more discreet to do the application, but nobody seemed to be watching and I was short on time. I then pulled on my wetsuit, yanking the legs up as far as I could to allow for more flexibility in my arms and shoulders. Then, as I reached around behind me to pull up the zip, the cord came away in my hand.

'Oh bollocks,' I said to myself, assuming that I had broken my wetsuit. I then looked down at my hand and discovered I was holding not the wetsuit cord, but my original timing chip. It had attached itself to the velcro on my wetsuit and been there all along.

After successfully doing up my wetsuit – this time finding the actual cord, which was still intact – I made my way sheepishly back to the penalty tent. I held up both of my timing chips to the lady and gestured to the velcro on the back on my wetsuit, and offered an apologetic grin. She just laughed at me, crossed out my number from the list and took the replacement timing chip from me, before wishing me 'bonne chance' again.

I turned and spotted Emily waiting in line to begin her swim.

'Oh my God, George,' she said. 'I'm about to start another IRONMAN! Is this really happening?'

'Yes it really is. It's crazy, isn't it? This time tomorrow you'll wake up and realise that you're an Ironman.'

'I hope so. You will too.'

'I hope so.'

I gave her a hug, wished her luck and went to hand my bag of 'street gear' into the bag drop. 'Street gear' is what Ironman call the bag of clothes that you change out of before putting your swim stuff on. My clothes are not 'street' in any way.

Five minutes later, my wave – the black hats – were asked to congregate by the water's edge. My emotions had fluctuated dramatically in the space of an hour. I had gone from extreme nausea brought on by my nervousness, to immense excitement after the music started playing, to enormous panic at the realisation that I didn't have a timing chip, and ending with a feeling of relief and calm. This was it.

A man next to me frantically tugged at his wetsuit cord, unable to do up the zip. I offered to help and saw the relief on his face too, once he was zipped up. I had assumed that the starting waves were assigned randomly, but looking around at the other competitors, it was clear that those donning the black swim caps – the final wave to start – looked slightly different to the swimmers in earlier waves. It was obvious that the majority of us were first-timers, presumably lumped together at the back so as not to annoy the more experienced triathletes.

'First time?' I asked a large man next to me.

'Yes. I'm shitting myself,' he replied in a Brummie accent.

The beginning of an Ironman swim is described as 'the washing machine'. It's a violent tangle of bodies, with arms and legs all fighting for space. It's common to receive several kicks to the face or elbows to the head. Swimmers will, without a second thought, swim directly over another if they are deemed to be in the way. For the elite racers, it's common for athletes to be deliberately targeted by their competitors and have a heel or elbow 'accidently' planted in their face. One of the reasons why triathletes are required to wear matching swim hats is so that, once in the water, each individual looks the same.

I had been advised by Simon to hang back at the swim start and allow others to enter the water first, in order to avoid this melee. The trouble was that most of the people in the black hat wave seemed to have been given the same advice. We were told by the announcer that we had three minutes before the start and should enter the water and make our way out to the start line. Rather than a scram of people all fighting to be first in the water in order to bag the best starting position, the majority of us were obviously trying to lurk at the back.

'Après vous,' I gestured, to try and encourage a pair of them in before me.

'Non non non, après VOUS,' they responded.

'Une minute! Une minute!' shouted the announcer.

There was no putting it off any longer. It was time for me to get in the water. After all the talk during the week about the high water temperature, I was expecting it to feel like stepping into a jacuzzi, but 23.6°C felt like a swimming pool; a slightly cold and far murkier swimming pool. I spat into my goggles, forgetting that I had recently swallowed a sticky sweet energy gel. I rubbed the sugary spit around the inside of the lenses and then gave them a quick rinse in the water before pulling them onto my head.

'Trente seconds!'

I waded out into the water until the ground disappeared beneath my feet and I swam out to join the others at the start line. This was my first time in fresh water with a wetsuit on and it was noticeably less buoyant than the seawater I was used to, but compared to how I would have felt without a wetsuit, it was like floating in the Dead Sea.

'Dix seconds!'

Four months ago I couldn't physically get off the sofa, let alone swim, bike or run. Here I was, ten seconds from the start of an Ironman. A huge smile spread across my face. Whatever happened during the rest of the day, I had made it as far as the start line.

I had positioned myself towards the far right of the starting line. The first buoy was about half a mile up the river and most people had congregated towards the left edge, forming the closest direct line to that buoy. I had read somewhere that to get more space you should position yourself on the outside edge, and the extra distance covered is minimal.

The horn sounded signifying the start. I can't be sure it was a horn. It might have been a cannon for all I know. Or maybe even a party popper. All I know is that one minute several hundred black heads were floating serenely in the water, like hypnotised seals, and the next an explosion of limbs were thrashing in all directions. I put my head in the water and stretched for my first stroke. I immediately made contact with the ankle of the person in front of me and lifted my head out of the water in shock.

'Pardon,' I muttered, as the swimmer behind me made contact with the back of my head with the palm of his hand, and then proceeded to continue to swim over the top of me, forcing me under. You would have thought I had learned my lesson after the Plymouth Breakwater swim. It was my own stupid fault for stopping to apologise to another swimmer. Who does that in a triathlon? Getting hurt goes with the territory.

I tried again. This time completing three strokes before making contact with another swimmer.

'Pardon,' I said again instinctively, this time not breaking my stroke. I received a few more elbows and kicks to the body, but it was not quite as bad as I feared.

I was making progress but something didn't feel right. My stroke felt frantic and rushed. I was hugely out of breath and gasping for air at every chance. I looked up ahead and could see hundreds of black hats disappearing off into the distance, which only made me try to swim harder and faster, compounding the problem. I was panicking. I needed to calm down, ignore the other swimmers and find my own rhythm. But I couldn't. Each time somebody swam past me I had an irrational fear that I was going to be left behind and miss the cut-off. *Relax*, I kept telling myself. *You know you can do this. You swam almost the equivalent distance in the sea with plenty of time to spare. Just relax.*

I started doing breaststroke to try and get my breathing under control. I glanced behind me and could see several black hats, which was reassuring, but nowhere near as many as were up ahead. So I wasn't last, but what if all the people behind me didn't make the cut-off either?

I knew the first leg was against the current. *Is it the current making me slower? Perhaps the current will mean that I don't make it inside the required time?*

Calm the fuck down! You can do this.

I started swimming front crawl again, this time attempting to ignore my speed and focus on the technique that I had spent so many hours in the pool trying to perfect. Long reach with the right hand. Drive the hip down, rotating the body and using that elusive core to propel my body forwards. Pull through the water and repeat with the other hand. It was working. My breathing felt less laboured and I felt like I was moving through the water much more efficiently.

What I thought was the buoy to mark the furthest point of the first lap turned out to be one only halfway there. I could now see a giant yellow buoy even further up the lake. I needed to forget about the distance, though. I knew rationally that I could cover it. Just focus on the here and now and I would get through it, eventually.

I looked over to the bank. Hundreds of people were walking and cycling along the shore level with us. Were they able to spot their loved ones amongst us, or were they just randomly watching the swimmers?

I was glad Rachel and the children hadn't made this trip though. The chances of being able to spot my black hat amongst the hundreds of others would have been almost impossible, and fighting for a viewing space by the swim exit with three children would have been tougher than the Ironman. They would be down to watch me hopefully finish the bike leg and be there for my four laps of the marathon. It was going to be a very long day for all of us.

I eventually reached the buoy that marked the point at which we turned around. This was roughly a quarter of the way through. We still had to swim the same distance in reverse, get out of the water, run/walk about 50 metres and then get back in and swim a slightly bigger loop.

I glanced at my watch. I had been in the water a little over 20 minutes. *Could that be right?* It felt like I'd been there over an hour. I did a quick calculation and realised that based on my current speed, I would complete the 3,800 metres well within the cut-off time.

As I turned the corner to start the return leg I could see all of the swimmers behind me, stretching back down the route I had just swam. There were many more than I had thought and I suddenly felt a lot better. I was doing ok.

I continued to swim using my bizarre hybrid front crawl/breaststroke. I was still unable to swim more than about 100 metres of crawl at a time, and the breaststroke gave me a chance to compose myself and look around. I was swimming breaststroke as I passed one of the race marshals in a kayak, whose responsibility it was to ensure swimmers didn't stray too far off course, or try to cut the corners.

'Bonjour, monsieur,' I said to him.

He looked surprised to hear one of the swimmers chatting to him.

'Bonjour,' he said hesitantly. 'Ça-va?'

'Oui, ça-va bien, merci. Et toi?'

'Bien.'

'Au revoir,' I said, putting my head down and beginning another stint of front crawl.

Drafting in swimming is the technique of tucking in behind or to the side of another swimmer to take advantage of the displaced water. Studies suggest you can conserve as much as 20% of your energy. It is commonly done in cycling, but during Ironman events it is strictly forbidden, and competitors face penalisation or possibly disqualification if caught.

Drafting in swimming is absolutely fine in an Ironman, though. The problem was that my crawl/breaststroke hybrid didn't allow me to draft behind anyone with any success. My front crawl – when I did it – seemed to be faster and more effective than those I was swimming with, so whenever I swam crawl I would start catching people's ankles with my hands. Then, when I reverted to breaststroke, I would be noticeably slower, and the person I was trying to draft behind would pull away from me. I focused instead on making sure I had plenty of space. Particularly for my breaststroke, to ensure that I didn't kick too many swimmers in the head.

At one point, I kicked out my legs during a spell of breaststroke and felt my timing chip slip out from under my wetsuit and slide down my ankle. I quickly rolled over onto my back and reached down to grab it with both hands before it slipped into the deep. I couldn't face another visit to the penalty tent to explain to the lady that this time I really had lost my timing chip. Wetsuits are supposed to aid buoyancy, but tucked on your back with both hands on your ankle, you sink like a stone. I flapped around like the world's worst synchronised swimmer and managed to tighten the chip and stuff it back under the leg of my wetsuit.

As I emerged from the water, a nearby kayaker was looking over at me anxiously.

'Ça-va?' she called.

'Très bien,' I replied.

My back had felt ok at the start of the swim, but the more breaststroke I did, the more uncomfortable it got. My incredibly buoyant neoprene bottom caused my back to bend unnaturally, placing a lot of strain on it. It was a great incentive to stick to front crawl as much as possible.

With the timing chip securely tucked under my wetsuit, I put my head down and concentrated on my stroke. I made it to shore at the end of the first lap and crawled out onto the side. A volunteer was there to take my hand but I was reluctant to accept any help in case it resulted in instant disqualification. Ironman rules forbid any 'outside help'. Perhaps the volunteers were there to test our mental strength; offer us an arm, and then the moment we make contact they laugh at us shout *'au revoir'* and disqualify us from the race. It seemed unlikely but you can never be too careful.

I stood up, expecting to feel the familiar dizziness that I had felt after all of my saltwater swims, but I felt pretty good. The warmer water clearly made a difference. The crowd lined the barriers on either side of the blue carpet as swimmers had to make their way about 50 metres to the start of the second lap. I glanced at my watch again. 44 minutes. The second lap was slightly longer, but I had plenty of time.

As swimmers ran past me and dived into the water to begin their second lap, I stood at the edge of the pontoon and took a moment to try and stretch my back. Another volunteer asked if I was ok, and I told him I was *'magnifique'*.

I felt a lot calmer during the second lap. My arms and shoulders were beginning to tire, but my breathing felt controlled and steady. The swimmers had spread out by this point so I had a lot more room. At one point I even felt like I was enjoying myself. At the turning point that marked the three-quarter mark, I could see swimmers still midway through the first lap. There seemed very little chance that they would complete the swim inside the cut-off, and it was disappointing to think of all the hard work they had put in. Or perhaps they hadn't put any work in at all, which was why they were struggling so much. Either way, I was delighted that I wasn't one of them.

The sun was now visible above the Vichy skyline to my right, and I could already feel the heat on my face as I turned to breathe. The sunlight was blinding, but it made me feel alive. I was approaching the end of my Ironman swim; something that before the Plymouth Breakwater Swim two weeks previously, I didn't think would be possible.

We had cycled to the dam at the end of Lake Allier earlier in the week on our hired quadracycle. Due to recent heavy rain, the water level was higher than usual and we had watched the water cascading viciously over the dam. The Ironman swim route was heading towards this dam. All that stood between us and certain death was a couple of young kayakers. After navigating the final buoy, we then had to swim back against the current to the swim exit. This section was particularly tough, and I was increasingly desperate to get out of the water. The idea of being on dry land, even if it meant cycling 112 miles, was preferable to any more time in the lake.

After 1 hour, 34 minutes and 5 seconds, I felt the solid ground touch my toes. Hundreds of spectators were cheering and shouting. I raised my arms in the air as I beamed from ear to ear. I felt a little lightheaded pulling myself out of the water, but my legs didn't feel too bad. I had read that you should increase your leg kicks in the final few minutes of a triathlon swim, to get the blood circulating and prepare your legs for the bike section. Due to the vast amount of breaststroke that I had swum, my legs were wide awake.

I had just completed the first, and potentially toughest, leg of an Ironman. *IN YOUR FACE, STROKE DEVELOPMENT 4!* I shouted to myself. *Who needs Dolphins? I've just completed an Ironman swim!*

I managed a slow jog along the blue carpet towards the bike transition. The swim was over. I couldn't stop smiling. I was on dry land for the rest of the day. Unless something went catastrophically wrong during the bike or the run, that is.

I had photographed the London Triathlon a few years ago for one of its sponsors and was positioned at the swim exit for a while. I became familiar with the site of swimmers reaching around to their back and pulling the zip cord, before peeling their arms out of the wetsuit as they ran, in order to save time in transition.

At the London Triathlon, the transition area is inside London's Excel Centre, and to get to it, swimmers had to walk up a metal staircase. In order to prevent this staircase getting too wet, swimmers were ordered to remove their wetsuits before entering the building, and place them in a plastic bag. One particular swimmer didn't seem to be making any effort to remove his wetsuit as he approached the building.

'Take off your wetsuit,' shouted the marshal as he approached.

'No, I can't,' he replied calmly.

'Take off your wetsuit!' she shouted.

He shook his head. The crowds squashed up against the barrier all ceased their cheering and looked over to see what the argument was about.

'You will not enter the transition area until you remove your wetsuit. It is against the rules,' she barked, stepping out into the middle of the gangway and blocking his path.

'I can't take off my wetsuit!' he shouted, trying to run past her.

'TAKE OFF YOUR WETSUIT! NOW!'

'I CAN'T!'

'Why not?'

'I'M NOT WEARING ANYTHING UNDERNEATH!'

A smile spread across the marshal's stony face.

'Well... in that case...' she said, as she stepped aside and gestured to the door.

Thankfully I had remembered to wear something under my wetsuit, but as I pulled it off my shoulders and tried to pull the arms inside out I got stuck. My left wrist was stuck on my stopwatch and the right on my security tag. Although I had worn my wetsuit a few times, I never had to get out of it in a hurry, and never without someone to help me. I stood by the transition bags unable to unhook mine from the rack with my arms like a pair of seal flippers flapping awkwardly around. I couldn't face the embarrassment of retrieving my bag with my flippered hands, so instead pushed my hands back through the wetsuit, turning it back the right way again. I grabbed my bike transition bag and was directed by a marshal into the changing tent.

Sitting down briefly on a wooden bench I was anxious not to get too comfortable. I attempted again to remove my wetsuit. This time successfully removing my arms, and then pulling my legs free with a combination of the classic standing-on-the-wetsuit-with-one-foot-while-removing-the-other-foot technique, and the lesser-known lying-on-your-back-while-frantically-doing-bicycle-kicks-in-the-air-shouting-fuckity-fuckity-wetsuit technique.

I emptied the contents of my bike bag onto the floor and stuffed my soggy wetsuit into the empty bag. I then removed my swimming shorts and added those too. Searching through the items on the floor, there was no sign of the tea towel I had asked to be added to the bag earlier that morning. The volunteer must have put it into someone else's bag by mistake. It was a sorry end to our favourite tea towel, but I smiled at the thought of the confusion that another swimmer would be feeling during transition when they emptied their bag to discover a tea-towel wedding invitation from two people he/she had never even heard of.

I smothered my arms, shoulders and neck with sun cream and applied some carefully to my nose and cheeks. I had been advised (by Simon, of course) to never put sun cream above the eyebrows as it just runs into your eyes once you start sweating, and once you have sun cream in your eyes, well, you have sun cream in your eyes.

With nothing to dry myself off with, I pulled on my cycling jersey and cycling shorts, pulling the shorts extra high – giving myself a wedgie in the process – to ensure they didn't slip down too much during the ride. I pulled the socks onto my wet feet and then tried to slip my feet into my cycling shoes. As I dropped my right foot into the shoe, I felt something squash up against my toes. Inside I found a bracelet that Layla had given to me before we left home with the word 'DAD' spelled out in wooden beads.

I had told her I would wear it during the Ironman, but had been anxious about losing it during the swim, so put it in my shoe so that I would remember it for the bike and run. I slipped it onto my wrist, put on my sunglasses, picked up my transition bag, uttered 'bonne chance' to the others on my bench and jogged towards the exit.

After handing my bag to a volunteer, I made my way to the bike area. It looked far less intimidating in the sunshine. Also, it was now mostly empty, making it much easier for me to locate my bike.

Triathlon rules dictate that you must put on your helmet and fasten it securely before even touching your bike. Failure to do so can result in disqualification. I'm not sure how much use a helmet would be to you as you push your bike towards the transition exit, but I didn't want to argue.

As I wheeled my bike along, I noticed that my dad's cycle computer was ticking along nicely. My last minute reset seemed to have done the trick. I broke into a jog because that's what others were doing, but I didn't have any experience of running whilst pushing my bike and it kept veering off at odd angles. A man with a flag stood by the line on which you are allowed to mount your bike. Having seen Jonny Brownlee receive a time penalty for mounting his bike a millimetre before the line during the triathlon of the London 2012 Olympics, I didn't want to take any chances, so pushed my bike a further two metres before clambering awkwardly aboard. I clipped both shoes onto the cleats and began pedalling.

I looked down to check that the cycle computer was still working. But it wasn't even there. Somewhere between picking up my bike and mounting it, the cycle computer had managed to detach itself from my bike. Due to the lack of space when I recently fitted a pair of aero bars, it had been a bit fiddly slotting it back into place after resetting it, and, in the darkness of the morning, it turns out I didn't attach it properly.

I considered turning the bike around and going back to look for it, but cycling the wrong way against a pack of fired up

Ironmen did not seem like a sensible idea. Besides, it had probably been crushed beneath the wheel of a bike or cycling shoe by now.

'Sod it,' I said out loud. Perhaps it would be a blessing in disguise, and allow me to ride at a speed at which I felt comfortable, rather than being dictated to by an electronic device.

It felt great to be on the bike. During the final half an hour of the swim I had fantasised about this moment. Swimming such a long distance was so unpleasant that the idea of sitting on a bike seat on dry land seemed magical. My legs felt good, and despite aching arms and shoulders and a slight discomfort in my back, I was raring to go.

I settled into a rhythm quite quickly as the route took us away from Le Centre Omnisports and out onto the ring road. It was several minutes before I remembered a key bit of advice that Simon had given me. *Make sure you eat and drink as soon as you get on the bike*.

I drank a few sips from one of my two water bottles and then unwrapped one of the two cheese croissants I had stuffed into my bar bag. It was sweaty and soggy and completely unappetizing but I knew I needed to eat it. Alternating between bites and sips of water, I managed to get the first one down before retrieving the second. This one had been wrapped so many times in cling film I was forced to play my own one-armed game of pass the parcel; tearing at the wrapping with my teeth while my fingers tried desperately to prise the damn croissant out, all the while terrified of dropping the wrapper. Littering during an Ironman is an offence punishable with instant disqualification. After months of training, failing due to a *freak croissant incident* would be fairly annoying.

I managed to stuff the second croissant into my mouth where it lingered for several miles. I was feeling slightly nauseous so just kept it stuffed inside my cheeks like a hamster. Not that I've ever stuffed a hamster inside my cheeks. Eventually, it all disappeared and I celebrated with one of the energy gels I had brought to tide me through to the first aid station. The sickly sweet syrup slid down my throat effortlessly. It was a taste I would grow to despise by the end of the day, but at that moment it was the greatest thing I had ever eaten.

It was only 9.30am but the day was already heating up. This was the first time I had ever taken part in a cycling event that didn't allow drafting. Not that I had much experience of drafting, but I had never had to concern myself with making sure I wasn't too close to other cyclists either.

Ironman rules state that you will face a time penalty if you are caught within 10 metres of another cyclist. If another cyclist passes you, it is your responsibility to drop back to create some distance. It gave me plenty to think about during those first few miles, as the route skirted through the suburbs of Vichy and then out into the countryside. The gradient was fairly flat, but the road had a corrugated feel to it and was peppered with potholes, which made it tough going. I had become used to the luxury of the French auto-routes, so expected every French road to be immaculately surfaced.

During the bike ride you are required to display your race number on your back. The number also shows your name and nationality. This was a nice touch and did result in most of the other Brits who overtook me offering an encouraging *'c'mon George, keep it up.'*

I was overtaken at about the 10km mark by another British rider named Ian. He was a giant of a man, atop a ridiculously expensive looking, yet surprisingly noisy, time trial bike. Time trial bikes differ from normal road bikes because they are built to be more aerodynamic, making key use of the aero bars, and often with aero wheels. Aero wheels are like normal bike wheels but noisy and annoying. They make a loud whirring noise, even if you are going slowly, to give the illusion that you are actually travelling very fast.

Ian flew past me, crunching away on his noisy expensive bike.

'Nice one, George,' he said with a London drawl. 'You're doing well, buddy.'

'Thanks Ian, you too,' I said, as I caught a glimpse of his name on his race number as he disappeared ahead of me.

A couple of kilometres later, we came to our first hill and I saw Ian mashing away in a big gear. I kept up my cadence and was alongside him in no time.

'Hello again,' I said.

'Oh, alright fella?'

'Any idea what speed we've been averaging?' I asked. 'My cycle computer fell off before I even got on my bike.'

He looked down at his complicated Garmin mounted to his handlebars.

'Err...' he panted. 'About 16mph, I think. We're doing ok.'

'Perfect, thanks.'

16 mph was exactly what I had been hoping for. If I kept that up, the 112 miles would take me 7 hours. 14mph would be 8 hours, and I wanted to complete the bike leg in somewhere between 7 and 8. Any quicker and I would be unlikely to have anything left to run a marathon, and any slower and I would be in real danger of missing the cut-off.

'I'm sure I'll see you again in a few minutes,' I said, as I slowly pulled away up the hill from Ian.

Sure enough, a couple of kilometres later, Ian passed me again on one of the flats. It was tempting to up my speed to try and match him, but I felt comfortable at my steady speed, and his erratic changes in pace didn't suit me.

'See you in a bit, no doubt,' he said, as he powered past.

Ian and I passed each other several times over the first 20 km. It was not a game of cat and mouse. There was no bravado and we weren't competing with each other. It was just two very different riding styles – a masher and a spinner – averaging out at identical speeds. We reached the first feed station at the 25km mark only seconds apart.

This was my first experience at a proper drive through feed station. The Dartmoor Classic feed station was like a leisurely lunch break, and RideLondon required deviating from the main route and filtering through a bottleneck where most then dismounted their bikes to refill water bottles and stock up on bananas.

The Ironman feed stations were like those experienced in organised running events. Volunteers stood with their arms outstretched into the road, and cyclists had to try to take something as they passed. A few metres before the aid station there was a huge metal basket where cyclists were required to discard any unwanted drinking bottles, before taking on new ones. I had become quite attached to my drinking bottles over the previous few months (well, as attached as it's possible to be over a plastic drinking vessel) but I reluctantly threw them both into the bin and gave myself a secret fist pump for landing both bottles, and felt like I should be awarded some Ironman time bonus for my efforts. However, any style points I would have been awarded were instantly undone when I completely misjudged the first volunteer handing out 'de l'eau'

I grabbed a bottle, shouted 'merci' but found myself in the wrong gear and unable to shift due to the bottle in my right hand. I somehow managed to unclip my shoes before almost running over the volunteer's feet and miraculously avoided crashing to the ground in a heap in front of her.

'Pardon,' I muttered, as I shuffled forwards with both feet on the ground and my legs still either side of the crossbar.

'Energy,' the next set of volunteers offered. These were identical bottles to the first table, but filled with energy drink rather than water. I hastily slotted my first bottle into one of my bike's bottle holders and then took a bottle of *'energy'* too.

Next up they offered energy gels. I took one and they offered me another so I took that too. The next volunteer offered me an energy bar. *Why not?* Then half a banana. *Yes please.* Some salty crackers? *Sure, hand it all over.* I resisted the Coke, tempting as it was, but I thought I would save that extra hit of sugar until later. With the back pocket of my cycling jersey squashed full of food, I clipped back in and cycled off.

We passed through many quaint villages, interspersed amongst the beautiful French countryside. Each village had clusters of locals gathered on the street corners to clap the cyclists through. Each time somebody clapped, I made a point of saying 'merci' and waving back. This always resulted in them cheering or clapping even louder.

On one section of road, an old battered Citroen 2CV sat randomly in a field of long grass that stretched to the foot of some imposing hills in the distance. It was a perfect French scene. Almost too perfect, and I half expected an old man with a beret to cycle past with onions on his handlebars. A few days later, I saw some of the official Ironman Vichy photographs, and several included this 2CV. So either the photographer had spotted this scene too as being particularly French and photogenic, or he had parked it there deliberately.

Plenty of cyclists were passing me. These were the weaker swimmers who excelled at cycling and were making up the precious time they had lost in the water to get back into contention. I did overtake the occasional rider but it was very rare. I felt quite happy and comfortable cruising along at my own pace.

At around the 60km mark, Martin from Kent – the guy from our campsite – shot past at a tremendous speed. He had told me he was a weak swimmer but a fairly competent cyclist so I had expected him to pass me at some point.

'Well done, George,' he said. 'You're looking good.'

'You too, Martin. Good luck,' I called as he sped off up the road. I didn't call him Martin from Kent to his face.

In the distance loomed Puy de Dôme, a dormant volcano that dominates the Auvergne skyline. This was the stretch of road that on paper looked like it should be really fast and easy. But the sun was relentless and there was no shade anywhere. It had been forecast to be in the high 30s, but reports later stated that it reached 40°C in places. To make matters worse, there was a significant headwind making progress very slow. I tried tucking down on the bike and using the aero bars, but the moment I leaned on them, they began slipping forwards towards the front wheel. The bike's handlebars had been too narrow when I fitted the aero bars, but I had bulked them out with electrical tape and hoped they were tight enough. They clearly weren't. I was so aero that I was almost upside down.

The first time I passed a cyclist lying on the ground under the shade of a tree I didn't think anything of it. Then I passed another. And another. Every lone tree that I reached on those exposed sections of the course seemed to have a cyclist lying in the shade underneath. None of them looked in a hurry to get up and back on their bikes. It was around the 70km point (still 110kms from the finish) that I saw my first ambulance. It screamed past me, lights flashing and siren wailing. I saw many more ambulances over the following few hours; a steady stream of cyclists being whisked off to hospital, presumably suffering from extreme exhaustion and heat stroke.

It made me change my focus. I still wanted to get around the course, but rather than speed or time, my main goal was to eat and drink as much as possible and try not to overdo the exertion.

After about 80km a motorbike pulled alongside me with a marshal frantically signalling from the back. I thought I was being served a penalty notice, but I was a long way behind the cyclist in front of me so couldn't see what I was doing wrong. Surely I hadn't dropped a croissant? The marshal then did the same gesture to the cyclist in front, who looked equally perplexed. Just then, a hum of aero wheels and a whirr of red Lycra went whizzing past.

Wow, he must have been one shit swimmer, I thought to myself, *to have been that far behind, yet such a fast cyclist.* And then it clicked. He was the race leader. I was being lapped.

I was only 50 miles into a 112 mile bike ride, and I had been lapped. That meant he was 62 miles ahead of me. The elite group had started their swim 40 minutes before me, but it was still phenomenal to see the speed they were able to maintain for such a long distance.

To begin with it felt slightly demoralising, but then I told myself that these were professional triathletes. They spend all day every day training and had probably been doing so for years. There was no point comparing myself to them.

I was enjoying myself. I mean, really enjoying myself. It was very tough going, but I felt pretty good considering, and I had eaten and drunk plenty and didn't have any noticeable pains. I was cycling through the French countryside. And I was taking part in an Ironman. It was completely surreal and the thought amused me for miles on end.

Your mind does strange things when you have to sit on a bike for many hours. There is only a certain amount of time you can spend appreciating the scenery, or eating or drinking. The rest of the time, your legs are just spinning around and the mind has a chance to wander. I kept looking at my watch and doing calculations in my head to try and work out what speed I was travelling at, and what my likely finishing time would be. My maths is dreadful at the best of times, but when tired, hot and cycling, it was completely irrational. To make matters worse, I was used to dealing with miles, yet all the distance markers were in kilometres. I knew that 10km was a little over 6 miles, but trying to calculate anything more complex proved too much for my brain to cope with. In the space of 30 seconds, I could go from thinking I was without doubt going to miss the cut-off, to thinking that if I kept up the current pace I might finish the bike leg in under 5 hours. The more I thought about it, the more confused I became. In the end I realised that it was futile trying to do any calculations. It was the same cyclists up ahead who had been there for miles (and kilometres) and I could see familiar cyclists in the distance behind me, who didn't seem to be gaining on me. I was doing alright. I just needed to keep doing what I was doing.

I continued to play leapfrog with Ian (not literally, that would be weird), until I passed him on a hill at about 80km and he didn't catch up with me again. He seemed to be struggling and didn't offer his usual 'I'll see you in a bit' response as I passed.

There were a couple of big hills towards the halfway point. The road climbed up, as tends to happen with hills, and it was actually refreshing to change gear and even get out of the saddle on a couple of occasions. When I had looked at the topography of the bike course beforehand, it was the relatively flat route that had appealed to me. What could be better than cycling on easy flat roads? When I told more experienced triathletes about Vichy's flat bike course, they all winced as though this was a bad thing. I didn't understand it at the time, but I did now.

Cycling along the flat is all well and good, for a while, but it can get very tedious. You start craving for some change in the terrain just to break things up a bit; a mountain, a hillock, a small incline, or even just a bloody speed bump, to put an end to the monotony.

Living in Devon I had grown to almost enjoy cycling up hills. I hadn't got to the stage where I would actively go out seeking hills, but there is something exciting about cycling up them. It requires a lot more thought than the flats; choice of gear, seated or unseated, slow and steady or as fast as possible to get it over and done with, push hard in a big gear or spin quickly in a low one? And the overall effect of hills on the average speed isn't too detrimental, because after every uphill slog, you are rewarded with a fast downhill, and the chance to either go for it to make up some lost time, or sit back and relax and let gravity do its job.

As the bike route headed up the hill through the woods, it also provided a few miles of much needed shade.

After descending a long hill into Vichy, the road forked and those still with a second lap to do were to stay right, and riders who had completed two laps turned left. I noticed a couple of cyclists who hadn't lapped me freewheeling down the left hand fork, with no intention to continue their race.

Within a mile of the second lap, I realised how quiet it felt. There had always been people within sight of me during the first lap, both in front and behind, but as I left the suburbs of Vichy for the second time, there was nobody in sight. The second lap was bound to be quieter because all those lapping me were now off the course, but there had not been too many of them. I later found out that many cyclists got to the halfway point and simply gave up. The heat and the wind had been too much for them and they couldn't face another lap.

I had cried several times during the day already. But none of the previous times had been because of genuine sorrow. I had just become overwhelmed on a few occasions by what I was undertaking, and the tears flowed as a release mechanism, almost in a euphoric way. I cried when I reached the halfway point of the swim and realised I had plenty of time. I cried when I got on my bike and discovered that my legs were still functioning. I cried when I remembered that I would hopefully be seeing Rachel and the kids soon.

But midway through the second lap I found myself crying again. But these tears were different. These tears had come out of nowhere and I realised it had all become too much for me. Up until this point, I had been extremely optimistic about my chances of finishing. But as the day got hotter, as my legs tired, and my body began to fall apart, I had a new understanding of the enormity of what I was undertaking. Perhaps the Ironman was too big a challenge for me after all. My dad was right – a half-Ironman would have been far more sensible. I would have almost finished that by now. On their own, the three triathlon disciplines had seemed achievable in my mind, but I had completely underestimated the cumulative effect that they have on the body. And I was only a little over halfway through the bike.

I began sobbing uncontrollably. Thankfully, due to the no drafting rule, there was nobody there to witness my breakdown. I started to question whether it was all worth it. I didn't have to prove myself to anyone. Nobody would be disappointed if I pulled out now. Plenty of other people had, so why shouldn't I?

I tried to snap out of the rut I had found myself in. I leaned down on my wonky aero bars and began pedalling harder. An annoying rattling sound broke my concentration. I couldn't work out where it was coming from. It wasn't coming from the chain or gears because it happened even when I wasn't pedalling. It didn't sound like it was coming from either of the wheels. It only happened when I leaned on the aero bars, and when I took my hands off them they were silent. When you have little else to think about, a rattling noise like that can really tip you over the edge.

I then found the culprit. It was the wooden beads of the '*DAD*' bracelet that Layla had given me, rattling against the metal bars each time I leaned forwards. It made me think of what she had been through yesterday. The IronKids was by far the toughest thing she had ever done. She struggled with it physically, and it tested her emotions. Yet she kept going, and she crossed that finish line. It was ok for me to cry. But I needed to keep going and do everything I could to cross my finish line.

But things continued to get worse. It was now 1pm and the temperature was unbearable. Never before had I experienced such relentless heat. Whenever I had visited hot countries previously, I had always been in the proximity of either water or shade, and never while undertaking an extreme endurance event. This was new territory for me and I was finding it incredibly difficult. I began routinely squirting water through the gaps in my bike helmet in a bid to cool down. My head throbbed with pain and the sweat and sun cream tasted bitter on my lips.

I was picking up two new drinking bottles at every 25km feed station, and they would both be empty before I reached the next one. I was making sure to pick up gels, fruit and bars at each feed station too, and eat as much as I could, no matter how hard it was, but it still didn't seem to be enough.

I was suffering really badly. At one point I genuinely couldn't remember whether I was on my first lap or second lap. I had promised Rachel and my mum that if things got too tough I would pull out. Things had got too tough.

Even the sunflowers had admitted defeat. Either side of me, fields of them stretched to the horizon, their leaves shrivelled and dried, and their once vibrant yellow petals now a shade of rusty brown. The heat was too much and they hung their heads in resignation.

I had not seen another cyclist in a long time. I had surely taken a wrong turn somewhere and was cycling off into the French countryside, away from the race and all the other competitors. Both of my water bottles were empty and the temperature had reached 40°C with a vicious headwind. I had been suffering from hallucinations on and off for about half an hour, my head pulsating in the heat. I kept seeing water stations in the distance, only for them to vaporise into nothing as I approached.

I thought of the many cyclists I had seen; their bodies littering the roadside, sheltering under the little shade they could find. I thought of the ambulances that had sped past, whisking away many of these competitors to receive further medical attention. That would soon be me. I would find a tree, lie beneath it, and wait for help to arrive.

A shape took form further up the road ahead. Shimmering in the heat. A mirage surely? It was a man. In his late fifties. Perhaps older. His weather-beaten face unfazed by the scorching heat. He stepped into the middle of the road, raised his arm in front, and pointed a gun at my head. This was it. There was nowhere for me to go, and I didn't have the energy to try to negotiate. I continued pedalling towards him, hoping that he was just another figment of my imagination and I would pass straight through him. But the closer I got the more lifelike he became. He was real, and there was no chance of an escape.

I took my hands off the handlebars and sat back in my saddle. I raised both arms in the air in defeat.

'Shootez moi, monsieur!' I shouted in Franglais, as my bike careered towards him. 'S'il vous plaît,' I then added, not wanting my final words on this earth to be considered impolite.

A toothy grin spread across his wrinkled face. He tilted his head back and roared with laughter. If this had been a film, his gold tooth would have glinted in the sunlight. But this wasn't a film. This was real life. He looked me straight in the eye. And then he pulled the trigger.

The blast from his hosepipe caught me right between the eyes. The icy chill of the water brought me straight back into the real world, and as the cool trickle seeped down my neck into my t-shirt I gasped for air.

I grabbed the brakes and brought my bike to a standstill right in front of the man, remembering to unclip from my pedals just in time. I wanted to eek out this moment a little longer. He stood there for a few seconds, still grinning as he drenched me from head to toe. He was enjoying it almost as much as me.

'Merci beaucoup, monsieur. Je t'aime.'

'De rien,' he said (it's nothing). But it wasn't nothing. Without realising it, he had saved me. Without the man and his hosepipe, I don't think I could have continued.

A little further up the road was a feed station. My head felt much better but my stomach had been feeling weird for the last few miles due to an influx of energy gels and bananas, and

I didn't want to risk 'doing a Paula' on the course. I propped my bike against a portable toilet and ventured inside.

I slumped down onto the toilet seat in the half light. An Ironman veteran friend of mine (not Simon, on this occasion) told me a story about when he was competing in an Ironman. He had gone way too quickly on the bike and had severely paid for it on the run. He went into a portable toilet and was horrendously sick several times. Determined to finish the race, but in no state to continue, he sat down on the toilet and had a sleep. For TWO hours. When he awoke, he felt much better, and carried on running, still completing the course in plenty of time.

I didn't have the luxury of two hours to spare to have a sleep. And the idea of napping in a portable toilet was not high on my bucket list.

I stood up to leave and glanced back into the plastic toilet bowl. Something wasn't right. Was it just the light inside the portable toilet deceiving me? No, it couldn't be. I squinted a little more, assuming my eyes were playing tricks on me, but the more I looked the more real it was. Everything I had passed was a dark pink colour. Almost red.

This wasn't good.

I had read stories of people taking part in extreme endurance challenges and pissing blood. It's often a sign of kidney failure caused by severe dehydration, and can be very serious and potentially fatal. I had been drinking as much as I could, but perhaps it still wasn't enough. It was tempting to ignore it and carry on regardless, hoping that my body would fix itself. As much as I wanted to complete the Ironman, I didn't want it to be at the expense of something more serious. I had made a promise to Rachel and to Mum to be sensible. The only rational solution was for me to tell an official. They would insist that I get seen by a race doctor, or possibly taken away in an ambulance, and that would be it. My race was over.

I left the portable toilet completely crestfallen. I knew I was making the right decision, but it was a cruel way to end my race. There was a group of race officials standing by the drinks station and I left my bike where it was and walked over to tell them about my condition. I was just metres away from them when a realisation hit me. The beetroot juice. The fucking beetroot juice! I had drank nearly a litre of the damn stuff the night before, and, as anyone who has ever eaten a lot of beetroot will know, it likes to make its mark when it leaves your body too.

'Ca-va?' asked one of the stewards, as she noticed me cackling away to myself.

'Oui madam. Je suis terrifique,' I said, turning on my heel and moving with a light jog back to my bike.

Ten minutes previously I had been on my bike, hallucinating, fatigued and suffering from heat stroke. I had then been brought back to life by a saviour with a hose pipe, before suffering an internal-bleeding scare. I now felt better than ever. The Ironman was back on. And, by my calculations – which admittedly weren't very reliable – I had less than a quarter of the bike course to go.

For the final 25 miles I felt like a different person. The heat was still unrelenting, but I knew that every pedal stroke now took me closer to Vichy. I still had the small matter of a marathon to run, but there was something appealing about getting off my bike and pulling on a pair of comfortable running trainers. During the bike leg I was constantly paranoid about getting a puncture, or suffering a mechanical failure of the bike. Running had no such worries, and was appealing in its simplicity. All I had to do was hope that my body could survive.

I began to overtake a lot of familiar names who had passed me earlier with such ease. Ricardo, the plucky Spaniard, Jean-Luc the Frenchman and Jens the giant Dane had all looked like experienced cyclists when they disappeared in a blur past me earlier in the day. Now here they were, slogging up the hills at little more than walking pace.

My cautious approach to the bike leg seemed to have paid off.

As I reached the fork where I had turned right for my second lap three and a half hours previously, it was an incredible feeling to fork left towards T2. The route followed the main road past our campsite, around the roundabout alongside Decathlon, where the day before I had made two trips; the first to buy Layla and Leo a new cycling helmet each, and the second to buy a new running top and visor. A running top and visor I would be putting on very shortly to attempt to run 26.2 miles.

I hadn't thought too much about the running leg of the Ironman. My running training had been almost non-existent, and I genuinely had no idea how my legs would feel after swimming and cycling such long distances. My plan all along had been to allow enough time to potentially walk the 26.2 miles, but I always knew there was a possibility that I might not make it as far as the run, so had tried not to think about it too much.

During the handful of 'brick sessions' that I did, I had suffered badly with stitches that were so painful that running was almost impossible. Simon recommended not eating for the final half hour of the bike, in order to avoid a stitch, and then wait until I've started running before eating. I managed to resist any food at the final feed station and descended into Vichy ravenous.

It was nice to be back amongst people again. The spectators out on the bike loop had dwindled considerably during the second lap, partly because of the heat, but also because most of those that were being supported had long since gone past.

Approaching T2, there were plenty of spectators lined up against the railings, clapping the cyclists in, congratulating us on completing two thirds of the Ironman.

I dismounted my bike and made an effort to run with it to the rack, but seemed unable to coordinate my legs, so opted for a brisk walk instead. I completed the 112 mile bike in 7 hours and 14 minutes. That's a fairly slow time by Ironman standards (the winner completed his leg in an astonishing 4h 31m), but 112 miles is a long way, and considering the conditions, I was extremely proud. Running a marathon, though? This was going to be an altogether different challenge.

I grabbed my run transition bag from the rack and sat down on a bench in the changing tent. My cycling jersey had become welded to my body, and proved almost as difficult to remove as the wetsuit. I eventually peeled it off and put on my brand new running vest.

In the past I had always just worn any old t-shirt to run in. I used to wear normal cotton ones, until I cottoned on (pun intended) to the fact that man-made fabrics didn't soak up the sweat and therefore made you look a little less grubby and sweaty when running. So I starting running in football shirts, as these were the only synthetic t-shirts I owned. I then got a couple of 'technical' t-shirts from taking part in runs, so these became my default running wear.

I was chatting to a friend just before the 10km run this year. I was wearing my t-shirt from the Berlin Marathon 2010 (soooo five years ago).

'Doesn't it annoy you running in sleeves?' he asked.

'What do you mean?'

'I would find running in sleeves really annoying.'

'But this is a short-sleeved t-shirt.'

'Yes, but even short sleeves touch your shoulder and flap around and generally get in the way.'

'What am I supposed to wear?'

'A running vest. Like most people,' he said.

'Most people? Yeah right,' I said, looking around at the assembled runners and noticing that the vast majority of them were actually wearing sleeveless running vests.

Until this point, I had never once thought about my sleeves whilst running. Every other part of clothing had annoyed me at some point – flappy laces, chafing shorts, t-shirt neck too tight, rubbing shoes, shorts riding up too high. But not the sleeves. Sleeves had never been a concern for me.

That was until this 10km. After that seed of doubt had been sown in my mind, all I could think about during the run were my fucking sleeves. They kept gently brushing my shoulder in a teasing way. My upper arms felt immensely hot all of a sudden. No hotter than they would normally be, but at that moment they felt like they were burning up. I wanted to rip the sleeves off my t-shirt there and then. I did try briefly at one point, but realised two things: firstly, I discovered that it is quite difficult to rip the sleeve off a t-shirt. Especially a technical one. Not to mention a little weird. And secondly, although it was five years ago, the Berlin marathon remains my finest hour, and I didn't want to damage my only memento.

I couldn't put myself through another 26.2 miles of sleeve hell, though, so on my way to hand in my transition bags I called into Decathlon (other sports superstores are available) and purchased their cheapest running vest. For such a massive shop, they had a surprisingly small selection of running vests. Does two even count as a selection? If I'd wanted horse riding boots, now that would have been a different story.

I also bought a visor. I know, I know – only dicks wear visors. But it was forecast to be incredibly hot, and I was happy to look like a dick if it meant shielding some of the sun from my face. They only sold golf visors so I had to purchase one that said *'how does my swing look?'* on the side. This did seem a little inappropriate if I wasn't even going to be on a golf course. It might as well have said *'how am I hanging?'*

The running vest felt amazing when I put it on. Light, airy and comfortable. How had I put up with sleeves for so long? I changed from my sweat soaked cycling shorts to a pair of running shorts. Again, just changing my clothes made a huge difference. It took a few more minutes than those wearing all purpose triathlon clothing, but I felt fresher and happier.

A Liverpudlian called Mark who had overtaken me during the first lap of the bike course was changing next to me. He must have had a difficult second lap of the bike as he had been really flying when he passed me.

'Do you want any of this, mate?' he asked, holding up a bottle of sun cream.

'Yeah, please. I'd better put a bit more on. It's so hot out there.'

'It's like a fookin sauna,' he said. 'I've heard it's even hotter out on the run course, cos the sun reflects back off the ground.'

'Oh great, thanks. I'll look forward to that,' I said, as I slathered some cream on my neck and shoulders.

My cycling shoes had felt fairly comfortable and my feet were in a far better state than they had been at the end of RideLondon, and I could at least still feel my toes. But my trainers felt like slippers in comparison as I pulled them onto my tired, weary feet.

This was the moment of truth. Was I going to collapse in a heap as I began to run? Were my legs going to seize up and not get going? Was my back going to go into spasm?

I handed my transition bag to a volunteer and took my first tentative running steps. My legs worked! It felt very weird, as I had expected, but they felt surprisingly good. The few bike-to-run brick sessions had dulled the shock for my body.

As I made my way out of the cool of the transition tent, I felt the immense heat of the air hit me again. It was after 4pm, but the temperature was still in the late 30s and, without the movement of air that you experience on the bike, it was even more stifling.

The barriers were lined with people and I kept a look out for Rachel. She had planned to find a spot near the centre, but I didn't know whether I would see her at the start of the first lap, or not until I returned to the start area after about 10k.

Then, just ahead, I spotted her by the barrier. She was staring anxiously at her phone in deep concentration. I ran up to her and stood less than half a foot from her. She glanced up briefly and looked back at her phone.

'Helloooo,' I called.

She looked up again.

'Oh my god! It's you. You're alive!' she said, throwing her arms around me.

'Daddy!' shouted the three children who were all sat patiently in the shade of the barrier on the floor.

'Of course I'm alive. What did you think had happened to me?'

'We didn't know. I've been trying to follow your progress on my phone, but your bike tracker stopped updating on the website after about 120km. We thought you must have given up, or had an accident.'

'No. I'm still going, just about. How are you all?'

'Good,' they said, jumping up at the barrier and grabbing hold of my arm.

'Aw, it's really great to see you,' I said.

'I can't believe you're here. How are you feeling? I didn't recognise you in your fancy new vest and visor. You almost look like an Ironman.'

'There's still a way to go before that. Just the small matter of running a marathon.'

'Well you look amazing considering what you've already done. How are you feeling?'

'Better than I thought I would at this stage. Just relieved to have done the bike ride. It was so much tougher than I was expecting.'

'Because of the heat?'

'Yes. The second lap was horrendous. I thought I was out of the race on a couple of occasions.'

'I don't know how you did it. It's bad enough here and we haven't had to cycle 112 miles.'

'No, but you have had to entertain three children for several hours. How have they been?'

'They've all been really good actually.'

'We've all been sad though,' said Layla. 'Mummy told us that you had probably had to pull out and we were worried that you had crashed.'

'Well here I am, and I didn't crash. Hopefully you'll get to see me a few more times before the end now. This might take a long while, so don't be surprised if I don't finish the first lap for ages.'

'Well you've got about 7 hours, so that should be plenty of time.'

'Yes, hopefully. We'll see how I get on.'

'Good luck. We'll try and find a spot in the shade over by the trees.'

'Ok, see you in a bit. I love you all,' I said, leaning over and giving them each a kiss on their head.

'Byeeeeee. Go Daddy.'

'You can win, Daddy.'

'Dad-dy, Dad-dy... Dad-dy,' I heard them chant as I headed off.

As I jogged slowly but sprightly alongside the beautiful lake, I kept reminding myself that this was the best I was going to feel for the next few hours and that it was only going to get much, much worse. There was a constant reminder of this fact everywhere I looked. It was like being on the set of a zombie movie. Runners staggered forwards, head bowed, and legs moving at a speed much slower than normal walking pace. It's a common sight, known in the triathlon world as the 'Ironman shuffle'. The legs have long since given up by this point, and they are being dragged along by pure determination alone.

Runners are given a different coloured wrist band after each lap, and you can't cross the finish line until you have four bands. Most of these Ironman zombies had two or three bands on their arms, meaning they were now on their final or penultimate lap before the finish. Some, however, had no wristbands yet and were in for a very long afternoon if this was the speed at which they were to try and complete the 26.2 miles.

I had already surpassed the achievements of German Silva, the two-time New York Marathon winner, who only managed 800 metres of the Ironman marathon, and I was soon upon the first aid station. Similar to the bike, it was split up into a series of tables with a variety of drinks and snacks on offer. But unlike the bike leg, I didn't have to worry about unclipping or running over a volunteer. I drank a cup of water, ate half a banana, and slowly began jogging again.

The feed stations on an Ironman run are generously spaced about every 2km. In a normal marathon they would be far more thinly spaced. But the body is already depleted of most of its energy and reserves, so eating and drinking regularly is essential to stand any chance of completing the course.

'Walk the feed stations,' Simon had advised. 'There's no point running through them as you can't eat or drink properly when you're running. Take a few seconds as you walk to get your breath back. Then try and make yourself run to the next feed station. It's as simple as that.'

This was the strategy that I planned to implement for as long as I could. It sounded simple. Rather than running a marathon, I was simply running a series of short 2km runs from aid station to aid station, where I could walk for a moment and have something to eat and drink. Then all I had to do was repeat it. Over 20 times. I tried not to think about the overall distance and concentrated on breaking it down into its 2km sections. Psychologically it made a huge difference.

The first section of the run course followed the western bank of the Lake Allier on the other side from Vichy heading up towards our campsite. There were some sporadic patches of shade along this side which eased the intensity of the sun slightly.

After about 4km the path passed underneath a bridge and then around a tight hairpin right hand bend and up a steep incline onto the bridge. It was only a very short section of uphill, but it was enough for the muscles to scream out in agony, and allow a moment of gratitude and reminder that the run route could have been a lot, lot worse.

The bridge spans the River Allier (it would be a bit of a shitty bridge if it didn't) and in my mind we just had to run back down the other side and over the other bridge, to complete the lap. I had forgotten that to make the distance of a lap equate to a quarter of a marathon, several detours were added. The first of these took me by surprise when we reached the other side of the bridge and turned right instead of left, heading still further away from the start. Still, it was a nice shady section through a tree lined path on a bank above the river. I still felt ok at this stage, but I knew there was a long way to go.

The path eventually led back down to the water's edge and the route doubled back on itself, this time by the water and away from the shade of the trees. And that's when I realised that the Liverpudlian I had chatted to in T2 had not been understating the heat. From relatively cool and comfortable conditions one minute, to running through a blast furnace the next, there was absolutely no escape along this stretch. The path was surfaced in fine sandy gravel that brutally reflected the sun back up, to ensure that it got us from every angle. My recently acquired new running technique had taught me to always look ahead, but on this stretch, even with sunglasses and a visor on, the glare and the heat were too much and I was forced to hang my head low to try and allow some relief.

After a couple of kilometres, the route left the lakeside and meandered around the city streets. It was a nice respite, and the cobbled pathways of Vichy city centre had plenty of shade, and more supporters than the rest of the route.

'Well done, George. You're doing great,' an English voice shouted.

'Thank you,' I replied, and it wasn't until I had passed him that I realised it was Emily's husband Pete. I completed a lap of the town square and as we headed back to the lake I caught sight of him again, standing by the side of the route with his baby daughter asleep in the pushchair.

'Pete! Sorry, I didn't recognise you before,' I said.

'That's ok. You're looking really good. Keep it up.'

'Thanks. How's Emily getting on? Have you seen her?'

'Not yet. I've been tracking her on my phone and she's about half an hour behind you. She's just got off the bike.'

'Brilliant. I'm glad she's still going. I didn't realise I'd passed her.'

'Yeah, I think you overtook her during the swim. Or maybe in transition.'

The liveliest of the feed stations was situated in this cobbled square. Loud music blared out of speakers and the volunteers all seemed to be high on life. The usual spread of fruit and energy bars were on offer, but this one had an extra stand at the end offering hot pieces of sausage with a mustard dip. They looked absolutely amazing, but I didn't think I was ready for it yet. I would hold off and use the sausage as an incentive to have on my final lap, if I made it that far.

'De l'eau?'

'Energy?'

'Banane?'

'Saucisse?'

'Biere?'

WHAT?

I looked up and a volunteer was pouring a bottle of Heineken into a cup and offering it to me. I couldn't work out if he was serious, or just fooling around. I paused slightly, and gazed longingly as the cold beer frothed in the plastic cup. It was so tempting. But I still had over 20 miles to run.

'Biere?' he said again.

'Non merci,' I smiled, and started running again.

The route left the shade of the town and rejoined the path along the lake in the blistering sun. Many bars and cafés lined the route, and the crowd were very vocal and enthusiastic as they sat down for drinks or dinner under the shade of their parasols. I looked on enviously for a moment but then felt incredibly self-satisfied. Yes, they were sitting down to a lovely-looking dinner, but tomorrow morning nothing would have changed. Tomorrow morning, there was a very good chance I would wake up an Ironman.

The pathway eventually looped round to the bridge that crosses the dam at the bottom end of the lake; the same dam that I had been worried about being swept over earlier in the day. *Was that really only this morning?* It felt like a week ago.

All along the far side of the river you could hear the music and the voice of the race announcer from the finish line. It was both inspiring and demoralising at the same time. Knowing that some people had already finished when I still had 20 miles to run was tough. But at least I was still running. As I approached the end of the first lap I still felt reasonably good. I was hurting all over, but it was bearable and my limbs seemed to at least be functioning.

After a brief section of off-road, where the route cut across the grass perimeter of Le Centre Omnisports in order to avoid the car park, barriers lined the route again (the rest of the run route was barrier free) and spectators stood lookout for their loved ones at the end of either their first, second, third or final laps. I spotted Rachel by the barrier again. She was looking directly at me, but seemingly oblivious. Again I ran up to within a foot of her and had to wave before she noticed me.

'Oh, there you are! Look kids, Daddy's here again.'

'I thought you're supposed to be looking out for me, not me trying to spot you?'

'I know, sorry, it's just I'm still not used to you wearing a white vest, sunglasses and that weird visor thing.'

'Yeah, it's not my normal look. Do I look like a bit of a dick?' I whispered.

'No, you look great. You look like an Ironman.'

'Cool, I might start wearing it more often then.'

'Please don't, Daddy,' said Layla. 'You look weird.'

'Ok, perhaps you do look like a bit of a dick,' whispered Rachel. 'But it's only for a few more hours.'

'So what have you been up to since I last saw you?' I asked.

'Getting these!' shouted Leo, and he and Kitty thrust two gigantic plastic cups at me, with fake palm leaves sticking out the top and a massive straw.

'Wow, what are those?'

'Slush Puppies. Want some?' said Leo as he pushed it towards my face.

Icy cold, sickly sweet, syrupy juice. I could think of nothing better and I desperately wanted to slurp down the lot. But I remembered about Ironman's 'no outside help' rule again and I thought receiving a disqualification for a slurp of Slush Puppie would probably be about the worst way to end a race.

'No thank you. Maybe I'll have one when I finish. What else have you been up to?'

'Nothing,' said Rachel. 'We've been queuing up for those since we last saw you. We've only just got here. You said you were going to be much longer.'

'I thought I would be. I'm sure I'll slow down lots for the other laps, so don't expect me back here anytime soon.'

'Well you're still looking great. Even with that visor. Did you hear about Simon?'

'No. What about him?'

'He had to pull out. He managed one loop of the bike course and then checked himself into the hospital tent.'

'Oh no, poor him. Is he ok?'

'Yes I think so. He was heading back to the campsite.'

'Such a shame. Glad he's ok though. He was in a pretty bad state this morning.'

'Yes. You'd better get going. We're very proud of you.'

'Thanks. See you in a bit.'

'Love you!' they shouted.

The runners then had to go through one of four different funnels, each marked with a different lap number, and a marshal put a coloured band onto our wrist to show that we had completed the lap. One down, three to go.

A further 50 metres on, the route split. Laps 1, 2 and 3 went into the left lane. Final lap went into the right. We all then entered the finish arena, regardless of which lap we were on. The arena was an impressive spectacle with a high grandstand packed with spectators, loud music and flashing lights. Those completing their Ironman stayed to the right and looped round and under the finish line. Those with more laps remaining stayed on the inside lane adjacent to the finishing straight.

The finish line was just there – literally within touching distance. It felt like it should be heartbreaking, but it was anything but. I was able to see the elation, the relief, and the pain etched onto the faces of other Ironmen as they crossed the line next to me on my first three laps. Although it would have been amazing to not still be out on the course, I didn't feel like I wanted to be there yet. My time would come. All I had to do was keep putting one foot in front of the other, and later that evening, it would be my turn and I would be the one forking right onto the finishing straight.

The heat showed no sign of diminishing. As well as all the food and drink, each aid station also had at least one volunteer with a hosepipe.

'Douche?' they would ask.

For any readers unfamiliar with French, 'douche' is the French word for shower. They were not verbally abusing me, or offering me a vaginal irrigation.

'Oui merci,' I said.

Simon had told me about the volunteers with hosepipes but cautiously suggested they were best avoided as wet trainers can cause blisters. I didn't care. The cold water on my face and body felt far too good. I stood there for a few seconds as the man soaked my head and t-shirt and then purposefully directed the hose at my shorts. Not just momentarily, but for a good few seconds, for no apparent reason. Perhaps he was offering me that sort of douche after all.

'Je t'adore,' I said, which only encouraged him, and all of the fellow volunteers laughed.

As I reached the steep incline to the first bridge, I saw a familiar face sitting by the path.

'Well done, George. Look at you. You're doing great.'

It was Martin from Kent's partner Sue.

'Thanks, Sue. How is Martin getting on? He whizzed past me on the first lap of the bike.'

'He's doing ok. He's walking a bit. According to the tracker he's just finished his first lap so he's about 3km behind you.'

I must have run past Martin from Kent on my first lap and not noticed him.

'Tell him to hang in there. I'll see him at the finish line.'

'Will do. Good luck.'

I could feel that my pace had slowed slightly, but I was still managing to run, and had only walked the feed stations so far, and stopped on a couple of occasions to chat to people.

The sun was a lot lower in the sky and soon it would dip below the tree line, but it seemed to be giving everything it had before disappearing for the day. I had never felt heat like it. It was 7pm and despite being soaked to the bone by a hosepipe at each aid station, and despite the amount of sweat I must have been producing, my clothes were always dry by the next hosepipe 2km later.

I saw Pete again near the town square. He told me that Emily was struggling and was walking. He was concerned that she might not make the cut-off.

I completed the second lap a few minutes slower than the first, but there was no sign of Rachel where they had been standing previously. I scoured the barriers, knowing that it was unlikely she would actually spot me. I couldn't see her anywhere so headed back out onto the lake path, disappointed that I hadn't seen them as that had been the main motivation for finishing my lap, but I knew that it meant the next time I saw them, I would only have one more lap remaining. I knew it was probably an emergency toilet visit for one of the children (or Rachel) that had caused them to leave, and I was still running a lot faster than I thought I would.

By the midway point of the third lap, the air finally started to feel like it was cooling down. I was still grateful for a hose down at each aid station, but the sections in between were a little less stifling. I had other concerns though. My body was severely feeling the effects of the day's exertion.

As anyone who has done any long distance running or walking will know, when you spend such a long time on your feet, any ailments or niggles become magnified. Old sports injuries that have long since healed and long been forgotten come back as if they were fresh injuries.

The first casualty was my right knee; a stabbing pain just to the left of the knee cap. I was instantly transported back ten years to a Sunday league football match between our team Abington Stanley and Piddington Saxons. Half an hour had been played and the score was 1-1, which was unusual for us, as we were normally at least 4-0 down at half time. One of the Piddington Saxons players caught my standing leg as we both went in for a challenge. There was nothing malicious in the tackle, but I felt something give way in my knee and an agonising pain spread through the joint. There was no way I could continue so I limped towards the touchline.

290

'You're going to have to stay on,' said the player/manager, as I hobbled from the pitch. 'We haven't got any substitutes.'

'I can barely stand on my leg, let alone run or kick the ball.'

'That's ok, nor can most of us. Just stand in the centre circle.'

So I did. I played the remaining 60 minutes without leaving the centre circle, only getting involved if the ball accidentally found its way to me, or if an opposition player was foolish enough to come too close to me.

I couldn't resist trying to get the ball as much as possible, and even had a shot at goal from the halfway line. The pain was so excruciating that it felt like my leg was going to detach itself at the knee. Needless to say, my shot barely even made it as far as the 18 yard box.

By the end of the match, my knee had swollen to twice the size and I couldn't put any weight on it at all. We lost the match 7-1, but at least we finished with 11 men.

Maybe if I'd left the pitch when I first injured myself it wouldn't be coming back to haunt me ten years later.

I plodded on. The crowds were beginning to thin slightly as more and more of their friends or relatives had finished the course. The course was noticeably quieter too with fewer runners still out there. The Ironman shuffle was the dominant mode of movement.

After receiving my third and penultimate wrist band, I spotted Rachel at the barrier.

'You made it! Well done, only two more to go.'

'Two more? That was my third lap. I'm about to start my final one.'

'But we didn't see you before. We just assumed you were walking slowly.'

'I'm still running. Just about. And I've definitely done three laps. Look!' I said, holding up my arm.

'I don't know how we missed you. I'm so sorry. You're doing amazingly. We've been here all the time. We had to nip off for about two minutes when Kitty needed a wee, but that was all.'

'That's ok. Are you all going to wait in the finish arena?'

'Definitely. We'll make our way there now.'

'See you there.'

'See you soon, Ironman.'

'Don't call me that yet!'

I had very little strength left in my legs, but the desire and excitement of finishing such a momentous day gave me renewed strength. I ran the first side of the lake at what felt like a faster pace than any of the previous laps. Crossing the bridge into what had been the hottest part of the course felt so much easier now that the sun had finally retreated.

Despite the significant reduction in the number of competitors on the course, each of the aid stations was still fully manned. There were as many volunteers at the end of the race as there had been during its peak. That is one of the ways in which endurance events are so special. Those finishing towards the end are treated with the same respect and admiration as those heading the field.

Having to choose which of the many volunteers to accept food and drink from was a challenge in itself. They were all fighting over the remaining athletes, trying to give away their wares. At the feed station in the town square, my decision was made easy. I went straight to the lady offering pieces of sausage dipped in mustard. It tasted hot and salty and delicious, and I foolishly washed it down with a glass of Coke – my first of the day. I was still doing sausage flavoured burps many hours later.

The next old injury to return was my left knee. This was from a snowboarding accident that I suffered 18 years ago. I was with a group of friends at a ski resort in Andorra. It was the first day, and we were taking advantage of some fresh snow. I was traversing across to my left when the front of my board dipped into a softer patch of snow and jerked to an abrupt stop. The rest of my body continued to move sideways and my leg bent awkwardly at the knee.

I made it down the mountain using my snowboard as a sledge and spent the rest of the day with my leg up with ice on it. I took the following day off too, and sat miserably in our apartment while my friends all went off for the day. It had improved marginally by day three and I could just about put weight on it. So I foolishly went back out onto the slopes and – adamant that I wasn't going to waste any more of the holiday – continued to snowboard for the rest of the week, despite the immense pain and the fact that I could no longer physically turn left. It has never been the same since.

For the remainder of the Ironman marathon, many more old injuries reawakened themselves. The pain in my left Achilles tendon – which I pulled one New Year's Eve many years ago when I slipped on some ice while drunkenly trying to chase a more sober friend – returned at the 20 mile point.

My sore left big toe, which has never been the same since I kicked the goalpost instead of the ball in a goalmouth scramble against Real Roochers Reserves in 2005 came back after 21 miles.

The little toe on my right foot, which I'm fairly certain I broke during my morning paper round at the age of 13 by stubbing it on Mrs Kennedy's front doorstep, came back to haunt me at 22 miles.

The recurrence of these injuries became more frequent the closer I got to the finish.

My right shoulder – an injury sustained playing tennis against a 9 year old girl when I was 15. I used this injury to justify many subsequent defeats, even once it was fully healed.

A pulled muscle in my upper back caused by putting out the recycling bins a couple of years ago – possibly the most middle-class injury that it's possible to get.

The scars on my right hand from my recent rucksack/bicycle injury started to sting again too.

My jaw felt bruised to the touch (presumably the side-effect of a freak childhood eating accident). My teeth ached.

Even my fingernails hurt.

But strangely, as my physical state deteriorated and my body fell apart, not once during the entire Ironman run did I experience any pain or discomfort in my lower back. The cause of so many problems over the previous 18 months, and the site of the surgeon's knife only months before, it caused me no issues whatsoever in the later part of the day. It had been uncomfortable for parts of the swim, and during the early stages of the bike, but as the day went on, the discomfort eased and my back seemed more than capable of facing the challenge that I had thrown at it.

The town square had been quite shaded, even during the heat of the afternoon, but now the sun had gone down it was very difficult to make out the route. At one point I caught my toe on a raised cobblestone and stumbled forwards, just managing to stay on my feet. Then shortly afterwards, I turned my ankle slightly by misjudging a curb. It hurt a bit, but it was thankfully nothing that was going to hinder my chances of finishing.

'George!' called a voice from the darkness.

It was Pete. I hadn't seen him on my third lap but it was good to see a familiar face again.

'How is Emily getting on?' I asked.

'Not great. She's only a couple of minutes ahead of you now, but she's a lap behind.'

'Is she running?'

'Not so much. Mostly walking now, I think.'

'She'll be ok. She's got plenty of time, hasn't she?'

'I hope so. She's moving at a very slow pace. She's going to be cutting it very fine, considering she still has 15km to go.'

'She'll get there. I know she will. Will you be at the finish?'

'Yes, hopefully. I'll wait until she passes here on her final lap and then drive over to the finish.'

Back alongside the water darkness had fallen, but the pathway was well lit. Less than a kilometre further on, I spotted Emily. She was unmistakeable in her bright pink t-shirt, and pink compression socks. She was walking very slowly, head bowed low.

'You're almost there,' I said, as I put an arm around her shoulder.

'Oh George. Am I glad to see you! Is this your final lap?'

'Yes,' I said guiltily. 'You're only 5km from your final lap too. That's just one Park Run.'

'I'm broken,' she said. 'I don't think I can do it.'

'Of course you can. You already have done most of it. Just a lap and a half to go and then you'll be an Ironman.'

'But I think I'll run out of time. I'm not going to make it inside the cut-off.'

She started crying which caused me to start crying.

'You are definitely going to make the cut-off. It's 9pm now, and your cut-off is 11.15pm, isn't it? So you've got over two hours to do 15km. Even if you keep walking you'll be able to make it.'

'But this isn't walking pace, is it?'

'Well, it's the Ironman Shuffle, that's what it is.'

'I promised myself I would never do the Ironman Shuffle.'

'It's the walk of kings,' I said. 'Ok, you're right, it's not quite walking pace but at least you are still moving forwards. Think of all the people who didn't even make it this far. Did you see all of those people collapsed at the side of the road during the bike? And all those ambulances?'

'I know. How we completed the bike leg in that heat I'll never know.'

'Because you're an Ironman,' I said, glancing at my watch and trying to work out the calculations in my head. She was going to be cutting it very fine.

'Don't wait for me,' she said. 'You've done brilliantly and I don't want to slow you down.'

'No, I needed a break anyway. Right, you see that lamppost up ahead?'

'Yes.'

'You're going to run with me to that lamppost, ok?'

'Ok, I'll try,' she said, and moved into a light jog.

'That's it. Well done.'

'My god this hurts.'

'Just think, every step is getting you closer to the finish line.'

'But then I have to go past the bloody finish line and do another lap,' she laughed for the first time.

'At least it's not hot. And there's no queue for the portable toilets at this time of night.'

We reached the lamppost and she reverted back to the Ironman Shuffle. After another minute I pointed out another landmark in the distance.

'You see that parked car? We're going to run to that.'

And so it continued for my final 5km, alternating running and walking. At the final aid station a lady pointed a hosepipe at me.

'Douche?' she asked.

'Non merci,' I said. I didn't need it this time. I only had a kilometre to go.

I looked at my watch again and tried to do the maths.

'If you keep up this pace for one more lap then you'll be fine, ok?'

'Ok,' said Emily. 'I'll try.'

'It's ok to walk, but make sure you do as much running as walking. Just alternate it.'

The music and the noise of the crowd had escalated, intensified by the darkness. The finish line – my finish line – was less than a kilometre away. Emily and I ran together up to the final wristband point. She went through the number 3 gate and I stepped up to number 4.

'You did it,' said the marshal. 'Congratulations.'

'Thank you,' I said, as he slipped the fourth and final band onto my arm. 'Thank you so much.' I gave him a big hug which took him by surprise.

'Enjoy the moment,' he called after me in perfect English.

'I will.'

Emily and I continued together until the point just before the finish arena when the two routes separated.

'You'll be here in no time,' I said, giving her a hug. 'Just keep moving.'

'Thank you so much for staying with me. Well done. Now go get your medal, you Ironman you.'

As we entered the arena the noise was deafening. Those that finish in the heat of the day don't get the same crowds and atmosphere that the Ironman finish has towards the end, as fellow athletes all gather to watch their comrades finish. The three grandstands on each edge of the finish arena were packed with people, and the barriers were stacked several people deep with spectators whooping and cheering and bashing inflatable Ironman batons together.

It's traditional to high five as many of the crowd as possible on the way to the finish line. Even the elite athletes do it.

Unless, of course, they are taking part in a sprint finish with another athlete. You wouldn't want to miss out on victory because you were too preoccupied high fiving. I ran along the edge of the arena with my right hand outstretched, whooping and cheering and high-fiving all of the reaching arms. Somewhere amongst the crowd were Rachel, Layla, Leo and Kitty. I tried to pick them out but on this occasion I didn't see them and I ran straight by.

Hormones and endorphins are funny things, and despite every inch of my body aching only moments before, the second I entered that finish arena my legs felt better than ever.

With less than 10 metres to go I had a realisation of how far I had come. A little over four months ago I had been in a hospital bed after having an operation to remove a tumour from my spinal cord. In the year preceding that, I had been able to do almost nothing in the way of physical exercise. Earlier that morning, I had stood on the banks of Lake Allier unsure of how the day would unfold. Now, 2.4 miles of swimming, 112 miles of cycling and 26.2 miles of running, and 13 hours, 56 minutes and 51 seconds later, I was about to become an Ironman.

I raised both hands in the air and looked to the sky as I crossed the finish line. As I did so, the sunglasses that I had tucked into the neck of my running vest bounced out and onto the carpet in front of me. I stumbled briefly to avoid treading on them, and then tried, unsuccessfully, to kick them over the finish line. I then had to embarrassingly walk back along the carpet, retrieve my sunglasses and cross the finish line for a second time.

I don't know if the commentator shouted *'George Mahood, you are an Ironman'* or not. My senses were doing weird things and a nuclear bomb could have gone off next to me and I wouldn't have noticed. Those had been the words that I had dreamed about, and longed for someone to shout, but in that moment, they didn't matter in the slightest. I knew it already. I was an Ironman. I am an Ironman.

The weight of the medal felt incredible around my neck, and several volunteers congratulated me as I made my way into the finishers' area where I had a picture taken and then picked up my finisher t-shirt. Inside the building, there were Ironmen everywhere. Some slumped onto tables. Others lying on the floor and some standing or walking around looking relatively spritely. Several tables of food were laid out with an assortment of sandwiches, cold pizza, pies and crisps. I reluctantly filled a plate, but had no desire to eat any of it yet.

'Crêpe?' asked a lady stood by two large hot plates.

Rachel had been talking about crêpes all week, but we hadn't managed to have one.

'Oui merci. Deux, s'il vous plait.'

With a plate in each hand, I made my way to the exit. Due to the logistics of keeping the running route free from pedestrians, events such as this often have to erect bridges so that people can get from one side to the other, without walking in front of competitors. The first obstacle that greeted Ironmen after passing through the security gate from the enclosure was one such bridge.

Twenty metal steps up (I counted them), then a short walk across the bridge, and then twenty metal steps down the other side. Despite the challenges we had all overcome during the day – judging by the manner in which people were ascending or descending these stairs – this was the toughest challenge yet. Men and women clung on to the railing like they were on the final ascent of Everest, edging inch by inch upwards. In a little while, I would have to do this all again carrying my bike.

Rachel and the kids were waiting for me by the entrance to the finish arena. When they saw me they all ran towards me screaming and shouting. With three children all squeezing my legs, I gave Rachel a big kiss and a squeezed her tightly.

'Well done, my Ironman. You're amazing,' she said. 'I don't know how you did it.'

'Neither do I,' I said. 'It doesn't seem real.'

'Look, I've got a medal like you two now,' I said to Layla and Leo.

'Yey,' said Leo.

Layla still clung to my leg, and I realised over the sound of the music that she was sobbing.

'What's wrong, sweetie?' I asked.

She looked at me for a moment and then carried on crying.

'She's been like this since you finished,' said Rachel. 'I think she's just overwhelmed by the whole thing and she had been really worried earlier that something bad had happened to you.'

'Come here,' I said, bending down and holding her close. 'Did you know that each time I finished a lap on the run they put a different coloured band on my arm, so that they knew how many laps I had done? You are not allowed to cross the finish line until you have all four.'

She smiled slightly between sobs.

'And do you know which was my favourite wrist band on my arm?'

She shook her head.

'This one. The one that says *'Dad'*. I kept looking at it all day and it's what got me through. Whenever I was finding it really tough, I looked at my wrist and remembered how hard you found IronKids yesterday but you just kept on going.'

She smiled and squeezed my leg even tighter.

'Daddy, we got you some pick 'n' mix,' said Leo.

'Wow, that's just what I wanted. Thank you. Oh, I nearly forgot. Rachel, I got these for you.'

'Crêpes? How did you manage to get those between the finish and here?'

'There were serving them to the finishers. I'd promised you a crêpe this week.'

'Thank you. That's very sweet of you.'

We sat on the bleachers of the finish arena for a few minutes, sharing the crêpes and the pick 'n' mix and chatting about the day. Leo and Kitty were both desperate to go to bed, but they agreed to stay to wait until Emily had finished. I took the opportunity to limp off to get my bike and transition bags and take them back to the car.

As I reached the bottom of the metal bridge there was a lady standing there with a baby in a pushchair. She was looking up at the stairs and looking around helplessly. There was nobody else about.

'Would you like a hand?' I asked reluctantly, gesticulating to the pushchair and the stairs and me, all with one international sign language movement.

'Ah, oui monsieur. Merci beaucoup.'

The next two minutes were two of the most terrifying of my life. Holding onto the end of that pushchair, and hoping that there was enough strength left in my limbs to make it to the other side without dropping it, we edged up and over the bridge. It could have been the most spectacular fall from grace. One minute an Ironman, the next a baby killer. Thankfully, we made it to the other side and I breathed an almighty sigh of relief.

'Merci beaucoup, monsieur,' she said.

'De rien,' I replied.

After retrieving my bike and bags and taking everything to the car in the car park, I went and joined the others in the finish arena. This had been the moment I had been looking forward to. Sitting, cheering, and clapping as others took their last few steps to becoming an Ironman. The familiar expressions of pain and elation carved into their faces. Each with their own story to tell, their own injuries overcome, and their own demons faced.

We watched Martin from Kent finish. This was his third or fourth Ironman, but he looked like he was enjoying the finish more than anything. Unlike me, he spotted his partner Sue at the barrier and they went and embraced, before he took those final steps across the line. I went down to the barrier and gave Sue a hug too. We had only spoken to each other a few times all week, but at this moment we seemed to have an awful lot in common.

'Isn't that Emily?' said Rachel, as a girl in pink socks crossed the finish line. I had been talking to Layla at the time, so didn't see her as she ran past.

'I don't know. Was it?'

'It looked a bit like her. She had knee high pink socks.'

I made the trip back out of the finish arena and over the metal bridge for the fourth time since finishing. I wandered around the finishers' hall and eventually found a lady in pink shorts and pink socks sitting at a table. But it wasn't Emily, so I hobbled back to the grandstand.

The minutes ticked by. Emily had been on the course for 15 hours and 40 minutes. She had 20 minutes to get back in order to be an Ironman.

There was no sign of Pete either.

'I really hope she makes it,' said Rachel.

'She will,' I said.

Another ten minutes went by. As each shape took form through the arena entrance, we sat up in anticipation to see if it was her. What if she finished a minute after the cut-off? What if she finished a couple of seconds after the cut-off? It wouldn't matter to anyone else. We would still know she was an Ironman. She would still have covered the required distance in the space of a day, so what difference did a few extra minutes make? In most other countries in the world, anything under 17 hours is an Ironman. But I knew Emily wouldn't be satisfied. To her the day would have been a failure. Those precious minutes or seconds meant everything.

And then I spotted Pete down by the barrier. Layla and I hurried down to join him.

'How was she doing when you saw her?' I asked.

'Not great. But she was still moving. It's going to be very close, but I'm confident she will make it,' he said, glancing at his watch. I looked at mine too.

10 minutes to go.

'Yeah, she'll make it,' I said.

5 minutes to go.

'Daddy, is Emily not going to make it in time?' asked Layla.

'I'm sure she will. Don't worry,' I said, and Pete and I looked at each other, the first glimpses of doubt in our eyes.

I started to feel guilty for encouraging Emily to sign up. Perhaps it was too soon for her. She'd only recently had a baby and had so little time to prepare. I shouldn't have been so persistent. I thought it would be the perfect way for her to overcome the disappointment of not completing Ironman Frankfurt. But how would she cope if she suffered a second *Did Not Finish*?

4 minutes to go.

We hadn't seen another finisher for several minutes. Most had either finished by this point, given up, or been told they would not make the cut-off.

'Is that her?' shouted Layla. 'Look, that's Emily.'

'I knew she'd do it,' laughed Pete, his stoic voice choking, as a familiar figure entered the arena.

'Never a doubt,' I said.

She was running. Sort of. Her arms were moving in the style of a run, and her legs were trying to do the same, but not really co-operating. It didn't matter. A giant spotlight was fixed on her and tracking her final yards around the arena. She had a massive grin on her face and raised a hand to the crowd in acknowledgement. She crossed the finish line in 15 hours 56 minutes and 22 seconds. She had over three minutes to spare. I felt far more emotional than I did for my own finish. Knee surgery, 15 marathons, a baby and now an Ironman with almost no preparation. It was a pretty incredible story.

We all waited a few minutes but there was no sign of Emily emerging from the athletes' area. As Pete wasn't allowed through, I offered to go and help her. I found her slumped face first onto a table – the rest of the hall almost deserted.

I eventually managed to persuade her to get to her feet, and I helped her hobble out, where I retrieved her bike and bags before tackling that bloody metal bridge for the seventh and final time.

'Promise me you'll never persuade me to do anything like that ever again,' she said, as we both limped towards Pete and Rachel.

'I promise,' I said, my fingers crossed by my side. 'Now go text your mum. Tell her you're an Ironman.'

It was 7.56am the following morning when I received a text message from Emily.

'It was brilliant wasn't it?'

Yes it was.

It was utterly brilliant. I'm not going to claim that I loved every second of it. In fact, there were only a handful of moments during the race that I can claim to have actually enjoyed. These were interspersed with a rollercoaster of feelings, fears and emotions that only served to heighten the positive moments when they did arise.

In the space of a day I had had a fear of being disqualified before the race had even started, a fear of drowning, fear of being shot, fear of kidney failure, and a fear of dying. I had suffered heat stroke, hallucinations, extreme fatigue, and more pain that I have ever experienced before in my life. I experienced new levels of hunger and thirst. During the darkest moments, I felt a love for those closest to me, more intense than I've ever felt before, and when I crossed that finish line, I discovered a feeling of elation that I had accomplished something incredible.

I had transformed myself from a hospital patient to an Ironman in a little over four months. I never thought I would be grateful for having a spinal cord tumour, but I undoubtedly was. Without it there is no chance I would have signed up for Ironman Vichy. I doubt I would ever have entered an Ironman. Before surgery, I had been the weakest – both mentally and physically – that I had ever been. I was now the strongest. It was a Transition Impossible. *(I'm sorry for shoehorning this pun in. Transition Impossible had been the working title of this book, until Rachel suggested the current one instead. She thought the triathlon reference might be a bit too obscure for some. And her title was way better than mine anyway).*

33

Back at the campsite we put the children into bed, and they were asleep before we had even zipped up the door to their sleeping compartment. I limped off to the shower block to wash off 14 hours worth of salty, sweaty grime that had caked every inch of my body. The lights in the shower block switched themselves off at 11pm, but there was something strangely magical about standing in the pitch black, as the thick ribbons of warm water trickled down my face and over my body. I was an Ironman. I couldn't stop smiling.

I bumped into Simon outside the toilet block. Simon, it seemed, was outside the toilet block whatever time of day or night.

'I'm really sorry to hear that you had to pull out,' I said.

'Yeah, it was a bit gutting but I shouldn't have even started today really. I wasn't in the best state.'

'No, it was impressive that you got through the swim and half the bike.'

'Well it was my own stupid fault really. I spent way too much time in the sun this week and shouldn't have pushed it so hard with the training. I think I'll just play crazy golf like you next time.'

'Well, after everything you've taught me about triathlon this week, it's nice to be able to offer some of my wisdom in return.'

'Ha! Congratulations on your race, by the way. I hear you finished in under 14 hours? That's incredible for a first effort. Especially in those conditions.'

'Thanks. How are you feeling now?'

'Lots better, thanks. I felt dreadful all afternoon, but I've had a few beers this evening and they have helped.'

'That's good. Next season will be here in no time.'

'I'm not waiting until next year. I've already signed up for Challenge Weymouth. That's another iron-distance triathlon.'

'Cool, when's that?'

'In two weeks. I managed to get a last minute spot. Hopefully I'll finish that and at least all my training this year won't have gone to waste.'

Simon took part in Challenge Weymouth two weeks after Vichy, and despite the horrendous conditions – not the heat like we experienced in Vichy, but typical British wind and rain – he completed the course in less than 12 hours.

I also bumped into Simon's friend Andy. Andy completed the Vichy course in 12 hours 29 minutes, which was slower than he had hoped. He had previously completed Ironman Wales, Nice and Lanzarote, which are considered three of the toughest in the world. But due to the extreme wind and heat, he rated Vichy as the toughest Ironman he had ever taken part in.

I woke in the early hours desperate for the toilet. Despite the litres of water and energy drink I had consumed throughout the day, I hadn't been to the toilet since the beetroot incident in the portable toilet in the middle of the afternoon. I knew I was dehydrated so made sure I drank plenty of water (and a couple of beers) before bed.

The walk to the toilet block took forever, as I inched along the gravel path, every part of my legs feeling like they had been crushed by a tank. But it was a satisfying feeling, and I was still smiling.

I was slightly disappointed that Simon wasn't at the toilet block at 3am, and I staggered back to the tent and slept solidly for another four hours.

In an ideal world, we would have had a few days in France to relax and recuperate. We had no such luxury, however. The children were back at school in two days and we were a day and a half from home. We had to be out of the campsite by 11am the morning after the Ironman.

'Do you want me to take the tent down?' asked Rachel, but in a way that came out of her mouth like, *'You don't want ME to take the tent down, do you? Please don't make me.'*

'No, I'll be fine,' I said in a way that meant, *'I won't be fine but I'm resigned to the fact that I'VE got to do it.'*

Taking the tent down was not as painful as I feared, but all of our possessions had quadrupled in size during the week, and my packing skills were a little haphazard. We stuffed every inch of the car and the roof box with our luggage and then slammed the boot closed before any of it could escape.

We had promised the kids a final swim in the campsite pool before the long drive back. And I secretly wanted one last go on the water slide.

The previous day I swam 2.4 miles, cycled 112 miles and ran a marathon. It was the hardest thing I had ever done. But standing there, the morning after the Ironman, a huge metal staircase stretching endlessly up to the top of the water slide, I had a new, far tougher challenge to conquer.

It took me a long, long time to reach the top, and I was lapped several times by my own children, but I eventually reached the summit, and the cool rushing water on my aching body was worth the pain. I climbed the stairs again. Then again. And again, getting faster each time, and recording negative splits for my four attempts.

'I'm going to drive,' said Rachel, after we paid our balance at the campsite reception and said our goodbyes and *au revoirs*.

'I'm fine to drive,' I said.

'No, I insist. You should rest. Sit in the passenger seat and stretch your legs out.'

'Thanks, that's really kind of you,' I said, climbing into the passenger seat. Only there didn't seem to be anywhere to put my legs. The passenger seat had been moved forwards to cram a few extra things behind, and then four bags had been squashed into the passenger seat foot-well. With the glove box door open for us to store a couple of coffees bought for the journey, it was an effort for me to even get my legs into the car.

'Stretch my legs out, you said?'

'Yeah, sorry about that. At least you can stretch your arms out a bit.'

After a few hours, Rachel and I swapped places. My legs were far more comfortable in the driver's seat.

We broke up the long journey home with another night at a 'futuristic' budget hotel near Le Mans, and enjoyed a delicious meal at an American steakhouse. When in France…

I felt a huge sense of pride as we boarded the ferry to Plymouth the following morning. Our first family holiday abroad had been a tremendous success. I couldn't help feeling that volunteers should meet all families at the ferry ports when they return home, and hang a medal around the necks of all the parents for surviving a week's holiday with young children. Family holidays are an endurance challenge of a very different kind, but it's one that Rachel and I will be desperate to sign up for again and again.

When I first received the diagnosis in November 2014 that I had a spinal cord tumour, I could not have entertained the idea that nine months later I would be an Ironman. It had been a crazy nine months. The first five of those months saw my strength and character diminish considerably; the final four saw me trying to build it back into something stronger.

I had learned so much during that time.

I learned to swim front crawl. I learned to cycle efficiently over a long distance. I learned to run in a way that causes minimum stress to my body. I learned how to keep going. I learned not to give up. I learned how to overcome adversity. I learned that it's ok to cry and admit you are scared. I learned the importance of love from friends and family on any journey. I learned that we are all capable of far more than we think. I learned that even if it feels like you have spent your entire life in Stroke Development, it is never too late to become a Dolphin.

Would I do another Ironman? Before and during the event itself the answer was always *No*. It was a one off. Just to see if I could. But since returning home, I won't pretend that I haven't thought about another. I don't think I could ever match the feeling of completing Ironman Vichy from the situation I was in. But I can't say that I will never stand on the start line of an Ironman again. I'm sure triathlon and I will meet again at some point in the future.

I want to continue to swim, bike and run, that's for sure. I have a new found fondness for all three, and I hope to continue each of them in some way.

A few days after returning home I spoke to my friend Mark on the phone.

'Your Ironman has really inspired me,' he said.

'Are you going to enter one too?' I asked.

'No chance. I haven't ridden a bike for 20 years, and I'm even worse at swimming than you.'

'Fair enough. So, what are you planning?'

'I'm going to sign up for an ultra marathon next year.'

'An ultra marathon? You mean like further than a marathon?'

'Yeah. A lot further. And a lot tougher.'

'Amazing. Good for you. Let me know when it is and I'll come along to cheer you on.'

'You won't be cheering me on.'

'Why not?'

'Because you're going to sign up for it with me.'

The End

Thank you so much for reading my book. I hope you enjoyed it.

I would be extremely grateful if you would consider leaving a short review on Amazon or Goodreads (it only needs to be a few words). Self-published authors rely almost exclusively on your reviews and recommendations to friends and family, so any way in which you can help spread the word would be massively appreciated. Thank you!

Please LIKE my Facebook page. Photos of the Ironman and my training will soon follow.

www.facebook.com/georgemahood

I have a website too, but there is really not much to see there. If you sign up to the newsletter you will be amongst the first to hear about any new releases

http://www.georgemahood.com/newsletter

You can also follow me on Twitter for general ramblings:

@georgemahood

Feel free to drop me an email with any comments, feedback or criticism. It's always great to hear from readers and I respond to every email.

george@georgemahood.com

I have written a few other books, too…

Free Country: A Penniless Adventure the Length of Britain

Here's what others have said about it:

'…spent last night laughing so much my coffee came out my eyes…'

'…this book is quite simply the best I've read in years…'

The plan is simple. George and Ben have three weeks to cycle 1000 miles from the bottom of England to the top of Scotland. There is just one small problem… they have no bikes, no clothes, no food and no money. Setting off in just a pair of Union Jack boxer shorts, they attempt to rely on the generosity of the British public for everything from food to accommodation, clothes to shoes, and bikes to beer.

During the most hilarious adventure, George and Ben encounter some of Great Britain's most eccentric and extraordinary characters and find themselves in the most ridiculous situations. Free Country is guaranteed to make you laugh (you may even shed a tear). It will restore your faith in humanity and leave you with a big smile on your face and a warm feeling inside.

Free Country is available on Amazon.

Every Day Is a Holiday

Here's what others have said about it:

"...had me laughing from beginning to end..."

"...loved the book – funny and engaging..."

George Mahood had a nice, easy, comfortable life. He had a job, a house, a wife and kids. But something was missing. He was stuck in a routine of working, changing nappies and cleaning up cat sick. He felt like he was missing out on a lot of what the world had to offer.

He then discovered that it was Bubble Wrap Appreciation Day. The day after that was National Curmudgeon Day, and the day after that was Inane Answering Machine Message Day. In fact, the calendar is FULL of these quirky, weird and wonderful events. He realised that somebody somewhere had created these holidays, believing that they were important enough to warrant their own official day. Surely he should therefore be more appreciative of their existence? So he decided to try and celebrate them all. As you do. He hoped that at the end of the challenge he would be transformed into a happier, more intelligent and more content person.

Follow George on his hilarious, life changing adventure as he tries to balance his normal life with a wealth of new experiences, people, facts and ridiculous situations. It's a rip-roaring, life-affirming, roller-coaster of a ride, where every day is a holiday.

Every Day Is a Holiday is available on Amazon.

Acknowledgements

Rachel, Layla, Leo and Kitty – thank you for everything. Sorry that I was a bit miserable during my back problems. I hope that I'm making up for it now.

Special thanks to Mum, Dad, Rachel, Angela Wright, Helena Azzam and Becky Beer for your help with the editing and kind words of encouragement.

Most importantly, thank you to Mr H and all south Devon NHS staff for helping to make me feel young again. You are all amazing.

Made in the USA
Lexington, KY
14 April 2019